Building

Continual

Improvement

Donald J. Wheeler

Sheila R. Poling

SPC Press
Knoxville, Tennessee

SPC Press, Inc.

5908 Toole Drive, Suite C
Knoxville, Tennessee 37919
(423) 584–5005
Fax (423) 588–9440

ISBN 0–945320–50-7

x + 320 pages
201 figures

2 3 4 5 6 7 8 9 0

Contents

Acknowledgments

Many thanks for the support and patience of everyone who has touched this book in some unique way. Among these are Fran Wheeler, who read and gave comments; Frony Ward, who read, commented, and provided the initial idea for creating the step-by-step guide for working with seasonal data; and, Henry Neave, who made suggestions for organization and content.

In addition, this book could not have been completed without the real-world examples supplied by our customers and friends. Those of you who recognize your stories should be pleased; those of you who don't should be relieved.

Finally there are the many customers who have patiently and persistently encouraged us to get this book finished—because they needed it yesterday. And our office staff, for wanting to get this book into the "patient" customers hands; so, they can keep them happy.

The many contributions of all of these individuals and more have helped us to build Continual Improvement.

Introduction

"I'm not in manufacturing. How can I use SPC?"

While this question has been asked by many, only a few have attempted to provide an answer. One immediate barrier that exists for those outside manufacturing is the very terminology itself. Statistical Process Control just doesn't sound like something that is needed in business. However, this barrier begins to disappear when one replaces the term "SPC" with the more descriptive phrase "the concepts and techniques of Continual Improvement." This book is our attempt to show some of the many different ways that the principles and techniques of Continual Improvement may be used in nonmanufacturing environments.

Since Continual Improvement requires a blend of concepts and techniques, this book must also be a blend. While the actual techniques are quite simple, the concepts of Continual Improvement are new to most people. This is why it takes time to create an environment where these techniques can be fully utilized. However, when the concepts and techniques of Continual Improvement (which are described in this book) are actively used throughout an organization, the results can be spectacular.

The foundation for the techniques of Continual Improvement was laid by Dr. Walter Shewhart, a physicist who worked with Western Electric and Bell Laboratories. His pioneering work in the 1920s was focused on quality in manufacturing. However, his approach is universally applicable, valid with all kinds of data, and useful in all types of organizations.

Dr. W. Edwards Deming extended Shewhart's work by developing and explaining its applications, first in the U.S., then in Japan after World War II, and finally throughout the world in the 80s and 90s.

We will make reference to the work of both of these pioneers throughout this book. However, this book is merely an introduction. It is not intended as an explanation of the work of these two men. When you embark on your own journey of Continual Improvement you will want to know more about the origins and development of this remarkable philosophy, and to that end, we recommend the books listed in the bibliography.

Chapter One

Why Continual Improvement?

Every organization has to generate revenues in order to continue to exist. These revenues must cover the expenses of the organization and also provide working capital for future operations. When an organization is "for profit" these revenues must also provide the profits expected by the shareholders. Because of this economic fact of life, all managers have to focus on the bottom line of the cash flow statement. From an executive's point of view the world consists of three things: income, expenses, and profits. The objective is clear: increase income and lower expenses in order to maximize profit. So how can you and your organization achieve this objective?

Managers commonly seek to meet this objective by setting sales goals, establishing quotas, having contests, launching advertising campaigns, creating new products or repackaging old products in different ways, or charging whatever the market will bear. At the same time, in order to lower expenses, managers cut back on inventory levels, lower the levels of service, decrease staffing, and slash all indirect expenses. As a result, we live in an age with decreasing levels of service; with a growing sense that everyone is increasingly harried as they are left to do more work with fewer resources. Every department, and often every person, is in competition for scarce internal resources, and cooperation is rare. As everyone scrambles to take care of his or her own turf, the organization suffers, and so new waves of cost reductions are put in place, continuing the downward cycle.

This downward cycle is seen in many different companies. It is the inevitable consequence of "management by results." When the corporate numbers are not good, the divisions get goals and targets. When the divisional numbers are not good, the departments get goals and targets. And when the department numbers are not good, the manager is reprimanded and individuals are given "stretch goals." This endless game of "making your numbers" leads to a "cover your anatomy" mentality in which the need to survive the internal competition becomes dominant, taking precedence over the needs of the company and the needs of the customer. The company becomes a financial football—a collection of assets to be reorganized, stripped, sold, and resold.

While the objectives of increased revenues, reduced expenses, and increased profits are legitimate, the real question is how this goal will be met. By far the simplest way to meet goals and targets is to massage the data—"Isn't there some way to show a five percent increase in productivity by the end of the year?" Of course, when the data are massaged they become distorted. While this distortion of the data requires the least effort, it has the disadvantage of coming back to haunt you later, requiring further distortions and resulting in unrealistic expectations.

The second way you can meet your goals and targets is to "work the system." This can take many forms ranging from simply shifting the blame to another person (or another department or another division), to changing the way the numbers are collected, to changing the actual processes to hide the problems. "Put the incomplete units in boxes and ship them—we'll let the service department finish assembling them in the field." Business becomes a game of tag where the objective is to avoid being "it" at the end of the month.

These "distort the data" and "distort the system" approaches are so common that many people have come to think that the major purpose for collecting data is to hide the problems. "We collect data to show how good things are, whether or not they are." This use of data to lie to the numerically illiterate has been a common practice for so long that "statistics" has come to be a synonym for obfuscation, distortion, and confusion.

There is a better way...

There is a way to simultaneously increase quality, boost productivity, and ensure an advantageous competitive position.

This better way does not consist of management by results.

Instead of focusing on outcomes, such as expenses and profits, this better way focuses on the processes and systems that generate the outcomes. Rather than trying to directly manipulate the results, it works to improve the system that causes the results. Rather than distorting the system or distorting the data, it seeks to use the data to understand the system as a basis for improving the system. This better way is known as Continual Improvement.

How is Continual Improvement different from "doing the same old thing" under a new banner? How can Continual Improvement have an impact upon the bottom line? Take, for example, the problem of reducing costs. Continual Improvement looks at costs as outcomes. In the traditional way of working we would focus directly upon reducing costs, and as a result we might well undermine the future to make the current numbers look better. Continual Improvement focuses on the causes of those costs—the processes that generate them. When this is done, it is common to find that a substantial portion of the costs are due to rework, things not done right, correcting errors and mistakes, and the complexity that these introduce. By working to eliminate these causes of poor quality, and thereby to reduce the complexity of our processes, we can reduce costs while improving our operations.

Continual Improvement is an approach that focuses on the processes which generate the business that is essential so we can have a profitable bottom line. The traditional focus upon income and expenses will tend to place different departments in competition, destroying cooperation, and undermining the delivery of products or services that the customers want. The objective has been to make your numbers by whatever means possible. In contrast to this, Continual Improvement seeks to build a system where the processes are integrated to deliver a product or service that will not only satisfy the customers but will delight them.

By encouraging internal *cooperation* instead of internal *competition* Continual Improvement releases the creative energy within your organization that was formerly devoted to survival. It encourages communication instead of secrecy, which builds trust rather than distrust, and thereby creates an organization that can respond to changes in the business environment. The alternative is to "continue the beatings" until your company goes out of business.

Of course, Continual Improvement requires a methodology for studying processes and systems, and a way of differentiating between the different types of variation present in processes and systems. There are techniques to be learned. But there is also a way of thinking to be practiced, and that is where it gets hard. Those who have traveled down this road universally proclaim the new way of thinking to be worth the effort, and the results do show up on the bottom line.

This book is intended to serve as an introduction to both the techniques and the way of thinking that comprise the approach known as Continual Improvement. And to that end, we shall begin with a definition of quality.

1.1 What Is Quality?

Karen, a sales representative of a printing company, was talking with one of her customers when the issue of quality came up. The customer was concerned about the quality of work turned out by the printing company. Karen's response was, "We don't have a problem with quality. We just have a problem with variation."

David, a consulting statistician in the United Kingdom, told a group from the postal service that their main problem was one of variation. "Oh, no," they responded. "We have no variation—our procedures are rigid!" "Okay," said David. "Perhaps you don't have any variation, but I wager that you have some chaos." "Oh yes," they said. "We have lots of chaos."

No matter what name it goes under, everyone struggles with quality. We want quality. We often fail to get it. Hence, a major question of the day is: "How can we get quality?" Of course, as soon as you ask this question you have to begin by defining quality:

- One definition of quality has been "fitness for use." This definition is clearly centered on an object rather than a service. Moreover, it implies a trade-off between that which is desirable and that which is merely acceptable.

- Another definition of quality has been "zero defects." While the physical origins of this definition are clear, it is possible to apply this definition to services—a defect would be an error or mistake on the part of the provider. However, since it should be self-evident that quality must be more than the absence of defects, this definition must be defective.

- Some would say that quality is a state of mind—if everyone simply does his or her best, then we will get quality. The naive simplicity of this definition is revealed by simply asking, "Would those who have not been doing their best please raise their hand?"

- Others say quality is a matter of reinforcement. Simply tell everyone how well they are doing, and do this often enough, and the result will be quality. While this may work with puppies, it sounds like wishful thinking here.

- Dreamers think of quality in terms of a goal. We need to have an impossible dream, and then fail, and then try again before we can achieve quality. "We have to have something to shoot for."

- And then there is the approach that is as old as Pharaoh and as common as dirt: "The beatings will continue until morale (and quality) improves."

What do these approaches have in common? While they may contain valid elements, in the end they depend upon wishes and hopes (or occasional threats) for achieving quality. Quality is reduced to a simple formula—"do this and you will get that."

W. Edwards Deming went beyond the simplistic level of wishes and hopes and defined quality in terms of a never-ending cycle of Continual Improvement—a process by which people could start where they are and work to improve their organization gradually over a period of time.

This is why Continual Improvement is different from all other approaches to quality. It provides a method for assessing the present and working to improve the future. While it can contain some of the elements mentioned above, it is more than goal setting, it is more than positive reinforcement, it is more than an appeal to an archetype, and it is much more than "everyone doing their best." Continual Improvement is not a magic formula that you can invoke. It is not a quick fix—"do this and you will get that." It is, instead, a way of thinking, a way of acting, and a way of understanding the data generated by your processes, that will collectively result in improved quality, increased productivity, and an advantageous competitive position.

1.2 Plan, Do, Study, Act

Continual Improvement involves a *cycle* of activities, which have been characterized as Plan, Do, Study, Act (PDSA). The PDSA cycle is a framework, a learning cycle that allows you to use all the various improvement tools and techniques to optimize your processes.

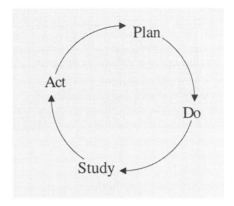

Figure 1.1: The PDSA Cycle

Plan: Determine the improvement to be made, the improvement method, and the method for evaluating the results. What do you want to accomplish? By what method will you achieve this objective? And how will you know when you have reached your objective? Until you have answered these questions you will not have completed the planning stage.

Do: Perform the activities defined in the plan. A pilot program is recommended. (Large starts lead to large consequences!)

Study: Compare the results with the desired results; learn from them. This step is sometimes referred to as "check" rather than "study."

Act: Take advantage of what you have learned. Make it part of your process, if appropriate, or decide what you will try next. Take action.

Implicit in the cycle is its repetition. After *Act*, it begins anew: *Plan* again, *Do* again, *Study* again, *Act* again; an unending cycle of learning, evaluating, and working on process improvement.

Of course, when you already have a system in place it might be good to begin with an evaluation of the current system before you begin to plan changes. In a case like this you might begin at the "study" portion of the cycle.

We learn one step at a time, and the PDSA cycle allows the organization, as a group, to learn about how to improve what is being done. Some people may know what we need to be doing. Others may know what we are doing. By bringing the objectives out into the open, and then studying the results of our efforts at achieving these objectives, we can continually update both our knowledge and our efforts. Thus, the PDSA cycle is a way to learn, to understand, and to improve. It may not sound dramatic, and it does not promise instant results, but when it is used consistently and repeatedly it will yield profound improvements.

As part of the PDSA cycle you will need to use various data analysis techniques that are described in this book. If you learn the techniques, but do not integrate them into an overall process of improvement, little will happen. If you attempt to make improvements and do not have the tools you need, then you will end up frustrated. The PDSA cycle will give you a framework for creating and implementing your improvement plan. The tools described in this book will give you the knowledge to make the plan work for you.

More will be said about the PDSA cycle in Chapter Fifteen. However, it is implicit in many of the examples and many of the techniques contained throughout the book.

1.3 Summary

So what is Continual Improvement? It is more than graphs and data. It is more than using the right bit of arithmetic. It is more than a technique. It is the ability to understand the messages contained in your data. It is the ability to differentiate between routine variation and exceptional variation. It is the difference between reacting to noise and understanding signals. It is ultimately an incredibly powerful way of thinking that will enable you to conduct your business more effectively.

How does Continual Improvement differ from traditional improvement programs? Rather than attempting to improve a process by throwing resources at the problems, Continual Improvement allows you to utilize your current resources to the fullest extent. Once you use Continual Improvement throughout the organization as the way of doing business you will discover that it allows you to get the most improvement from the least effort.

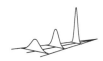

Part One

Context is the Beginning of Improvement

Chapter Two

Visualize Your Process

In most cases the PDSA cycle should commence with a careful and thoughtful analysis of the current system. To this end it is helpful to visualize your process, and the tools for doing this are flowcharts and cause-and-effect diagrams. While both of these techniques are simple, they are also profoundly useful.

These graphic techniques are profound in the way they clarify relationships between individuals, between departments, between causes and effects, and between suppliers and customers. But the chief value of flowcharts and cause-and-effect diagrams is the way they highlight those places in which the system or process breaks down. If a branch of the chart cannot be connected back to the main flow, then the process has not been completely defined. If some simple cause is the source of problematic effects, then the process has not been completely de-bugged.

The tools that are taught in this chapter are best used by groups or teams of people who feel secure in openly discussing their work. The people working in the process are the most qualified people to diagram or document the process. They are the only people who really know what is going on. Diagrams constructed by supervisors or managers are more likely to depict wishes and hopes than to be true pictures of the process.

2.1 Brainstorming

To construct a flowchart, it is necessary for employees to discuss how they do their jobs. In many work situations, people are afraid to talk about their work in front of others—particularly if supervisors are in the group. Without a free flow of information, it will not be possible to construct an accurate flowchart or cause-and-effect diagram. Important steps or components may be hidden. One way of getting this free flow of information is to train people in the use of brainstorming.

Brainstorming is an effective way of getting people to speak freely. It may be helpful to practice this technique with an innocuous topic before using it to construct·flowcharts of work processes or cause-and-effect diagrams. The rules should be explained to everyone (and enforced throughout the activity). They are:

1. A recorder is selected to write the ideas on a chalk board or flip chart. It is important for everyone to have a clear view of this record.
2. The group leader will clarify the topic (and enforce the rules as needed). It is very important that the topic be clearly defined in such a way that everyone in the group understands it.
3. All members of the group should be encouraged to participate.
4. It will be helpful to encourage people to use five words or less to express their ideas.
5. All ideas should be recorded verbatim without interpretation by others.
6. All group members must understand that every suggestion, however unusual or unexpected, has possible value. No one should be ridiculed in any way.
7. Statements should not be evaluated, organized, or criticized in any way.

In the beginning some may not feel comfortable with the brainstorming process. One way to minimize this discomfort is to take a few minutes at the start to have the group members privately write down their ideas before anyone begins to share them. Then the group leader can ask each person in turn to share items from their list. After a couple of circuits of the group it is usually much easier to get participation in the free flow of ideas that is the essence of the brainstorming technique.

After the brainstorming session is completed group members can work to organize the ideas, evaluate their accuracy or usefulness, construct a chart, or use the input in various ways.

Brainstorming not only helps to visualize your process, but it can be a powerful way to generate new ideas and suggestions for improvement, while facilitating the improved communication that is needed to make any organization work effectively.

2.2 Flowcharts

Flowcharting became important in the 1950s with the increasing need to write computer programs. Since the details involved in writing thousands of lines of code were so great, some way to obtain an overall view of the process was needed, and the flowchart was invented. Because of the simplicity and power of this technique the use of flowcharts has spread far beyond the writing of software.

Flowcharts allow you to visualize your process from the point of view of how the work is done. They allow you to characterize your current processes, to design new processes, to streamline existing processes, to assess weaknesses in your current system, and even to spot those places where the system has broken down without your knowledge. Flowcharts help to identify internal suppliers and internal customers, and they allow you to eliminate duplication of effort.

Since flowcharts give you a graphical representation of your process, they help you to share this process with others, making training easier and creating greater consistency in your operations.

Conventions have been developed to symbolically show different types of operations. While these conventions are helpful, the real power of a flowchart resides in the overall picture itself. A few of the more common symbols will be explained on the following pages. These conventions may work for you, or you may develop your own methods of flowcharting.

Flowchart Conventions

Boxes with rounded corners are commonly used to denote starting points, input points, and ending points.

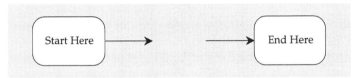

Regular boxes are used for ordinary steps and transactions.

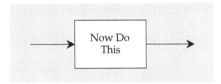

Diamonds are commonly used to denote decision points. Decision points are points where the flowchart will branch. The branch you take will depend upon the answer to the question posed in the diamond.

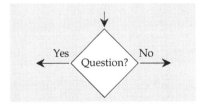

Circles are used to denote connections to remote portions of the flowchart. They allow a large flowchart to be shown as a sequence of smaller flowcharts. They also minimize the spaghetti effect of a large flowchart.

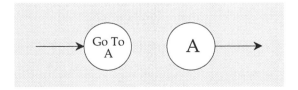

And, of course, arrows are used to show the direction of the flow.

The simplest type of flowchart is a block diagram.

Figure 2.1 shows a block diagram for taking a turn in the game of Monopoly. This block diagram is expanded into a full blown flowchart in Figure 2.2. The flowchart in Figure 2.2. contains thirteen decision diamonds—this simple game has a fair degree of complexity.

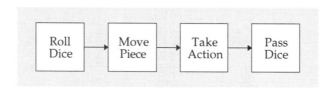

Figure 2.1: Block Diagram for a Turn in Monopoly

Your turn begins when you receive the dice.

If you are in jail, you may pay your fine, you may play a "Get Out Of Jail" card, or you may try to roll a double. If you have not rolled a double after three turns you must pay your fine and move your piece.

When you move your piece you will either land on a property or on one of the eight "special" spaces. If your piece lands on a property which you own, you may choose to improve it. If your piece lands on a property which someone else owns, you are liable for paying rent. If your piece lands on a property which no one owns, you may buy it from the bank.

If your piece does not land on a property, then you may be required to take some action. If you pass "Go," you get to collect $200. If you rolled a double, you get a repeat turn. However, if you used the double to get out of jail, you do not get this repeat turn. If you happen to roll three doubles in succession, you will have to go to jail. Your turn ends when you pass the dice to the next player.

The flowchart in Figure 2.2 outlines 122 possible ways for a turn to be played, and it does this using only 27 steps. By concentrating on the sequence of decisions and actions, and allowing the reader to progress one step at a time, the flowchart makes complexity comprehensible.

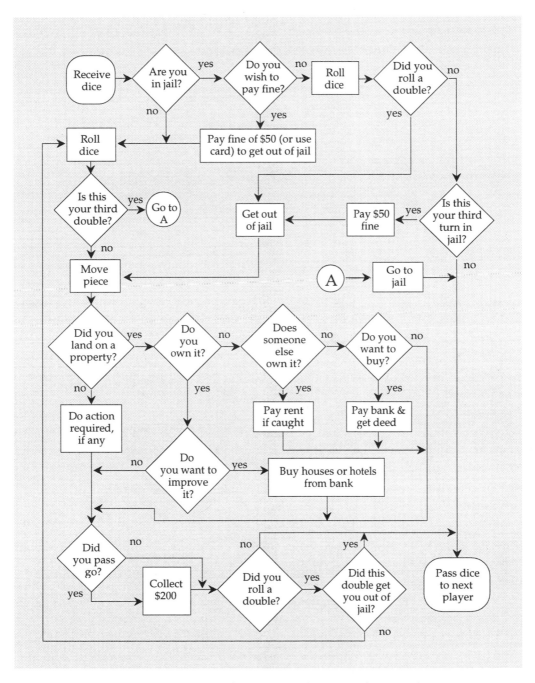

Figure 2.2: Flowchart for a Turn in the Game of Monopoly

2.3 Constructing Flowcharts

A block diagram which shows the process on a large scale (with few details) may be helpful as a starting point for the construction of a flowchart. A small mail order company created the block diagram in Figure 2.3 for their order process.

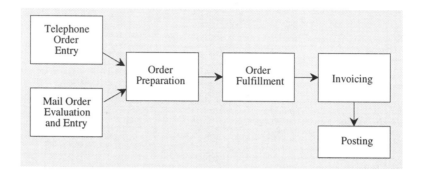

Figure 2.3: Block Diagram for Order Process

A block diagram allows you to break the overall process down into subprocesses and thereby simplifies the job of creating the flowchart. Furthermore, the block diagram for your process can be a useful way to organize your data about problems when you do a Pareto chart in the next chapter. Notice that the six blocks in Figure 2.3 define the major portions of the overall order process. Given the complexity of this process, they began by constructing a flowchart for each portion of the process shown in the block diagram.

When you move beyond the level of the block diagram, the key task is to correctly identify the decision points. The decision points define the branches on the flowchart. If you miss a decision point, you will be leaving out a portion of the process. In between the decision diamonds, you may place more or less detail as appropriate. However, be sure to consider each branch carefully in order to spot any embedded decision points that might lead to sub-branches.

Avoid ambiguity. All arrows are one-way streets.

Since the sequence of the steps is the focal point of the flowchart, the actual form of the chart is secondary. As long as the overall picture is not too crowded, or too hard to follow, the chart will be satisfactory.

The flowchart for the "Mail Order Evaluation and Entry" portion of the block diagram of Figure 2.3 is shown in Figure 2.4.

The flowchart in Figure 2.4 is the second page of a five page flowchart. This flowchart was constructed as a first step in improving the order process. This company was preparing to change from a manual order entry system to a computerized system. Before they implemented a new system the managers wanted to fully understand the current system, with all of its accumulated problems, so that they could be sure that the new system would be better than the old one.

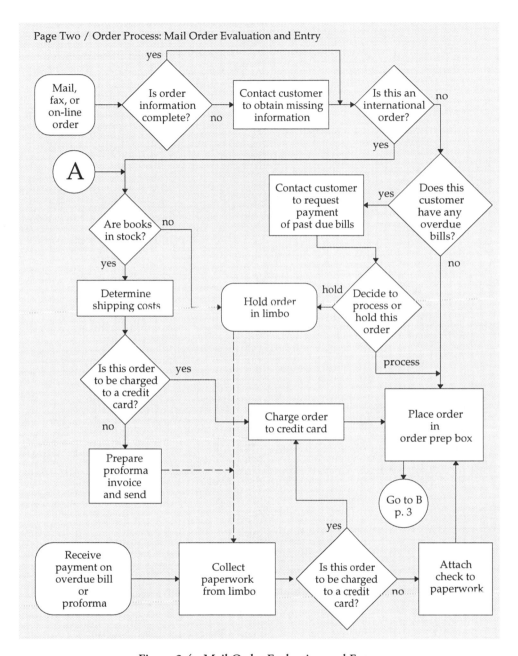

Figure 2.4: Mail Order Evaluation and Entry

While many employees will have some knowledge of the process, few individuals will have the global perspective provided by a flowchart. This is why you always want to create a flowchart by talking with the people who actually perform the work. Flowcharts drawn by those who do not do the work have no contact with reality. They commonly depict nothing more than wishes and hopes. "Make-believe" flowcharts do not provide the foundation needed for Continual Improvement. The objective is not to create a "glamour shot" of your process, but rather to spot the problems and inconsistencies which exist. Therefore, if your current process actually contains "limbo boxes," be sure to include them. The objective is to understand the *actual* process. Honesty is a prerequisite for *useful* flowcharts.

It is helpful to use sticky notes as the different steps in the flowchart are discussed. Their use makes it easy to move steps around as new branches are added. The final flowchart will be a revision of many rough diagrams, and may even take more than one session to complete. (The Monopoly flowchart went through four revisions before it was finished.)

To construct the flowchart in Figure 2.4 the managers of the mail order company sat down with those who did the work in each part of the process shown in the block diagram of Figure 2.3. They created a five-part flowchart, one page of which is shown in Figure 2.4. Not only did this help the managers, it also gave the workers a global view of the process in which they worked. It gave the managers a chance to discuss and design the new system with the workers and allowed the workers to "buy into" the changeover.

Following the creation of the flowchart the managers proceeded to look for opportunities for improvement—places where the flowchart could be streamlined, or where the process could be automated. This knowledge was then used as the basis for purchasing and organizing a computerized order entry and accounting system that would fit the needs of their business.

Next a dummy set of records were created on the new system, and workers were given practice exercises to perform each day using the new system. As they did these exercises they found problems with their own understanding, and occasionally, problems with the system. Based on this experience the new system was tweaked, and after two months of practice, the company was ready to change over. The supplier of the new computerized accounting system was amazed at how few troubles this company had with the transition.

The original five-page flowchart had 50 steps and 25 decision diamonds. The new flowchart, shown in Figure 2.5 and made after the new process was fully operational, contained 49 steps and 20 decision diamonds. The gray boxes in Figure 2.5 show the steps that were automated: of the 49 steps, 12 were automated; of the 20 decisions, 10 were automated. So the new process contained 37 manual steps and 10 manual decision diamonds. While this may not sound like a major reduction in work, the benefits were spectacular.

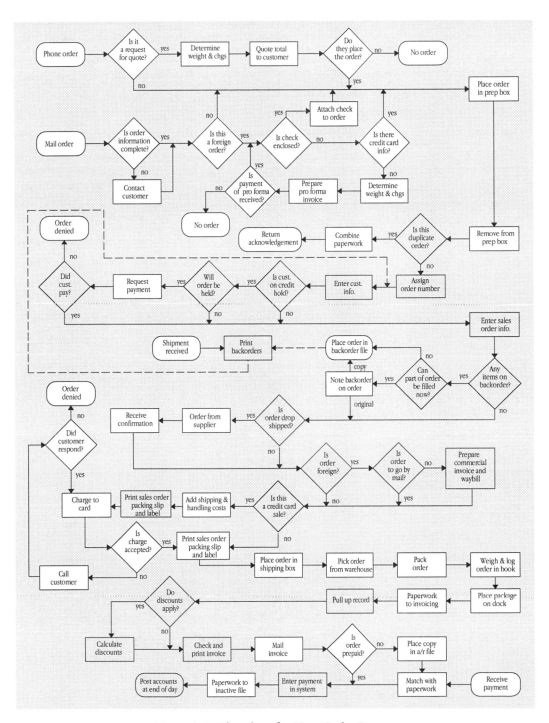

Figure 2.5: Flowchart for New Order Process

It previously took about one-half man-hour to process a single order from receipt to posting, and because of the interface between the different phases of this process, this 30 minutes was spread out over a 15-day period. With the new system, the time was reduced to under 10 minutes, including order picking and packing. In most cases the new system allows orders to be completely processed on the same day they are received.

Previously invoicing had a two- to three-day backlog. Now invoices go out on the same day as the shipment. The posting of accounts receivable had previously been running 10 days behind. With the new system the journal entries are automatically made at the end of each day.

Since the company was understaffed at the start of this improvement project, some things were simply not getting done. Now, with the increased productivity of the new system, the personnel have more time to spend on these formerly neglected areas.

The automated system provides much more effective inventory control, better accounting information, and more timely sales information than was formerly available. The personnel love the new system. When asked, no one wanted to go back to the old system. The customers get their orders faster, with fewer errors. The workers can respond to customer's questions more quickly, more completely, and with greater consistency. Finally, the new system allows the workers to respond to the special requests of the customers more easily.

Those who have used flowcharts have found that there is a lot of "low hanging fruit" out there. These items that are easy to fix are made visible by the flowchart. After using flowcharts successfully some practitioners have even taken a vow that they will no longer start a project without first creating a flowchart. It seems extraordinarily simple, but it works.

Flowchart Summary

The process of creating a flowchart is a process of discovery…

> "You mean we do that?"
> "What happens after this?"
> "How does an order ever get out of Limbo?"
> "What kind of follow-up is needed here?"

The advantages of flowcharting should be self-evident. Flowcharts provide a structure to use in understanding complex processes. They communicate the options and branches more effectively than words on a page will do. They provide a bird's-eye view that makes it easy to spot inconsistencies.

So why don't more people use flowcharts? Perhaps it is because they work in an environment where the truth is hard to accept, where complexity is thought to be profound, or where communication is strictly forbidden. It may be dangerous to point out that the Emperor is wearing no clothes.

PRACTICE: Read through the flowchart in Figure 2.4. It is a picture of a portion of a real process as it existed at that time and place. Since it is a real process it has the problems that are common to real processes. Can you spot some of the flaws, or shortcomings, in this process? While the existence of boxes marked "Limbo" in these figures is very convenient as a description of the process, what do you think they mean for the customer? What do they cost this company?

2.4 Deployment Flowcharts

Deployment flowcharts break the overall process up into pieces: each piece is performed by one department, one area, or one person. The pieces for each department are then shown side by side, and the arrows from one zone to another depict the hand-offs between departments or people, and in some instances, the transactions back and forth between them.

The example in Figure 2.6 is based on a deployment flowchart created by Myron Tribus and shown in his book, *Quality First*. It shows the process for producing a newspaper. Across the top are nine categories—the people dimension. From top to bottom we have the work sequence. Horizontal relationships show customers and suppliers. Vertical lines entering a box indicate who has responsibility for that activity. Horizontal lines indicate a shift in responsibility. The lack of horizontal lines between the editorial side of the process and the advertising side show the relative independence of these two different parts of the operation.

Of course the various activities shown on a deployment flowchart may need to have their own detailed flowcharts. Yet there is a distinct advantage to having a deployment flowchart for your process—it shows the overall process and makes visible some very important relationships that are not obvious on block diagrams. At the same time, the excessive detail of a more extensive flowchart can obscure those interrelationships that are made visible by the deployment flowchart. It is this visualization of these interrelationships between departments that is one of the chief advantages of the deployment flowchart—barriers cannot be removed until they are perceived.

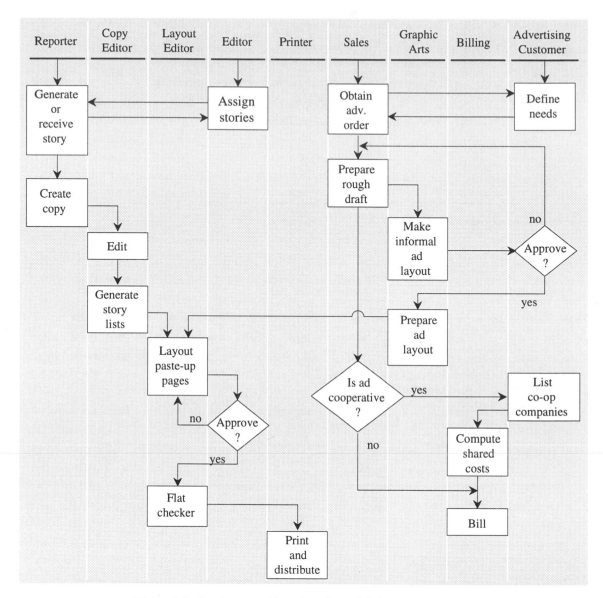

Figure 2.6: Deployment Flowchart for Publishing a Newspaper

2.5 PERT Diagrams

PERT networks or diagrams are flowcharts of the work in a project. PERT stands for Process Evaluation and Review Technique. The heart of a PERT diagram is a flowchart which shows the steps in a project. The emphasis of a PERT diagram is on showing which steps can be done concurrently and which steps depend on others. Figure 2.7 shows the

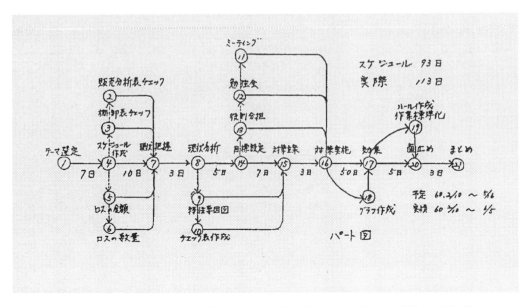

Figure 2.7: PERT Diagram for "Let's Reduce Losses on Beer and Sake Sales"

PERT diagram from a project carried out by waitresses at the Esquire Club, a nightclub in Osaka, Japan.

In this project the waitresses and their supervisor followed the Plan, Do, Study, Act cycle. In the "Plan" phase we might place Steps 1 through 7, as shown in Figure 2.8.

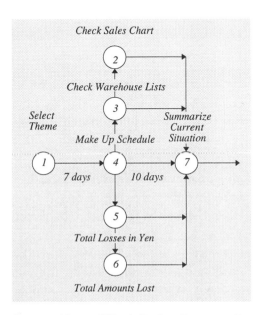

Figure 2.8: The Planning Phase of "Let's Reduce Losses on Beer and Sake Sales"

The selection of a theme was followed by the collection of the relevant information. Source documents were checked, losses were quantified, and this information was gathered into a summary of the current situation. From other parts of the story, it appears that this planning phase was primarily carried out by the supervisor of the waitresses and the managers of the club. This portion of the project was scheduled to last a little over two weeks.

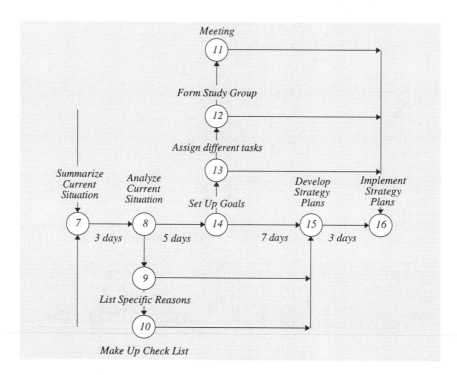

Figure 2.9: The Doing Phase of "Let's Reduce Losses on Beer and Sake Sales"

The "Do" phase of this project consists of Steps 8 through 16. In a two-week period the team of seven waitresses, along with their supervisor and the club managers, went to work to identify reasons for the losses, to set up a check list, to identify areas where improvement was feasible, and to look at ways of making these improvements. Finally they came up with a plan and put it into effect.

The "Study" phase of this project consists of Steps 16, 17, and 18. This phase was planned to last 50 days, during which they would collect data to use in before-and-after comparisons. Notice that Step 18 is "Make Up Graphs." This is where they summarize their accomplishments and improvements.

The "Act" phase of this project is contained in Steps 19, 20 and 21. Here they plan to make certain changes permanent, and assign responsibility for follow-up in the future.

The rest of this story will be given later. For now it is sufficient to ask, "When was the last time you were part of an improvement project that was this carefully planned?"

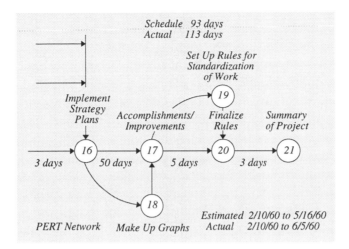

Figure 2.10: The Study and Act Phases of "Let's Reduce Losses on Beer and Sake Sales"

2.6 Do People Really Do This Stuff?

One large automotive supplier, having discovered the power of flowcharts, began to use them with all sorts of administrative processes. One flowchart which they constructed was for the budget process. They already knew that they were spending an average of 190 working days on the preparation of each budget, and they knew that the uncertainty created by this long lead-time was not good. However, over the years, the process seemed to have gotten longer rather than shorter.

After they constructed a flowchart for the budget-planning process, they went through each step of the process and asked the all-important question: "What value is added by this step?" By cutting out those steps that did not add value they streamlined the process, and the time required to complete it, down to 109 working days. With this shorter lead-time, the budget process was not only easier, it was also better—a savings of both time and money.

The maintenance department at a chemical plant created the flowchart in Figure 2.11 to show the steps required to obtain a tool from the Central Tool Room.

While this flowchart is not legible at this scale, it contains 66 steps, including 19 decision diamonds. After they created this flowchart it became obvious that they were treating every tool as if it were a major piece of equipment. They created two categories of tools, depending upon their value, and then created a simplified process for the cheaper tools.

23

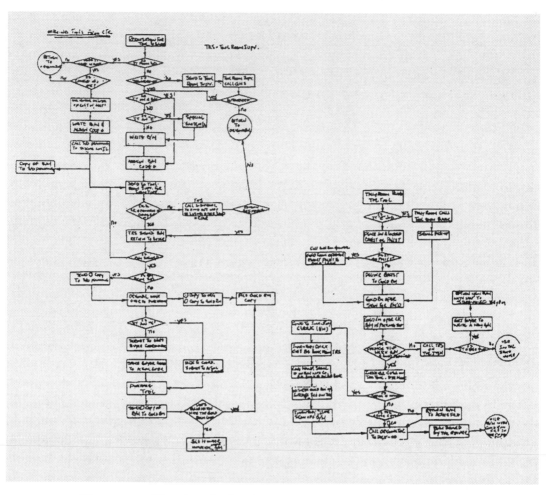

Figure 2.11: Flowchart for "Ordering Tools From Central Tool Room"

Another manufacturing company, upon discovering the advantages of flowcharting, decided to apply them to their service functions. One of the flowcharts they constructed covered the process for responding to a "request for quotation" (RFQ). This process involved the Sales, Engineering, Purchasing, and Manufacturing departments. Each department created its own flowchart for their part of the RFQ process. In spite of this organized approach, and in spite of well-defined processes within each department, they were still having a problem in responding to RFQs. So they used a deployment flowchart to look at their overall process across departmental boundaries. That is when they discovered that while everyone knew how to do their own job, they did not know who their customer was—they did not know where the paperwork should go next. There was, in essence, a box marked "No Longer My Responsibility" between each department. The RFQs were being dropped at the hand-off between departments. By dovetailing the different departmental flowcharts, they could eliminate these areas of uncertainty. When they did so, they reduced the average time to respond to an RFQ from 3 months to 2 weeks.

Based upon this company's success, one of their customers decided to examine its RFQ process. The block diagram for this (larger) company had 17 steps. However, when they began to fill in the details and outline the many different branches, they found that their RFQ process contained over 400 steps, and that fully 70% of these steps did not add value. Immediately, there were 280 steps that were candidates for removal! It was not hard to make dramatic improvements in the processing of RFQs.

Improvement does not have to be hard. Improvement does not have to be profound. In many cases it is just a matter of identifying the opportunity and then doing what you know you need to do.

2.7 Processes and Systems

Everything we do can be described in terms of processes and systems. Taking an order, making an appointment, scheduling a delivery, selling an item—and virtually every transaction we are involved in—are all processes and are parts of systems. We may not give much thought to these processes, at least not until they go wrong, but they do exist.

While it may help to think of "systems" as a collection of "processes" it is not our intent to be overly precise here. Systems and processes have to be defined according to your own needs. However, fuzzy thinking here can get you in trouble, so you should begin by characterizing your process or system graphically by using a block diagram.

Figure 2.12 shows a generic block diagram for a production process. This is the diagram used in Dr. Deming's lectures in Japan in 1950, and is Figure 1 in his book, *Out of the Crisis*.

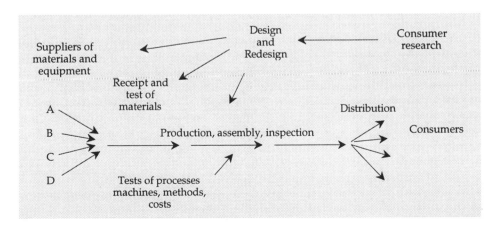

Figure 2.12: Production Viewed as a System

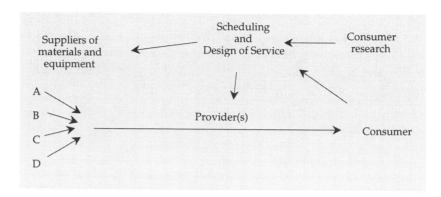

Figure 2.13: A System for the Delivery of a Service

Figure 2.12 may be adapted to fit many different environments. To suggest how this might be done, Figure 2.13 shows a block diagram for the delivery of a service.

The purpose for these block diagrams is not so much as a framework for creating detailed flowcharts as it is to provide an alternative to the traditional hierarchical view of the organization. These block diagrams show the flow of work that keeps the organization in business. They help everyone to think in terms of their customers, instead of the hierarchy.

While the delivery of a service, or the delivery of a product, may not be quite as complex as a manufacturing operation, each has its own sources of complexity. Each involves several different streams of information, and each has multiple points at which this flow of information can break down. When the organization is viewed as a system the complex web of relationships becomes visible, facilitating understanding and efforts at improvement.

2.8 Cause-and-Effect Diagrams

Quite often, a large number of factors will be involved in a problem. When this happens an organized approach is necessary in order to reduce the effect of the problem. One of the simplest tools for this organization is the cause-and-effect diagram.

The cause-and-effect diagram was first applied in conjunction with statistical process control in Japan. Dr. Kaoru Ishikawa found that most plant personnel were overwhelmed by the number of factors that could influence a particular product or process. Thus, in 1950 he began using a "fault tree" as a tool for organizing the attack on a particular problem. This practice proved to be so effective that it spread rapidly throughout Japan. The versatility of a cause-and-effect diagram makes it a useful tool for organizing problem-solving efforts in every area of the manufacturing and service industries.

The versatility comes from the way in which a cause-and-effect diagram is created. Its power comes from the graphic representation of the relationship between problems and their sources. The general procedure for making a cause-and-effect diagram follows.

1. Choose the effect to be studied, and write it at the end of a horizontal arrow.
2. List all the causes that influence the effect under consideration.
3. Arrange and stratify these causes. Choose the principal causes and show these as the major branches off the horizontal arrow.
4. Draw the sub-branches for the various subsidiary causes. This process of sub-dividing is continued until all causes are included on the diagram.
5. Check the diagram to make sure that all known causes of variation are included on the chart.

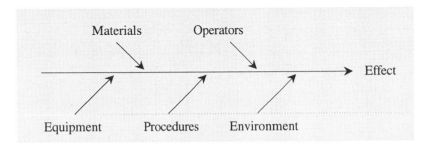

Figure 2.14: A Typical Framework for a Cause-and-Effect Diagram

A common guideline for creating cause-and-effect diagrams is to use five major branches: Materials, Equipment, Operators, Procedures, and Environment. This approach is shown in Figure 2.14. Other ways of organizing cause-and-effect diagrams are possible. The key is to make the cause-and-effect diagram fit the problem.

A simple cause-and-effect diagram for delays in delivery is shown in Figure 2.15. In this case the two major branches were taken to be the responsibilities of the two partners in the sale.

Since the intent is to use the diagram to conceptualize the process, it is best if the diagram reflects the perspective of the many different individuals who are closely connected with the process. Diagrams drawn by only one or two individuals are usually rather poor because they lack this broad base of observation of the process. For this reason, cause-and-effect diagrams are often drawn during brainstorming sessions that include the workers.

After a cause-and-effect diagram has been generated, it may need to be modified and realigned to show the causes in their proper relationships. There should be many sub-branches and even some sub-sub-branches. Even though this kind of chart has been called a fishbone diagram, the finished chart should not look like the skeleton of a fish. Such a cause-and-effect diagram would not effectively show the relationships between the various causes and sub-causes because every factor would appear to be a primary factor, making it difficult to decide where to start.

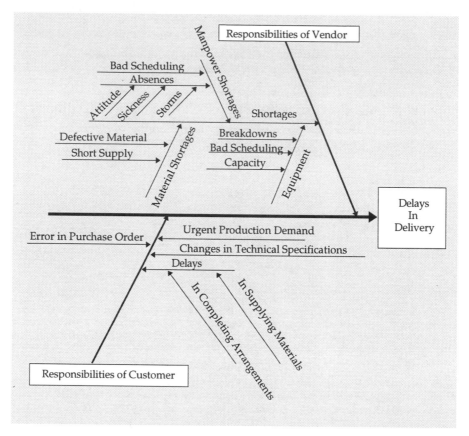

Figure 2.15: Cause-and-Effect Diagram for Delays in Delivery

After the cause-and-effect diagram has been drawn, and rearranged if necessary, the group which generated the diagram should analyze each of the causes to see if there are any obvious things that need to be done, if there are any data that could be collected, and if not, if there is any indirect way of characterizing whether or not this cause is changing. If these things are noted directly on the cause-and-effect diagram it will help to highlight those areas needing immediate action. Following the initial changes resulting from the use of a cause-and-effect diagram, plans should be made for using it on a continuing basis.

The cause-and-effect diagram provides a framework for collective efforts. In Chapter Six we shall make a distinction between processes that are predictable and those that are not predictable. When a process is predictable, the cause-and-effect diagram will help organize efforts to make the process better. When a process is unpredictable, the diagram will suggest areas for investigation.

A second way to use a cause-and-effect diagram is to review what has already been accomplished. The diagram often prevents personnel from overlooking various aspects of the problem. Vast improvement for one principal cause may have only a slight impact on the quality characteristic, while modest improvements on several principal causes may result in dramatic improvements in product quality.

The third way that the cause-and-effect diagram can be used on a continuing basis is to orient new personnel to the problems in a given area. Then they can be smoothly integrated into the work force, without repeating the mistakes of their predecessors.

A fourth way to use the cause-and-effect diagram is in the integration of operations in different areas or different departments. This can be especially important in administrative applications, since the delivery of a service is often quite hard to visualize and coordinate.

At one steel mill the appropriate operators and supervisors were called into the plant manager's office during their lunch hour and asked to produce a cause-and-effect diagram on the problem of "Cracks" (lunch was catered). Cracks had been the number one problem in this mill for the past six months, and nothing they had done had really had an impact on this problem. Everyone had their own unique ideas about what caused Cracks, and the cause-and-effect diagram combined all of these perspectives into one global picture. When everyone could see the big picture, and could put the potential causes down in an organized manner, it was much easier to work together to reduce the occurrence of Cracks. Out of these efforts the incidence of Cracks was cut in half each month for the next four months. A sixteen-fold reduction in their major problem—after months with no progress.

The cause-and-effect diagram is effective in the various areas and ways listed above because the process of producing the chart is a thought-provoking and informative process. It helps all involved personnel systematize their thoughts. Yet it is so easy that virtually anyone can understand and participate in its construction.

PRACTICE: Continual Improvement is not a spectator sport. You learn by doing. So if you do not have experience in constructing flowcharts or cause-and-effect diagrams, you should begin with the following practice exercises.

- Draw a block diagram for some process with which you are connected either at home or at work.

- With the input of those who actually do the work, convert your block diagram into a reasonably complete flowchart, showing all the relevant decision points.

- If appropriate, convert your flowchart into a deployment flowchart. Remember the people dimension of a deployment flowchart can be individuals, groups, departments, or organizations.

- Select a process characteristic or a problem and construct a cause-and-effect diagram showing those causes that have an impact upon the effect chosen.

Chapter Three

Visualize Your Data

The human brain does not easily absorb large sets of numbers. That is why a page full of tabular data is so hard to assimilate.

If you want to impress your audience
>   show them page after page of numbers in tables—
>>   you will either intimidate them or alienate them.

But if you want to *really communicate* with your audience,
>   use *good graphs* which reveal the information contained in the numbers
>>   in a clear and concise manner.

You have about thirty seconds to communicate the content of your data to your audience. After that, their eyes glaze over. The only way that you can consistently beat this thirty-second deadline is to use effective graphs.

This chapter will introduce some of the basic graphs you can use to make sense of data. You will learn how to effectively construct and use running records, bar charts, Pareto charts, histograms, and stem-and-leaf plots.

3.1 Running Records

Data tend to be associated with time. When was this value obtained? What time period does that value represent? Because of this association with time there is information contained in the time-order sequence of the values. To recover this information you will need to look at your data in a time-ordered plot, which is commonly called a running record or a time-series graph.

A running record is a simple graph where one scale represents time and the other scale represents values of the measure of interest. Traditionally the time scale is horizontal and the value scale is vertical. To illustrate a running record we will use the data shown in Figure 3.1, which are the Quarterly Sales for Region D over the past five years.

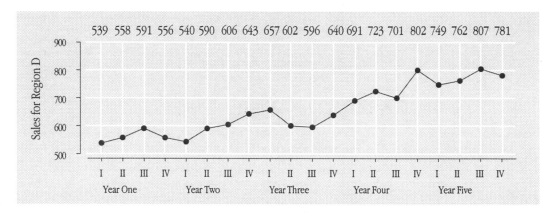

Figure 3.1: Running Record for the Quarterly Sales for Region D

The running record in Figure 3.1:
1. conveys the overall level of sales by the vertical scale,
2. shows the amount by which the sales vary from quarter to quarter,
3. shows the overall trend in sales over the past five years, and
4. places the current value in context;

which is a lot to accomplish with such a simple graph!

The lines on a running record draw our eyes and help us to instantly comprehend the message contained in the values. The points without the lines do not create as powerful a graph. However, there are situations where the graph can be improved by the judicious deletion of certain line segments. In Figure 3.2, gaps are left between the years. These gaps give our eyes visual anchors and allow us to know which quarter is which without even consulting the horizontal scale.

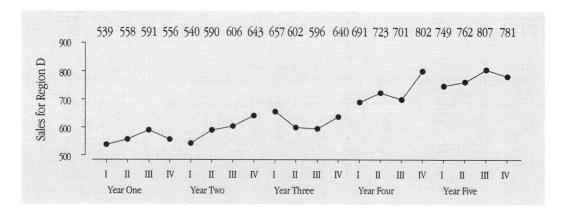

Figure 3.2: Running Record for the Quarterly Sales for Region D

By including the values in the margin of the running record you make the graph even easier for your readers to use. If they want to know a particular value, they do not have to hunt it up on some table on another piece of paper, but can simply look it up in the margin of the plot.

In constructing a running record the value scale only needs to represent those values which are present in the data. A glance at the values in Figure 3.1 shows values ranging from the 500s up to the 800s, so a scale from 500 to 900 should be sufficient. By using a vertical scale that ranges from just below the minimum value to just above the maximum value, you will end up with a running record that uses the vertical space on the graph effectively.

An example of what a poor choice for the vertical scale can do is seen in Figure 3.3, where all of the values are crowded into the upper 20% of the graph and most of the graph is empty.

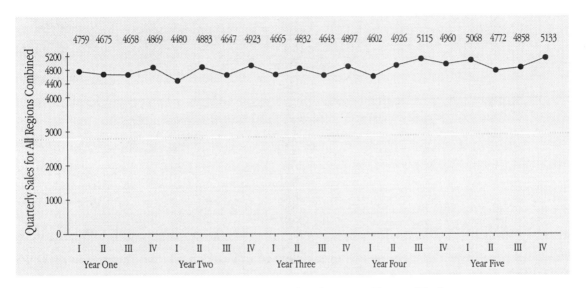

Figure 3.3: A Running Record with a Poor Choice of Scale

Occasionally you may combine two or more running records on a single graph. One executive routinely plotted the inventory level, accounts receivable, and the cash reserves for his company. Since these were all measured in the same units (dollars), he used the same graph for all three records with a different colored ink for each time series. As long as you can easily distinguish between the different running records, this practice is acceptable.

Figure 3.4 shows two of these three running records over a seven year period. The heavy line represents the cash reserves, while the light line shows the inventory levels. Both curves use the same vertical scale, which, in this case, starts with zero. The breaks in the lines show the ends of each year, and the arrows at the bottom show new product release dates.

This pair of running records tells a dramatic story. At the end of Year Three this company launched two new products. At that time their inventory levels began to climb while their cash position began to erode. Since these graphs made the change in status so obvious, actions could be taken in a timely manner to avoid a crisis. Steps were taken to hold the line on inventory. New manufacturing and stocking policies were adopted, allowing

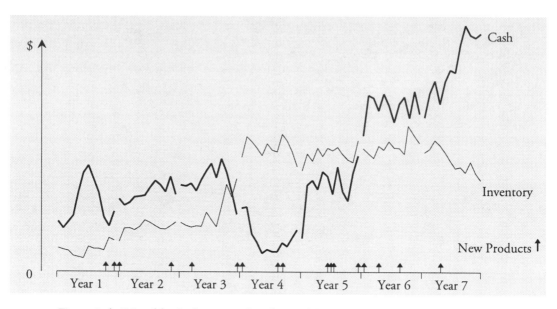

Figure 3.4: Monthly Cash on Hand and Monthly Inventory Levels for Seven Years

tighter inventory control. At the same time, steps were taken to conserve cash and to reduce or defer expenses.

With these corrective actions in place they still had to endure a cash crunch during Year Four, but it was not so severe as to prevent them from launching two new products during the middle of the cash crunch. Since one of these products proved to be very popular, its introduction was the beginning of the turn-around. During Years Four, Five, Six, and Seven the inventory levels remained fairly steady in spite of the fact that the company introduced ten new products during this period. At the same time the cash position of the company has steadily grown. After a two-year sojourn in the land of the inventory-rich-but-cash-strapped, this company returned to the land of the cash-rich and inventory-lean.

Much of the interesting information available in your data is tied up in the time-order sequence of the values. The running record unlocks this interesting information. Of all the different types of graphs that exist, this simple plot of the values in their time-order sequence is one of the most useful, one of the most powerful, and one of the most easily interpreted of them all.

The beauty of a running record
is that
the lines draw your eye
in the direction
that your mind wants to go.

3.2 Bar Charts

The purpose of a bar chart is to compare values or amounts across different categories.

One Monday morning in the restaurant of a large hotel, one of the authors attempted to pay for breakfast with a twenty-dollar bill. Since the amount of the check was under ten dollars the cashier asked if the author had a smaller bill.

"I'll bet you get a lot of twenty-dollar bills on Mondays." I said.

"Oh yes. I never have enough change on Mondays and Fridays."

"Have you ever asked your boss for more change on those days?"

"Oh yes, but he won't ever give me any more. I always have the same amount of change each day."

"Here's an idea. Keep a tally of the number of twenty-dollar bills offered each day. That way you will have some data to back up your request for more change."

"Oh wow! What a great idea!"

If the cashier did keep a tally, her data might have looked something like the following:

Sunday	₩₩ ₩₩ ₩₩ III	18
Monday	₩₩ ₩₩ ₩₩ ₩₩ ₩₩ ₩₩ ₩₩ ₩₩ ₩₩ ₩₩ ₩₩ ₩₩ ₩₩ ₩₩ ₩₩ II	77
Tuesday	₩₩ ₩₩ ₩₩ ₩₩ ₩₩ ₩₩ II	32
Wednesday	₩₩ ₩₩ ₩₩ ₩₩ ₩₩ ₩₩ III	33
Thursday	₩₩ ₩₩ ₩₩ ₩₩	20
Friday	₩₩ ₩₩ ₩₩ ₩₩ ₩₩ ₩₩ ₩₩ ₩₩ ₩₩ ₩₩ ₩₩ ₩₩ ₩₩ IIII	69
Saturday	₩₩ ₩₩ III	13

Figure 3.5: Number of Twenty-Dollar Bills Presented

While tally sheets such as this may be converted into other graphs, they are already a powerful and graphic representation of the data. The magnitude of the problem is thus presented in a form that everyone—including the manager—can immediately grasp: the cashier needs more change for big bills on Mondays and Fridays.

Simple tally sheets like Figure 3.5 are a primitive form of a bar chart. A bar chart is a two-dimensional plot where one dimension consists of a list of categories and the other dimension consists of frequencies or amounts for some measure. A bar is constructed for each category where the length of the bar represents the value of the measure for that category. If we were to construct a bar chart for Figure 3.5, the days of the weeks would be the categories, the other scale would list the possible numbers of twenty-dollar bills presented, and the length of each bar would be the number of twenty-dollar bills presented each day.

—◆—

The data in Table 3.1 are from a telephone service center. These data came from a report which was generated by a computerized monitoring system. The Call Lengths are the times in minutes for calls that came during one hour and which lasted longer than 15 seconds.

Table 3.1: Hourly Call Summary for Service Center Five

Operator I.D.	10:00 to 11:00 am on February 12 Call Lengths (in minutes)								No. of Total Calls	Time
1	10.0	10.7	11.4	10.7	9.8				5	52.6
2	9.1	7.4	6.6	5.8	2.8	16.9			6	48.6
3	13.2	12.3	10.8	10.1					4	46.4
4	10.9	12.2	10.6	12.4					4	46.1
5	14.2	22.0	13.9						3	50.1
6	11.7	10.4	9.7	8.0	6.8	6.1			6	52.7
7	5.4	3.1	16.8	3.2	3.1	5.8	6.3	6.0	8	49.7
8	6.9	7.6	9.0	13.4	15.3				5	52.2
9	6.1	10.3	10.4	7.0	11.2				5	45.0
10	7.5	11.5	12.0	8.1	12.7				5	51.8
11	13.1	9.3	15.0	6.1					4	43.4
12	10.0	19.7	6.6						3	36.3
13	11.0	1.1	2.0	12.5	9.1	5.7	15.3		7	56.7
14	10.0	6.2	6.6	7.3	1.4	2.1	3.2	5.4 5.7	9	47.9
15	15.8	18.3	6.1						3	40.2
16	24.7	11.3	7.6	3.2					4	46.8
17	5.6	9.3	10.3	7.0	8.0				5	40.2
18	9.2	6.1	6.7	8.5	10.5				5	41.0
19	17.8	7.7	9.7						3	35.2
20	16.0	9.2	3.2	7.4	9.3				5	45.1
21	11.3	12.8	11.4						3	35.5
22	10.2	9.6	8.7	1.9	6.4	7.2			6	44.0

Table 3.1 is already a pseudo bar chart: each row shows the number of calls taken by each of the 22 operators during this time period. While some operators logged only three calls, others logged seven, eight, or nine calls. However, these simple counts do not take into account the duration of the calls. We could construct a bar chart to show the Total Connect Time for each of the 22 operators for this hour. This bar chart is shown in Figure 3.6. The Operator IDs are the categories along the bottom and the Total Connect Time is the measure along the vertical scale.

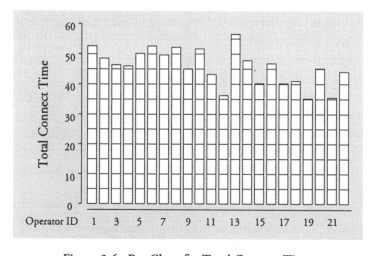

Figure 3.6: Bar Chart for Total Connect Time

The purpose of a bar chart is to compare amounts across categories. The emphasis is upon the length of the bars in the graph, and this is the essential mechanism for the comparisons. The categories may be people, regions, countries, companies, departments, or any classification that makes sense for a given collection of data. Since the purpose is to compare the lengths of the bars, it is customary to begin the scale of possible values with a value of zero. If this scale started with some value other than zero, or if some the intermediate values were suppressed, then the lengths would be distorted and the comparisons would be skewed. The integrity of the comparisons depends upon the lengths of the bars representing the values of the measure of interest.

—◆—

In 1786, William Playfair produced the first known bar chart. It showed the exports and imports for Scotland for the 12-month period from Christmas 1780 to Christmas 1781. A facsimile of this chart is shown in Figure 3.7.

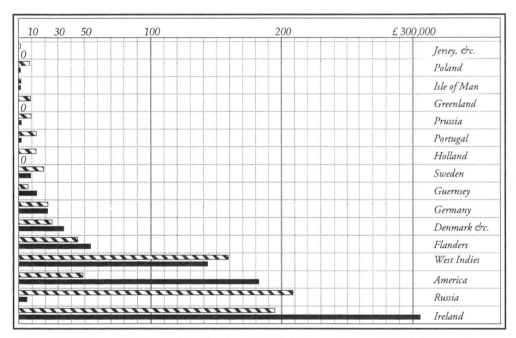

The upright divisions are Ten Thousand Pounds each.   The Black Lines are Exports.   The Ribbed Lines are Imports.

Figure 3.7: The First Known Bar Chart

The categories in Playfair's bar chart consist of those counties, countries, and colonies who were Scotland's trading partners.* He arranged them, in a general way, in order of increasing levels of trade. In this he anticipated a particular form of the bar chart which is in use today—the Pareto chart.

---

* This bar chart was in Playfair's book *The Commercial and Political Atlas*, London, 1786. Several of the interesting graphics in this landmark book were resurrected by Professor Edward R. Tufte in his lovely book *The Visual Display of Quantitative Information*, Graphics Press, Cheshire, Connecticut, 1983.

3.3 Pareto Charts

The Pareto chart is named after an Italian economist, Vilfredo Pareto, who observed in 1897 that 80% of the wealth of a country was held by 20% of the population. Over time it was observed that many different sets of data display this same type of behavior. Most of the problems, most of the defects, most of the costs are due to a minority of the categories. This idea came to be known as the Pareto principle. Therefore, if we can identify the few categories that contribute the greatest amount toward the total number of problems, defects, or costs, then we will know where to concentrate our efforts for improvement.

Whenever possible, costs are the preferred scale to use with the Pareto chart.

The Pareto chart is a bar chart in which the categories have been arranged according to their values. The chart begins with the category having the greatest amount, and then proceeds in the order of progressively smaller amounts. If we rearrange the export data from Playfair's bar chart (Figure 3.7) we get Figure 3.8. This chart shows at a glance that the bulk of Scotland's exports are purchased by three trading partners: Ireland, America, and the West Indies. But does the Pareto principle apply?

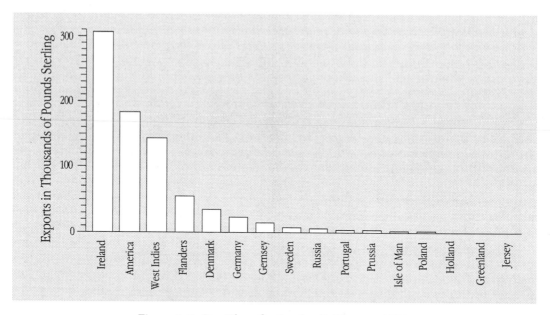

Figure 3.8: Bar Chart for Scotland's Exports, 1781

While some consider Figure 3.8 to already be a Pareto chart, it is easier to interpret the plot if we add a few elements. We begin by extending the vertical scale upward to cover the total amount of all bars combined. In this case, the total amount of Scotland's exports in 1781 was, approximately, £ 783,000. This value will be represented as 100%. In many cases a second scale marked in percentages will be placed on the right-hand side of the Pareto chart. These scales are shown in Figure 3.9.

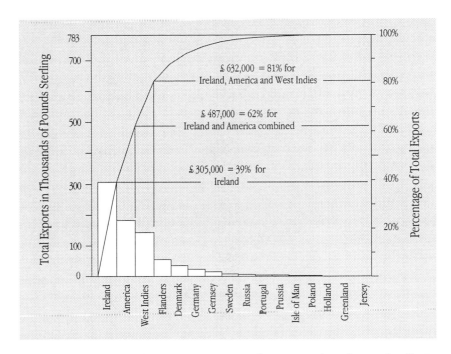

Figure 3.9: Plotting Cumulative Percentages on the Pareto Chart for Scotland's Exports

Next, a cumulative percentage curve is added to the plot. To obtain these cumulative percentages you proceed in the following manner. Beginning with the category on the left, the percentage of the total represented by this one category is computed. For Playfair's data, Ireland bought £ 305,000 out of the £ 783,000 of exports, which is about 39% of the total. This percentage defines the first point (after zero) on the cumulative percentage curve (see Figure 3.9).

Next, the combined amounts for Ireland and America are used. These two countries bought £ 487,000 worth of goods, about 62% of the total. This amount defines a second point on the cumulative percentage curve, which is plotted directly above the right edge of the second bar in Figure 3.9.

Ireland, America, and the West Indies bought £ 632,000 worth of goods, about 81% of the total. This defines the third point on the cumulative percentage curve, and is plotted directly above the right edge of the third bar on the graph.

The points on the cumulative percentage curve are then connected with lines to get the full Pareto chart shown in Figure 3.9.

PRACTICE: Scotland's exports to Flanders amounted to £ 55,000. What is the cumulative percentage that you would use for the fourth point on the cumulative percentage curve in Figure 3.9?

PRACTICE: Scotland's exports to Denmark amounted to £ 35,000. What is the cumulative percentage for the fifth point on the cumulative percentage curve in Figure 3.9?

In Figure 3.9 we see the Pareto principle at work, even though Playfair's bar chart pre-dated Pareto's observation by 116 years. Ireland, America, and the West Indies were three of Scotland's 16 trading partners in 1781. Three out of 16 is about 19 percent, and they accounted for 81 percent of Scotland's exports.

The extra scales and curves added to the bar chart are intended to facilitate the determination of whether or not the Pareto principle applies. While we may be content with Figure 3.8, Figure 3.9 is the preferred form for a Pareto chart.

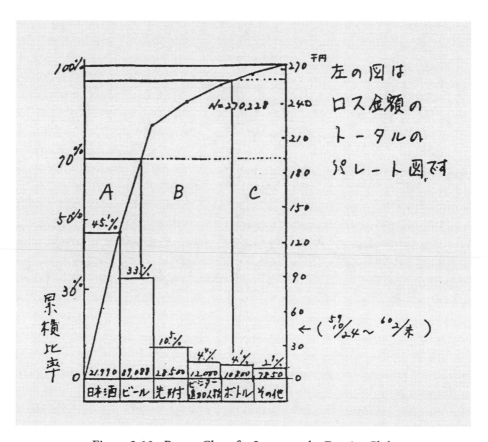

Figure 3.10: Pareto Chart for Losses at the Esquire Club

Figure 3.10 is a Pareto chart prepared by the members of a QC (quality control) Circle whose members were seven waitresses and their supervisor. This chart is an analysis of the sources of monetary losses at the Esquire Club, a nightclub in Osaka, Japan.

The six categories on this Pareto chart are, respectively from left to right: sake, beer, side orders, latecomers, bottle losses, and others. The scale on the left shows the cumulative percentage of total losses. The scale on the right shows the total amount of losses in thousands of Yen. These losses were accumulated over the period from October 24 to the end of February and totaled ¥270,228.

They clearly broke the categories into three groups. Group A contains the losses on beer and sake sales. These two categories accounted for over 70% of the losses. Group B included side orders and losses on service charges due to latecomers. Finally, Group C consisted of the last two categories, which accounted for less than 5% of all losses.

Based on this analysis, the QC Circle began a project to find ways to cut down on the losses on beer and sake sales. They created a flowchart for the various steps in their project, planned the work for a 93-day period, and were able to complete the work in a 113 days, including a 50-day evaluation period. They cut the losses on beer and sake sales by almost 90 percent, and could document these gains.

The Pareto principle, that a minority of categories will account for the vast majority of the problems, is another facet of what has been called the law of diminishing returns. It is a phenomenon that occurs in all types of endeavors, and is therefore seen in all kinds of data. The major use of a Pareto chart is to make that law visible. To deal effectively with problems, we must know where most of the problems occur. When looking for opportunities for improvement, what areas have the greatest (negative) impact upon the operation? Which problems cause the majority of the complaints? Which steps in the process create the majority of errors?

It does not matter whether you are dealing with problems in manufacturing or service processes. Both types of work involve a series of transactions. Each transaction may or may not have a problem. If a transaction has a problem, then the type of problem it has must be determined. Keeping track of the types of problems that you encounter, and the number of times that each problem occurs, will provide the raw data for a Pareto chart.

Flat Pareto Charts

If 20% to 30% of the categories do not account for 70% to 80% of problems, then you have what is known as a flat Pareto chart.

This problem was encountered by a tax collection agency that was attempting to determine which of their problems should be tackled first. They put the problems that they found in a weekly audit of 1260 tax returns on a bar chart and created Figure 3.11.

In Figure 3.11 the third largest count corresponds to the category labeled "Other." If you decide that this category

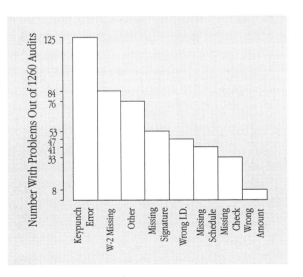

Figure 3.11: Problems with Tax Returns

is one of the "critical few," what are you going to do about it? Because of this problem, catch-all categories are, by convention, placed at the extreme right hand side of the category scale on a Pareto chart. When this is done, and the cumulative percentage curve is added, we see a *flat* Pareto chart in Figure 3.12.

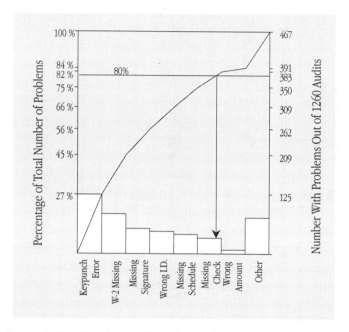

Figure 3.12: Flat Pareto Chart for Problems with Tax Returns

In Figure 3.12 six of the eight categories account for 80% of the problems. This is hardly the Pareto principle at work! The *flat* Pareto chart is usually telling you that *all* the categories are problems. You cannot identify a critical few because they are all alike. This was made apparent the next week. When the data for the next weekly audit were used to construct a Pareto chart, the two leading problems were "Wrong Amount" and "Wrong I.D." And just where were these two categories in Figure 3.12?

This month-to-month rotation of the categories is itself a signal that all of the categories are problematic. When the leading problems one month fade away the next, and former cellar dwellers take over the lead, then all the categories are in need of attention.

One day the Quality Director of a company was describing to one author the Pareto analysis they performed on their warranty claims each year. He complained that the Pareto chart was always flat. Nothing stood out. To which the author replied, "Of course the Pareto is flat, Joe. Your processes are unpredictable, and over the course of a year, every problem has its fifteen minutes of fame! By the end of the year they all average out, giving you a flat Pareto chart."

The rotation of categories from month to month and flat Pareto charts are ways that your process can tell you that it could be a mistake to concentrate on a critical few of the categories. When the same categories persist in the lead position on a Pareto chart month after month, and when the Pareto principle seems to be at work, then you can benefit by concentrating on the critical few.

A patient survey at one hospital included a space for write-in comments. A tabulation of these comments from 73 surveys was used to produce the Pareto chart in Figure 3.13.

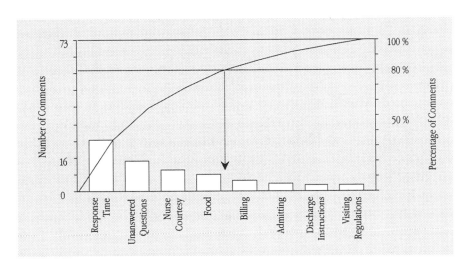

Figure 3.13: Pareto Chart for Patient Complaints

Here it takes 50% of the categories to account for 80% of the complaints. This is hardly the same phenomenon that Vilfredo Pareto described!

The 73 surveys in Figure 3.13 were all surveys on which someone took the effort to write in a complaint. If this is 73 out of one or two hundred surveys, then perhaps these issues need to be addressed. If this is 73 out of one or two thousand surveys, then there may be little merit in this ranking of problems. (Some people will manufacture complaints just because they think they are supposed to fill in the blank space on the survey form; others are just plain troublemakers.) When dealing with count data it is critical to know the "area of opportunity" for the count in order to interpret the count correctly. See Chapter 10 for more about this important concept.

In general, if the vast majority of the problems (say 70% or more) are not attributable to a minority of the categories (say 30% or less), or if the categories take turns "leading the parade," then it will be a mistake to tackle the critical few categories. You will only be chasing the wind. When there are only a few dominant categories, the Pareto chart will help to make them known. When no categories dominate the others, it becomes obvious that all the parts of the process need work.

The power of graphic communication is demonstrated in the Pareto chart. It is especially useful in developing a consensus about which categories to tackle in a problem-solving mode. However, Continual Improvement requires more than merely working on isolated problems. Many problems are built into the system and can only be addressed by changing the system. While it may help to remove the "things gone wrong," it will take more than that to *delight* the customer.

3.4 Histograms and Stem-and-Leaf Plots

Histograms and stem-and-leaf plots are simple ways of organizing large amounts of data to convey a sense of how a collection of values vary. For example, we shall again use the data from the Hourly Call Summary shown in Table 3.1.

Table 3.1: Hourly Call Summary for Service Center Five

Operator I.D.	10:00 to 11:00 am on February 12 Call Lengths (in minutes)									No. of Calls	Total Time
1	10.0	10.7	11.4	10.7	9.8					5	52.6
2	9.1	7.4	6.6	5.8	2.8	16.9				6	48.6
3	13.2	12.3	10.8	10.1						4	46.4
4	10.9	12.2	10.6	12.4						4	46.1
5	14.2	22.0	13.9							3	50.1
6	11.7	10.4	9.7	8.0	6.8	6.1				6	52.7
7	5.4	3.1	16.8	3.2	3.1	5.8	6.3	6.0		8	49.7
8	6.9	7.6	9.0	13.4	15.3					5	52.2
9	6.1	10.3	10.4	7.0	11.2					5	45.0
10	7.5	11.5	12.0	8.1	12.7					5	51.8
11	13.1	9.3	15.0	6.1						4	43.4
12	10.0	19.7	6.6							3	36.3
13	11.0	1.1	2.0	12.5	9.1	5.7	15.3			7	56.7
14	10.0	6.2	6.6	7.3	1.4	2.1	3.2	5.4	5.7	9	47.9
15	15.8	18.3	6.1							3	40.2
16	24.7	11.3	7.6	3.2						4	46.8
17	5.6	9.3	10.3	7.0	8.0					5	40.2
18	9.2	6.1	6.7	8.5	10.5					5	41.0
19	17.8	7.7	9.7							3	35.2
20	16.0	9.2	3.2	7.4	9.3					5	45.1
21	11.3	12.8	11.4							3	35.5
22	10.2	9.6	8.7	1.9	6.4	7.2				6	44.0

The values shown in Table 3.1 are Call Lengths in minutes for 108 calls received during a period of one hour. In order to learn something about the behavior of the Call Length data we could quickly place these 108 values in a "stem-and-leaf plot." To begin this plot we need to obtain a rough idea of what range of values is present in these data. The left-hand portion of the numbers will be used to make up the "stem" of our plot. A quick glance at the data, plus knowledge that these values are minutes, suggests that we can begin our stem with 0 and extend it out to 20 or so. (If we grouped the data in ten-minute intervals we would basically end up with two groups, 0 to 9 and 10 to 19. This would obscure too much detail, so we use one-minute intervals instead.) Thus the stem for our plot would start out like:

0 1 2 3 4 5 6 7 8 9 10 11 12 13 14 15 16 17 18 19 20

Since it is generally easier to create stem-and-leaf plots in a vertical format, we shall rotate the stem as shown in panel (a) of Figure 3.14. Next we read the data and place the right hand portion of each value as the "leaves" on the stem. The first value is 10.0, so we place a "0" leaf beside the 10 position on the stem to mark this value. Moving down the first column of Table 3.1 the second value is 9.1, so a "1" leaf is placed beside the 9 position on the stem to mark this value. These first two values are shown in Panel (a) of Figure 3.14.

The next two values in the first column are 13.2 and 10.9. The placement of these two values is shown in Panel (b) of Figure 3.14.

Continuing in this manner the next 104 values are added to get the stem-and-leaf plot shown in Panel (c) of Figure 3.14:

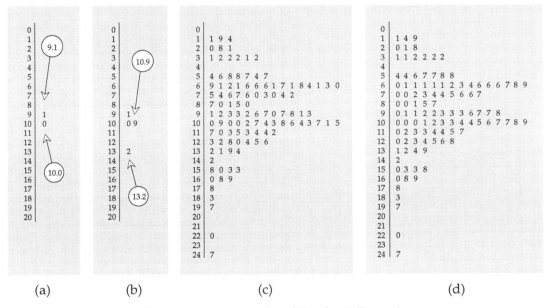

Figure 3.14: Stem-and-Leaf Plot for Call Lengths

PRACTICE: In Panel (c) of Figure 3.14, draw a circle around the next two values (following the 10.9) to be placed on the stem-and-leaf plot.

Finally, by numerically sorting the values on each row of Panel (c) of Figure 3.14, we can completely order the data into the form shown in Panel (d) of Figure 3.14. This last graphic is an elegant combination of table and graph. Each value is preserved, the data have been ranked, and the shape of the histogram is revealed all at the same time. A glance at Panel (d) reveals that the gap around 4 minutes is actually over two minutes long (from 3.2 minutes to 5.4 minutes). The interpretation of this gap would be that any call that lasts much beyond three minutes is complex enough for it to take over five minutes to complete.

For the calls that last more than 5 minutes there are two mounds, one centered around 6 minutes and another centered around 10 minutes. While there is no distinct gap at 8 minutes, there is a distinct valley. There may even be another dip at around 14 minutes, but we would need this dip to persist before it would be worth interpreting. Thus, these data have three or four distinct clusters within the histogram, and all of this is revealed by one of the simplest of graphs.

If the data in Figure 3.14 were reproduced as a histogram, Figure 3.15 would result. Histograms are like the stem-and-leaf plot, but bars replace each stack of "leaves." Thus the main difference between the stem-and-leaf plot of Figure 3.14 and the histogram of Figure 3.15 is that the stem-and-leaf plot preserves the values, while the histogram is a form of a bar chart.

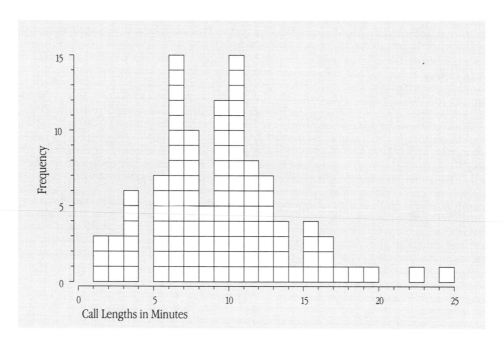

Figure 3.15: Histogram for the Call Lengths

But a different grouping of data could be used. For example, we could use intervals centered on whole numbers. Or we could change the width of the intervals. As the "groupings" for the data become larger, the histogram will become less detailed. For example, if the Call Lengths were grouped in five minute intervals (e.g. 0 to 4.9, 5.0 to 9.9, etc.) then the rather disappointing histogram in Figure 3.16 would be the result. The wider intervals obscure the interesting details in these data.

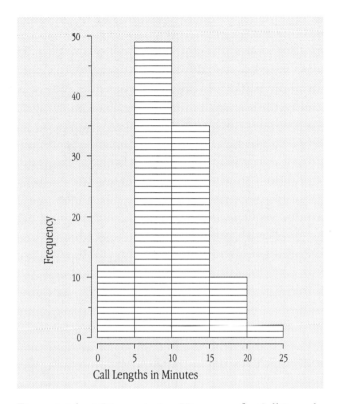

Figure 3.16: A Disappointing Histogram for Call Lengths

The art of creating a histogram lies in selecting intervals that are:

1. easy for the reader to interpret,
2. narrow enough to reveal the interesting details, and
3. wide enough to show how the data "pile up."

Thus, the art of creating a useful histogram involves finding the right balance between the simplification of the overall picture and the loss of detail that is necessarily part of that simplification. This balance point will differ with different data sets. It will depend upon the structure present in the data, the amount of data, and the purpose of the histogram. Constructing a stem-and-leaf plot is one of the best ways to get this feeling for the data, and so the stem-and-leaf plot can be considered to be a preliminary step in preparing a useful histogram.

If the data consist of fewer than 20 or 30 values, the stem-and-leaf plot will generally suffice. When the data consist of hundreds of values, some grouping will generally improve the picture. One common guideline is that there should be about 20 categories, or fewer, in the region where the bulk of the data occur. In the past, elaborate formulas were given as guidelines for establishing the intervals for the horizontal axis of the histogram, but today it is usually simpler to try different sized intervals and let a computer do the work.

Decorated Histograms Are Dangerous and Misleading

Computer programs for histograms bring their own problems—they tend to give you more than you can use. First, they overwhelm you with numerical summaries. Then, they tend to superimpose extra curves on the histogram. To see the impact of these extra curves consider what they do to the histogram of the Call Length Data. The top panel of Figure 3.17 shows the simple, undecorated histogram for these data; the middle panel shows the most common situation where a bell-shaped curve is superimposed on the histogram; and the bottom panel shows a more complex curve fitted to the "shape" of this histogram.

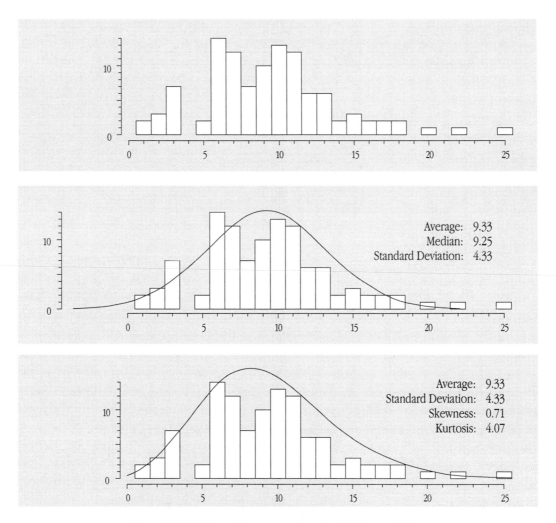

Figure 3.17: Three Histograms for the Call Length Data

The first problem with these superimposed curves is that they are not real—they are purely imaginary. At best, they are a mathematical approximation of reality. They should never be confused with reality itself. At the worst, these curves can be totally misleading.

The second problem with these superimposed curves has to do with the way we see things—notice how your eyes tend to follow the smooth curves. In each case the curves draw your attention away from the gaps at 4 minutes and 8 minutes, while in the top panel your eye tends to follow the tops of the bars. Thus, superimposed curves actually distract, interrupt, and distort the message of the graph.

Finally, which of these superimposed curves is right? You can always come up with many different curves to fit any one histogram. When you have a few hundred observed values, or less, you simply do not have enough information to make an informed choice between the different mathematical approximations. This means that the particular curve which your computer program may display on a histogram is more of a reflection of the assumptions of the programmer than a revelation of the characteristics of the data. Edward R. Tufte coined a technical term for these superimposed curves—he called them "chartjunk." And that is exactly what they are—a waste of ink. So if you use a software package to create histograms, turn off the chartjunk options!

In addition, the computer-generated histograms shown in Figure 3.17 contain another triumph of computation over common sense—who on earth knows (or even cares) about the "skewness" and "kurtosis" for these data? So be careful. It is easier to get much more than you want or can use from computer-generated histograms.

By creating a histogram of the Call Lengths from Table 3.1 we have gained some insight into the system. With an average call length of 9.3 minutes it is unreasonable to expect operators to average more than about 6.5 calls per hour. Therefore, 22 operators will be able to handle an average of 130 to 140 calls per hour. Higher volumes will require more operators. Of course, such generalizations depend upon the degree to which this one hour's worth of data is representative of the way the system performs at other times, with other operators, and with other supervisors.

You should consider using a histogram whenever you want to see how the values for some measure vary. Variation is present in every measure. In subsequent chapters you will learn more about characterizing variation as a way to improve a process. In that context histograms are one of the basic tools for visualizing routine variation.

3.5 Summary of Bar Charts and Running Records

Histograms and Pareto charts are special types of bar charts.

Bar Charts: The distinguishing characteristics of bar charts are:
- One scale is a list of categories.
- The other scale shows the possible values for some measure.
- Each bar displays the value of the measure for a particular category.
- The lengths of the bars make the comparisons between categories.

Pareto Charts: Pareto charts begin life as bar charts:
- Categories are organized according to the height of the bars, except that a miscellaneous category is placed last.
- Costs, rather than counts, are the preferred measure for use in a Pareto chart.
- A cumulative percentage curve adds perspective to the chart and allows you to check to see if the Pareto principle is present.
- The stair-step of the bars and the cumulative percentage curve make the comparisons.

Histograms: The distinguishing characteristics of a histogram are:
- One scale consists of possible values for the observed measure. (Traditionally this scale is on the horizontal axis.)
- The other scale consists of frequency values.
- Each bar on the histogram shows the frequency with which the observed measure falls into the relevant interval.
- The bars show the mounding of the data and the taper-off toward each extreme.

Time-series plots are fundamentally different from bar charts.

Running Records: The distinguishing characteristics of a running record are:
- One scale consists of possible values for the observed measure.
- The other scale consists of time periods.
- The values of this one measure are plotted in their time-order sequence.
- The variation of this measure over time is displayed, and the comparison is a comparison of a single measure *with itself* at different time periods.

Bar charts, by their very nature, use the bars to make comparisons. For this reason the value scale of any bar chart should always begin at zero. Baselines other than zero will distort the comparisons. Additionally, the value scale should have no breaks—all the possible values between zero and the observed values should be represented on the value scale. Finally, the value scales should be linear—that is, one unit at the top of the value scale should represent the same range of values as one unit at the bottom of the scale.

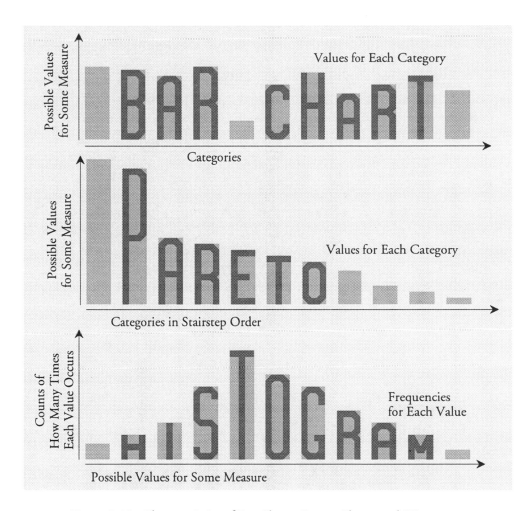

Figure 3.18: Characteristics of Bar Charts, Pareto Charts, and Histograms

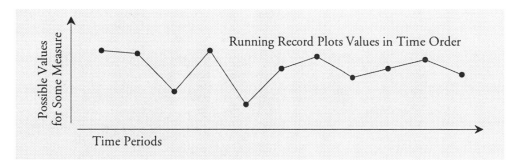

3.19: How a Running Record Differs from Bar Charts, Pareto Charts, and Histograms

Bar charts and running records do different jobs. Bar charts are useful for comparing different categories, at a single point in time, using a single measure. Histograms compare the frequency with which the different values of a single measure occur without respect to their time order. A running record uses a single measure, for a single category, and compares this measure with itself at different points in time.

It is important that you recognize the different roles for these different graphs, otherwise you cannot use them effectively.

The bar chart in Figure 3.20 uses a common measure, quarterly sales, to compare six regions. It is a snapshot taken at one point in time. While a common measure is apparently being used, there are no guarantees that the measure is computed in the same manner from region to region. Neither is there anything that says that the regions should be comparable. This graph merely shows the relative contributions of the different regions to the total sales of the corporation. The emphasis in Figure 3.20 is upon the height of each bar. It is the amounts that are being compared, not the trends over time. The time element in Figure 3.20 is static. While the comparisons of Figure 3.20 may allow us to rank the six regions, they do not provide any insight into what is happening to the sales in each region.

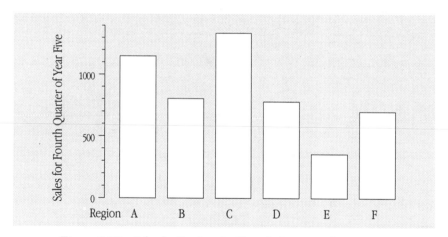

Figure 3.20: Sales by Region for Fourth Quarter of Year Five.

Unlike the bar graph above, the running record in Figure 3.21 shows how the sales in Region D have varied over the past 20 quarters.

When the emphasis is upon the amounts for different categories, bars make the interesting characteristics apparent and easy to grasp. But when the emphasis is upon the variation over time, the use of bars is distracting and inappropriate. Consider what happens when the time-series of Figure 3.21 masquerades as a bar chart in Figure 3.22.

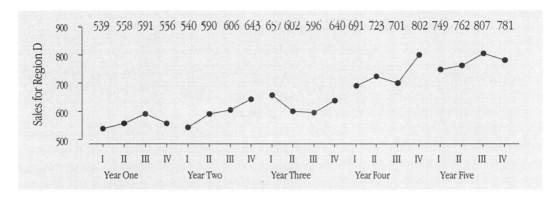

Figure 3.21: Running Record Quarterly Sales for Region D

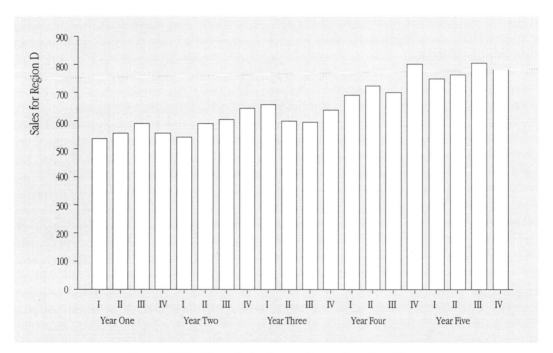

Figure 3.22: Time-Series Pretending to be a Bar Chart

Figure 3.22 contains the same information as Figure 3.21—it presents the time-order sequence of the quarterly sales values, but it does so in an awkward and inefficient manner. Over half of the vertical scale is wasted. All of the variation is crowded into the upper portion of the vertical scale. So while the overall trend is visible, the details are obscured by the use of bars rather than connected points. Our eyes get lost in the "clutter" of the skyline and the vertical emphasis of the graph itself. While you may get away with the graphs like Figure 3.22, the use of a bar graph to represent a time-series is not good practice. It is not exactly incorrect, but it is a sign of naiveté.

3.6 Pie Charts

Pie charts perform a job that is similar to that of a bar chart. They compare the amounts for various categories at a fixed point in time. However, rather than dealing with the actual amounts, they convert these amounts into percentages of the total amount, and then show these percentages as pieces of pie.

Pie charts are not easy to construct by hand, but today's software makes them available at the click of a button. They show the relative proportion due to each of several categories. For example the data in Table 3.2 consist of a breakdown of the operating expenses, in thousands of dollars, for two months. The pie charts for September and October are shown in Figure 3.23. There you can see which categories amounted to the biggest proportion of the total expenses for each month.

Table 3.2: Operating Expenses

	September		October	
Compensation	127.6	36.6%	125.2	36.5%
Benefits	17.0	4.9%	17.0	5.0%
Depreciation	36.0	10.3%	18.8	5.5%
Advertising	64.4	18.5%	121.2	35.3%
Travel	67.5	19.4%	19.3	5.6%
Operations	36.2	10.3%	41.5	12.1%
Total	348.7	100 %	343.0	100 %

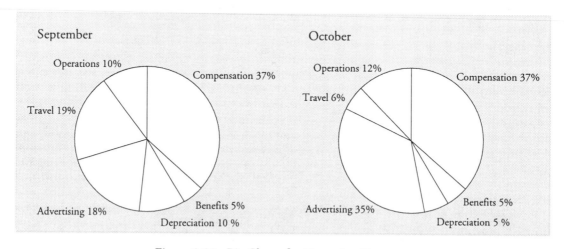

Figure 3.23: Pie Charts for Operating Expenses

While the advertising expenses went up in October, the travel expenses declined. While pie charts provide a visual breakdown for the data, they do not provide a comparison between the totals for each month. Can you tell from Figure 3.23 which month had the greater total expenses? No—you will need to look in Table 3.2 to answer this question. This is why pie charts should always be presented with a table of values—so they do not obscure more than they reveal.

Pie charts provide interesting and useful descriptions of the data. And if all you are trying to convey is a general impression of the relative contributions of different categories to a total, the pie chart will suffice. But if you are trying to compare amounts, or make careful distinctions between similar values, the pie chart will be unsatisfactory. This is because people have more difficulty in distinguishing differences in angles than in distinguishing different heights of bars. And this problem becomes more severe when the circles are distorted into ellipses, as is commonly done with pie charts.

Therefore, while you may use pie charts for simple descriptions, you will need to go beyond pie charts to really understand your processes.

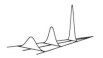

-

Chapter Four

Graphical Purgatory

Unlike William Playfair, who drew his graphs by hand using India ink, today we have the ability to generate many different graphs almost instantaneously using any of the popular spreadsheet programs. But not all change is progress. Along with the proliferation of graphing options has come an abundance of chartjunk, decoration, and inappropriate graphics. This chapter is intended to help you create good graphs by taking you on a guided tour of "graphical purgatory"—a territory in which many of you live and work.

Throughout this chapter we will make use of the data in Table 4.1. The values shown are the quarterly sales figures for each of six regions. Each column pertains to a single region, and within each column the first four values are the average quarterly sales for each year, while the last four values shown are the actual quarterly sales for Year Five.

Table 4.1: Average Quarterly Sales and Last Year's Quarterly Sales

Year		Region A	Region B	Region C	Region D	Region E	Region F
One	Averages	1007	1251	1076	561	402	443
Two	Averages	929	1130	1145	595	422	511
Three	Averages	1076	1030	1200	624	425	405
Four	Averages	941	902	1342	729	431	556
Five	Quarter I	1,041	939	1,330	749	420	588
	Quarter II	1,020	834	1,003	762	454	699
	Quarter III	976	688	1,197	807	447	743
	Quarter IV	1,148	806	1,337	781	359	702

4.1 Computer-Generated Bar Charts

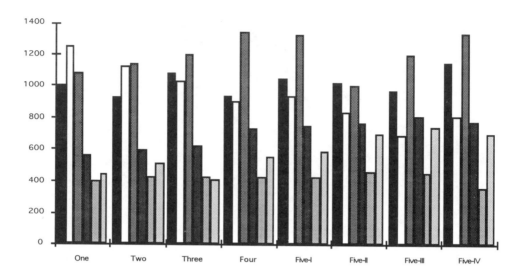

Figure 4.1: A Simple Bar Graph

The default option for many programs is a bar chart. When the values of Table 4.1 are plotted using this option the result might look like Figure 4.1.

The bar chart in Figure 4.1 can hardly be said to be an improvement on the table. In the table we at least had rows and columns to differentiate the region-to-region variation from the year-to-year variation—reading across each row showed the variation between regions, while reading down a column showed the variation over time for a single region. Figure 4.1 shows both the year-to-year information and the region-to-region information along a single (horizontal) axis—which makes this graph harder to use than the table!

But wait. Did not Playfair (Figure 3.7) show imports and exports for each region on his bar chart? Yes, but while a bar chart with two values for each of 16 categories may be complex, it is still comprehensible. A bar chart such as Figure 4.1 which has six values for each of eight categories is merely confusing.

Good graphics should amplify and clarify a table of values, not compete with it.

Another problem with Figure 4.1 is the horrible (automatic) shading. The solid black bars catch your eye. The white bars disappear, and the gray bars simply vibrate. This vibration is essentially an op-art effect that is the result of high contrast, narrow bars, and the heavy black lines outlining each bar. All in all, Figure 4.1 is a failure to communicate combined with bad art.

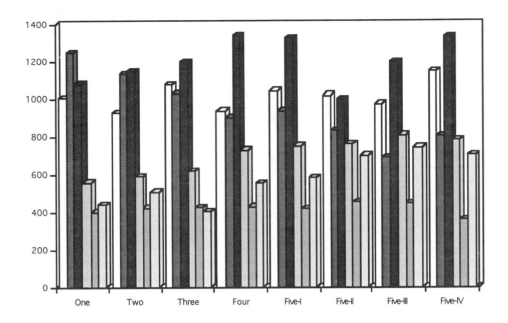

Figure 4.2: A Three-Dimensional Bar Chart

But things can get worse. Figure 4.2 is a decorated version of Figure 4.1.

While this bar chart still has two dimensions (regions and years) compressed onto a single horizontal axis, it adds a third dimension for the sake of decoration. Making the bars of Figure 4.1 into three-dimensional sticks does not improve things any.

The problem with Figure 4.1 is confusion about what is being represented. The problem with Figure 4.2 is that it is decorated confusion.

Both Figures 4.1 and 4.2 use different shades for the different bars. With six regions for each time period, six different shades are used. While you may get away with using two shades or colors, three or more shades tend to create so much visual confusion that they hurt the overall graph. In general, if you have to use different shades for the bars of a bar chart you are probably trying to present too much information in a single graph.

The objective of using graphs
to communicate numerical information
is to make it easy for your readers
to understand the information.

If the graph is not easier to understand
than the table of numbers,
then the graph is a failure.

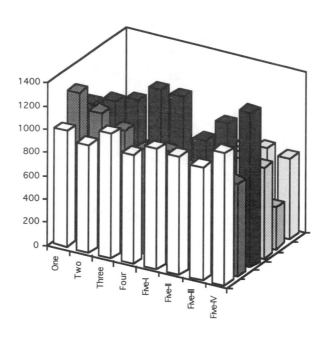

Figure 4.3: Another Three-Dimensional Bar Graph

Figure 4.3 might be considered to be an improvement over Figure 4.2 because it does at least use the third dimension to represent the different regions.

While this graph is very pretty, only 25 of the 48 values in the table are visible. If we make a distinction between ink used for decoration and ink used to represent the data, the problem of Figure 4.3 is that some of the data-ink is hidden behind the bars. For this reason this plot is also less useful than the table of values. This graph calls more attention to itself than it does to the data it is supposedly trying to present. When ornamentation overwhelms the message, the result is pure chartjunk.

4.2 Computer-Generated Running Records

Figure 4.4 displays the same shortcoming that was seen in Figure 4.3: most of the values are hidden.

Figure 4.5 removes the solid volumes under each time series in Figure 4.4, which does clarify the situation some. However, the limitations of projecting three dimensions into two dimensions results in some confusion as to which ribbon belongs to which region. Is it obvious that the black ribbon is Region C? To which region does the lowest ribbon belong? In fact, which is the lowest ribbon?

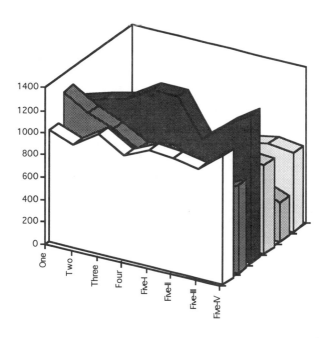

Figure 4.4: A Three-Dimensional Running Record

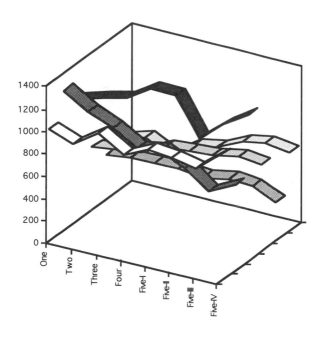

Figure 4.5: A Three-Dimensional Ribbon Chart

Perhaps we should abandon efforts at decorating our graph. Let's try a simple graph with six running records.

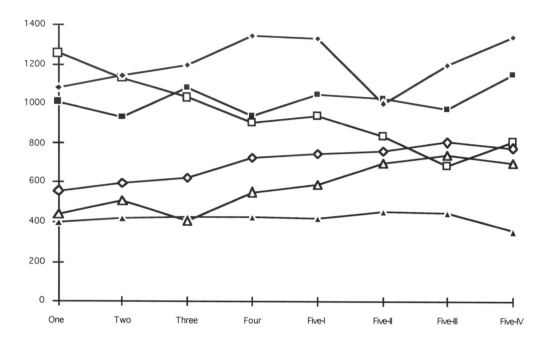

Figure 4.6: Running Records for Six Regions

While Figure 4.6 may not be as colorful or as decorated as the preceding figures, it is intelligible, it is useful, and it communicates clearly, without distortion.

The different sizes for the "dots," and the heavy black lines combine to make this graph look very amateurish, but it is still a vast improvement over the five preceding graphs. In fact, out of the six different graphs considered so far, only this graph is an improvement upon the table of values. With the addition of a legend, Figure 4.6 could essentially replace Table 4.1.

No matter how decorated, no matter how colorful, no matter how traditional, a graph that does not clearly and honestly present the data is worse than useless. When the graphs are simple enough, some decoration may be acceptable, but it is very easy for the decoration to overwhelm the data...

Decoration is not analysis.

4.3 Stacked Bars and Linear Pie Charts

Another way that the data of Table 4.1 might be plotted is as a set of segmented bars.

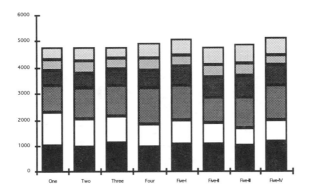

Figure 4.7: A Stacked Bar Chart

Figure 4.7 does overcome the basic problem of Figure 4.1. Seven time series (six regions plus the total) are shown stacked up on top of each other, while the regions are compared within each bar. However, bars are still a poor way to show time series data.

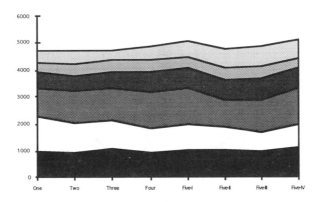

Figure 4.8: A Linear Pie Chart

Figure 4.8 is a linear pie chart. It is a definite improvement over Figure 4.7.

Of the eight different ways of plotting the data of Table 4.1 which have been considered, only Figures 4.6 and 4.8 are friendly to the reader. Only these two, which are the least decorated, least busy, and least splashy of the lot communicate the information of Table 4.1 to the reader.

4.4 Radar Plots

Finally, there are graphics which are so far from being useful that they are positive snares—graphics that are guaranteed to entrap, confuse, and alienate the reader.

Radar plots belong in this category. The radar plot presents the same information as a traditional graph, but it uses polar coordinates to do so. For example compare Figure 4.6 with the radar plot in Figure 4.9. The six points for Year One are plotted on the 12 o'clock axis of the radar plot; the six points for Year Two are plotted on the 1:30 axis; the six points for Year Three are plotted on the 3 o'clock axis, etc. So a horizontal line in Figure 4.6 becomes a "circle" in Figure 4.9. Which of these two plots is easier to interpret correctly?

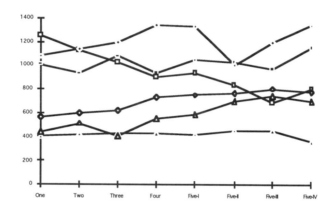

Figure 4.6: The Regional Sales for Six Regions (repeated)

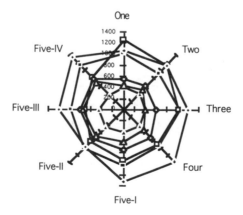

Figure 4.9: The Regional Sales for Six Regions as a Radar Plot

If we change the perspective, and let each axis on the radar plot represent a region we get Figure 4.10.

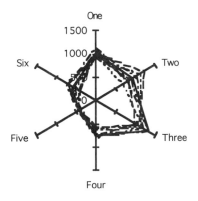

Figure 4.10: Radar Plot for Regional Sales

This plot attempts to compare the six regions. (As if they should be the same!) (In case you have difficulty interpreting the radar plot in Figure 4.10, the same information is shown in an unwrapped form in Figure 4.11.) These figures might be interpreted as follows: Region One (A) is consistently near 1000; Region Two (B) is highly variable; Region Three (C) is also variable, but at a higher level; Regions Four (D) and Five (E) are consistent at a low level, and Region Six (F) is variable at a low level. While this may seem like interesting information about the six regions, you can learn more about each of these regions by using Figure 4.6. Figure 4.10 does not produce any insight that cannot be obtained more easily some other way, and it can be misleading.

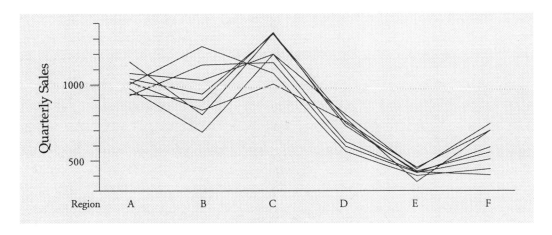

Figure 4.11: The Radar Plot of Figure 4.10 Replotted

Figures 4.10 and 4.11 connect the points from region to region, rather than showing the variation over time. They connect things which are known to be different (and therefore are not comparable), while they fail to reveal the time ordered sequence that exists in these data. This is why Figures 4.10 and 4.11 are meager and unsatisfactory plots.

Radar plots also distort the data they present. Consider what happens to the pair of parallel lines shown on the left of Figure 4.12. On a radar plot they become a pair of spirals which, segment by segment, are definitely not parallel.

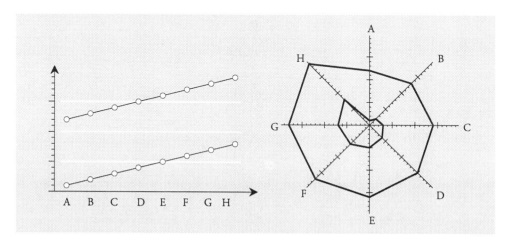

Figure 4.12: What a Radar Plot Does to Parallel Lines

Thus, by replacing the customary rectangular coordinates with polar coordinates, the radar plot substitutes angles for parallel lines, distorts the relationships between levels, and in general, plots simple data in a complex manner which is virtually guaranteed to confuse the reader. Radar plots are pure obfuscation, and should not be used under any circumstances.

4.5 Improving the Two Best Computer Graphs of Table 4.1

Figures 4.6 and 4.8 are the two best computer-generated representations of the data in Table 4.1. These two graphs are reformatted in Figures 4.13 and 4.14.

Figure 4.8 was already much better than most of the other computer generated graphs, but it could still be improved. The first improvement is to lose the shading. The different intensities of the different shades distracts the eye. Next the heavy lines are replaced with lighter lines. The result is Figure 4.13, which shows the total sales for the eight time periods, and shows the relative contribution of each region to these totals.

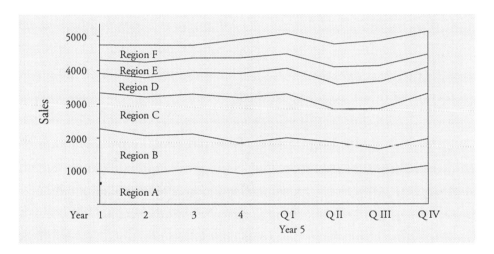

Figure 4.13: Improved Version of Linear Pie Chart

In Figure 4.13 the stacked bands show the total sales, but the stack makes it more difficult to interpret the information about any one region. For example, is it clear from Figure 4.13 that Region D's sales are growing? Is it clear from Figure 4.13 that Region C's sales are essentially unchanged?

While Figure 4.13 attempts to provide information about seven time series, six of these series are represented by the width of a band, rather than a simple curve. On the other hand, Figure 4.14 shows the six time series as six curves.

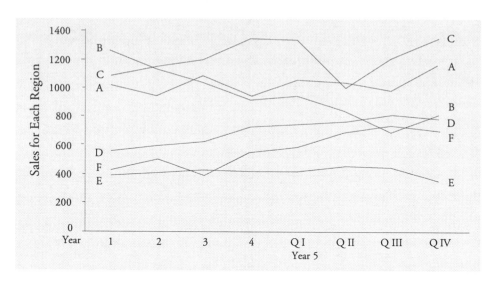

Figure 4.14: Improved Version of Running Records for Six Regions

In Figure 4.14 we modify Figure 4.6. One way to improve Figure 4.6 is to replace the heavy lines with lighter lines. It is the continuity of the line that attracts our eye, and with a time series the lines are merely connectors to lead our eyes to the points, therefore light lines are more friendly than heavy lines. Another way to improve Figure 4.6 is to lose the awkward points on the curve. In this case we can leave the points out. This is possible because the six "curves" are sufficiently easy to follow (they do not overlap too much). Also, because of the low amount of overlap we can label each curve to enhance the interpretation of the graph. Finally, the graph is improved by moving the vertical scale over to the left so that it does not compete with the data.

So while Figure 4.13 provides a neat representation of these data, Figure 4.14 reveals more real information.

4.6 Summary

Less is more.

Chapter Five

Some Arithmetic

In the previous chapters we looked at graphical summaries of data. Before we continue we need to spend some time discussing some computations and concepts that will be used in the remainder of this book.

First we will look at the common numerical summaries used with collections of data. Then we will make some observations on the relationships between ratios, percentages, and proportions. Next is a discussion about the number of digits to use. Finally the problem of using the right tools in the wrong way will be discussed.

5.1 Measures of Location

The first class of numerical summaries consists of measures of location. These statistics characterize the "location" of the "mid-point" of the data in different ways. We shall be concerned with only two measures of location: averages and medians.

Averages

The simplest measure of location for a set of values is the arithmetic average. This is the first statistic taught in school, and is widely used. It is found by adding up the values and dividing the sum by the number of values.

For the data { 3, 5, 2, 6, 2, 1, 9, 1, 7 } the arithmetic average is:

$$\frac{3+5+2+6+2+1+9+1+7}{9} = \frac{36}{9} = 4.0$$

If we use the symbol X to denote our values, then we denote the average of a set of X values by placing a bar over the X to create the symbol:

$$\bar{X} = \text{average of the } X \text{ values}$$

The arithmetic average is the balance point for the data. If we constructed a simple histogram for our data, the average would be the balance point for the histogram. The nine

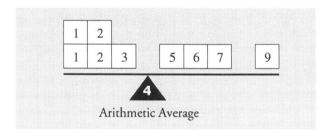

Figure 5.1: The Average as Balance Point

values $\{3, 5, 2, 6, 2, 1, 9, 1, 7\}$ are shown in this way in Figure 5.1.

For simplicity in this book, whenever the word average is used we will be referring to the arithmetic average.

Medians

A second measure of location is the median. A median divides a set of values into two halves, thus a median defines the fiftieth percentile for the data.

If we use the symbol X to denote our values, it is customary to denote the median for these values by using a tilde (~) above the X, creating the symbol:

$$\tilde{X} = \text{median of the } X \text{ values}$$

To find the median for the nine numbers

$$\{3, 5, 2, 6, 2, 1, 9, 1, 7\}$$

we begin by arranging them in ascending order:

$$\{1, 1, 2, 2, 3, 5, 6, 7, 9\}$$

Since this data set contains $n = 9$ values, the median will be the middle value in this ordered listing:

$$\tilde{X} = 3$$

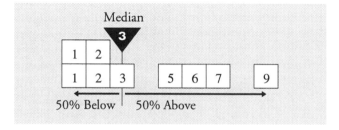

Figure 5.2: The Median as Fiftieth Percentile

*Whenever n is an odd number
the median will be the middle value
from the ordered listing of the set of values.*

To find the median for the six values in the data set

$$\{ 12, 15, 18, 19, 14, 16 \}$$

we again arrange the values in ascending order:

$$\{ 12, 14, 15, 16, 18, 19 \}$$

Since this data set has $n = 6$ values the median will be the average of the two middle values from this ordered listing:

$$\tilde{X} = \frac{15 + 16}{2} = 15.5$$

*Whenever n is an even number
the median will be the average of the two middle values
from the ordered listing of the set of values.*

Because of the possibility of several values being equal to the median, we have to interpret a median in the following way:

- Fifty percent, or more, of the data will be greater than, or equal to, the median;

- and fifty percent, or more, of the data will be less than, or equal to, the median.

In Figure 5.2, five out of the nine values are less than or equal to 3, while five out of the nine values are greater than or equal to 3.

5.2 Measures of Dispersion

Once we have summarized the location of the data by characterizing the balance point (by using an average) or the fiftieth percentile (by using a median), our next question concerns how the data are spread out around this location.

Ranges

The first, and simplest, measure of dispersion is the range. It is defined to be the difference between the *maximum* value and the *minimum* value. It characterizes the total spread of the data, and is commonly denoted by the capital letter R:

$$R = \text{Maximum} - \text{Minimum}$$

For the data set $\{ 3, 5, 2, 6, 2, 1, 9, 1, 7 \}$ the maximum value is 9, the minimum value is 1, so the range is $R = 9 - 1 = 8$ units.

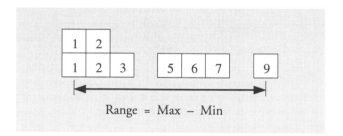

Figure 5.3: The Range is the Spread for the Data

If all the values are identical, the maximum value will be the same as the minimum value and the range will be zero.

The range is intuitive and natural to use. Therefore we shall use it throughout this book. Along with the range you should also report how many values were used to compute the range. To see why this is the case consider what would happen if we were to add more data to the histogram in Figure 5.3. Some values would fall in between the values of 1 and 9, and these values would not change the range. But some values might fall above 9, while some values might fall below 1, and these values would affect the range. Therefore, as the number of data points in the histogram increase, we expect to see larger values for the range. This is why we will always need to know just how many values are spanned by the range. In Figure 5.3, the range spans $n = 9$ data. This value for n is needed to properly interpret any range value.

There are several other measures of dispersion in use today. For small data sets they offer little advantage over the range. However, with the computational power now available, you are likely to encounter some of these other measures of dispersion. Therefore, even though we will not explicitly use them, it is necessary to describe the most common alternatives to the range: the root mean square deviation and the sample standard deviation.

Root Mean Square Deviations

The root mean square deviation is denoted by many different symbols. We shall use the symbol s_n to represent this measure of dispersion. When taken in reverse order the four words "root mean square deviation" define the four steps required for the computation of this measure of dispersion. They are:

1. Find the *deviations*: measure the amount by which each point deviates from the arithmetic average.

2. *Square* the deviations from Step 1.

3. Find the *mean* of the squared deviations: i.e., find the *average* of the squared deviations.

4. Find the square *root* of the average of the squared deviations.

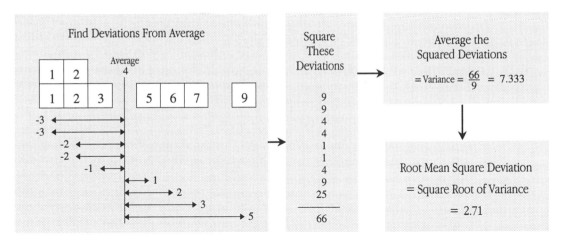

Figure 5.4: The Root Mean Square Deviation as a Measure of Dispersion

These four steps are illustrated in Figure 5.4. For the data set { 3, 5, 2, 6, 2, 1, 9, 1, 7 } the root mean square deviation is $s_n = \sqrt{7.333} = 2.71$ units.

There is no simple physical interpretation for the root mean square deviation. It is technically the square root of the rotational inertia, but this interpretation is too esoteric to be of any practical use.

Sample Standard Deviations

A measure of dispersion more commonly used today is the sample standard deviation, s. This statistic for dispersion is quite similar to the root mean square deviation, except that in Step 3 you divide by $(n-1)$ rather than n. This makes a slight difference in the value obtained, but it still contains the same basic information about dispersion.

For the data set { 3, 5, 2, 6, 2, 1, 9, 1, 7 } the sample standard deviation would be:

$$s = \sqrt{\frac{66}{8}} = \sqrt{8.25} = 2.87 \text{ units}$$

While the notation used here is the mainstream notation for these statistics, the advent of computers and calculators has seriously undermined this notation. The only way to be sure just which number you may be getting is to check out the divisor in the formula. This inconsistency of notation, along with the fact that some calculators allow you to compute both the sample standard deviation and the root mean square deviation, are two more good reasons for using the range.

Using Numerical Summaries

Numerical summaries are simply the result of some arithmetic—do *this* with your data and you will get *that* summary value. Since arithmetic cannot create meaning, the interpretation of any numerical summary will depend upon the original data used in the computation. This means that you must think about the nature of your data and make sure that the numerical summary you are computing makes sense for the data you are using. For example, a spreadsheet program does not have any inhibitions about computing the average for a set of telephone numbers—but hopefully you know better than to do this.

This obvious concept that the meaning of any numerical summary depends on the context for the original values is increasingly important because of the computational power available to us today. In order to avoid a "triumph of computation over common sense" it is important for you to think about the nature of your data. Not all data are suitable for the computations above. Numbers which are used as labels should not be summarized numerically. Numbers which quantify some process characteristic may be suitable for a numerical summary. The presence of numbers does not mean that numerical summaries need to be computed. Think first, and then think "statistically."

5.3 Ratios, Percentages, and Proportions

Many of the measures used in business are ratios. Some of these ratios are percentages, and some of these percentages are proportions. In the interest of clear thinking it is helpful to distinguish between these different types of ratios.

Ratios

If you want to know your gas mileage you have to record more than the number of miles between fill-ups; you also need to know how many gallons were used. To characterize fuel consumption, we divide the number of miles driven between fill-ups by the number of gallons needed to fill the tank.

$$\frac{\text{number of miles driven}}{\text{number of gallons consumed}} = \text{miles per gallon}$$

This is an example of a measure that is a ratio. Many management numbers are ratios—frequently the value for one measure is adjusted by dividing by the value for another measure. Ratios such as these will be described by the units attached. In the example above, the label "miles per gallon" describes the ratio—miles go in the numerator, while gallons go in the denominator. This label also helps to prevent an accidental inversion of this ratio; you are not likely to confuse "miles per gallon" with "gallons per mile." Another example of this type of ratio would be the number of dollars spent by a school system divided by the average daily attendance (dollars per student).

Many aspects of operations require the use of ratios. For example, consider a bank with branch offices throughout a city. A small branch office in a residential area is not likely to have the same number of transactions, or the same dollar volume, as a larger branch office located in a commercial district. So how can you compare the two offices? How can you decide on the appropriate level of staffing? If you divide the number of transactions in a week at a branch by the number of teller-hours worked that week you obtain the ratio of transactions per teller-hour. The adjustment of some direct measure of activity by a measure of opportunity is common in all types of businesses. In order to understand fully such ratios it is necessary to understand each measure and the assumptions used in the calculation of each measure.

The ratios described above have the following characteristic in common. The units of measurement for the numerator are different from the units of measurement for the denominator. When this is the case the ratio may be conveniently described by the units as [numerator units] per [denominator units]. But what happens when the numerator and the denominator are measured in the same units? It would be strange to talk about "miles per mile," or "dollars per dollar." So in this case, we express the ratio as a percentage.

Percentages

Percentages are a type of ratio. A ratio is commonly expressed as a percentage when the numerator and the denominator have the same measurement units. A percentage is therefore a ratio where the two measures have the same measurement units, and which has had the decimal place shifted over two spaces to the right. This shift of the decimal is similar to the conversion from dollars to cents, and is merely a matter of convenience. Which is easier to say: "Auto imports constituted 21 percent of the trade deficit last month." or, "The ratio of the auto imports to the total trade deficit last month was 0.21." More importantly, which is easier to understand? If you want to communicate the ratio of two measures which have the same measurement unit, use percentages.

Ratios   Percentages

Figure 5.5: Percentages Are a Subset of the Class of All Ratios

In another chapter an example will use a set of accounts receivable data. Rather than looking at the accounts receivable values in their raw form, these values will be adjusted— they will be divided by the total sales over the past three months. Since both numerator and denominator are measured in dollars, we will express this ratio as a percentage.

Proportions

All percentages are ratios. But only some percentages are proportions.

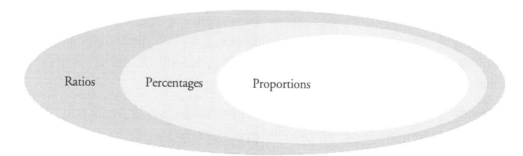

Figure 5.6: Proportions Are a Subset of the Class of All Percentages

A percentage becomes a proportion when the denominator limits or restricts the numerator in some way. For example, for a given time period, the ratio of

$$\frac{\text{the sales for one region}}{\text{the total sales for the whole organization}}$$

would be a proportion because the sales for one region cannot be any greater than the sales for the whole organization. The denominator places a limit on the value of the numerator. This is why proportions must always fall between 0.00 and 1.00 (0% to 100%).[*]

Another example of a proportion would be the ratio of

$$\frac{\text{number of transactions at the drive-in window}}{\text{total number of transactions}}$$

for a given time period at a single bank office. Once again, the numerator is restricted by the denominator. However, the ratio of

$$\frac{\text{accounts receivable in dollars}}{\text{three month sales in dollars}}$$

would not be a proportion. If a company had some large invoices go uncollected for more than 90 days, their accounts receivable could exceed the total sales for the past three months. Thus, the denominator does not limit the numerator, and this ratio is not a proportion.

There are several ways of expressing this special relationship between numerator and denominator that is the hallmark of a proportion. One way is to say that the denominator represents the "area of opportunity" for the numerator. Another way is to say that with a proportion "numerator plus something equals denominator." Both of these expressions characterize the limitation that is the essential characteristic of all proportions.

---

[*] At this time we are not making a distinction between the alternate expressions of a proportion as a dimensionless ratio or as a percentage. In Chapter Eleven some calculations require the use of proportions as dimensionless ratios.

While this distinction between ratios, percentages, and proportions will not be critical with regard to the methods of analysis given in this book, it will help you to avoid the embarrassment of confusing one type of ratio with another. Moreover, clear thinking about the nature of various ratios will help you to construct ratios that will be useful in your work.

5.4 How Many Digits Do You Need?

How many digits should you use with your percentages? The sentence "Auto imports constituted 21.0 percent of the trade deficit last month" works, but "Auto imports constituted 21.0526 percent of the trade deficit last month" is more than our minds want or need to absorb. The extra digits are visual clutter, providing unwanted information. Because of our familiarity with decimal monetary systems it will usually suffice to report percentages to the nearest whole number (21 percent). Occasionally one decimal place will be acceptable (21.2 percent). More than one decimal place will be excessive in most situations.

When it comes to making sense of numbers it is generally sufficient to use three-digit or four-digit values. Consider a measure that we all come in contact with—our own weight. Weights may be recorded in various units. In England, for example, one stone is equal to 14 pounds, so a 200 pound man would be listed as being "a little over 14 stone." In this system of measurement a one-unit increment would amount to one part in 14, or about 7 parts per hundred (also known as 7 percent). While your weight in stones may be sufficiently precise for a general description, think about how absurd it would be to say: "I've starved myself for two months and still haven't lost a stone." (Which is presumably why the English also use pounds to measure their weights.)

By recording our weight in pounds we get values that commonly use three digits. For a 200 pound man a one-pound increment is one part in 200, or about one-half of one percent of the total. The use of pounds gives us a "parts-per-hundred" precision in the value reported.

But newborns are not weighed in pounds! They are weighed in pounds and ounces. Why do we do this? Because, for a typical newborn baby, an increment of one pound is one part in six or seven and this is not sufficiently precise. By using pounds and ounces we change the precision. There are 16 ounces per pound, so six pounds is equal to 96 ounces, and by recording the weights of newborns to pounds and ounces we once again have characterized weight to the nearest parts-per-hundred level of precision. But with adults, the use of ounces would be excessive. A 200 pound man would be 3,200 ounces, and so a one-ounce increment would consist of one part per 3200, or about 3 parts-per-ten-thousand.

Finally, if you were to record your weight in grams, of which there are about 28 per ounce, a person weighing approximately 14 stone would be about 90,000 grams. A one-gram increment would therefore be about one part-per-hundred-thousand. Excessive precision indeed! However, since 90,000 grams is 90 kilograms, recording weights to the nearest kilogram is again sufficient to give approximate parts-per-hundred precision.

What about heights? Do we measure how tall we are to the nearest foot or the nearest meter? No, we use inches or centimeters. For most individuals the use of inches gives a precision of one part in 60, while the use of centimeters gives a precision of one part in 150.

These common approaches to measuring weights and heights give us a clue to the way we use and interpret data. In most cases we are content with knowing a value to the nearest parts-per-hundred or parts-per-thousand level. Rarely do we need greater precision than this. When our measurement unit is so large that it does not allow for approximate parts-per-hundred precision, we tend to shift to smaller increments. When our measurement unit is sufficient to allow better than parts-per-hundred precision we begin to round off the values in the interest of simplicity.

To achieve this level of precision in our measures we will generally need to record values to at least three or four digits. Since arithmetic operations can introduce round-off errors, it is always better to err on the side of slightly more digits than fewer. Therefore, four or five digits will suffice for most routine business computations. While there is nothing wrong with letting your computer or calculator work with eight-digit numbers, you will commonly find it helpful to round such numbers off to three or four digits when communicating with others.

5.5 Comparing Apples and Oranges

You can pick the best graphic format, and compute the best numerical summaries, and still end up with nonsense because you are comparing apples to oranges.

In Chapter Four every graphic was created using the data of Table 4.1. The first four rows of Table 4.1 consist of averages. The last four rows of Table 4.1 consist of quarterly values. And while it might be nice to compare the current value with some historical average value (so you can be happy about half the time), there is a problem in placing averages and individual values side by side. Averages can never vary as much as the individual values will vary.

This difference between the variation of individual values and the variation of averages is the result of the arithmetic of computing an average. It will happen in spite of extraneous issues such as seasonal effects and yearly trends. To illustrate this effect Table 5.1 contains 192 counts obtained from a bead box. Each of these counts is the number of yellow beads in a sample of 50 beads drawn from the bead box.

If we think of each count as a "monthly value," we could average each group of 12 counts to obtain an average for each "year." The histograms for the 192 counts and the 16 "annual averages" are shown in Figure 5.7.

Table 5.1: Monthly Counts and Average Counts

Counts												Averages
11	4	6	4	5	7	5	4	7	12	4	2	5.92
4	5	6	4	2	2	5	9	5	6	5	9	5.17
8	6	5	7	3	2	5	8	6	7	6	5	5.67
5	4	2	7	11	5	6	4	5	7	6	2	5.33
8	3	6	5	5	5	4	8	5	7	7	8	5.92
6	6	3	5	7	4	6	6	4	6	3	6	5.17
9	4	4	3	4	6	7	5	10	5	7	3	5.58
5	4	5	10	4	8	5	4	3	2	4	4	4.83
4	7	6	6	4	5	4	8	4	8	3	8	5.58
6	4	6	4	6	3	9	4	5	2	3	7	4.92
7	2	8	4	7	7	6	5	6	5	9	3	5.75
8	3	9	4	4	7	4	5	6	6	3	6	5.42
3	4	4	6	4	6	5	6	6	10	1	7	5.17
8	4	4	4	8	7	5	4	3	8	6	4	5.42
4	6	4	10	5	5	1	6	7	6	8	9	5.92
6	5	7	3	4	6	9	2	8	7	6	4	5.58

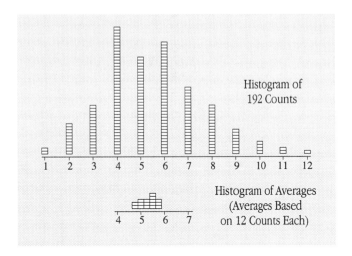

Figure 5.7: Histograms of Monthly Counts and Average Monthly Counts

The histogram of averages does not vary as much as the histogram of the individual counts. It never has, and it never will. Moreover, the averages can take on values which are impossible for the individual values. These two properties of averages create a problem when people compare averages with individual values. The most common way in which this happens is seen in Figure 5.8 where the average monthly counts for the first 15 years are followed by the monthly counts for the current year.

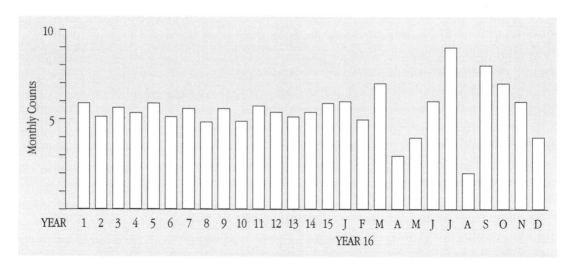

Figure 5.8: A Bar Chart Used to Compare Averages and Monthly Values

The error of using a bar chart to represent a time series was discussed in Chapter Three. Figure 5.9 corrects this misuse of a bar chart, but it cannot correct the mistake of comparing apples to oranges.

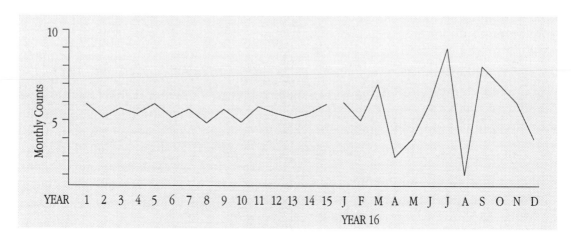

Figure 5.9: Averages Compared to Monthly Values

The problem with Figure 5.9 is a subtle one. It occurs when you try to understand a current value in the light of the previous averages. The average values show the general level for these counts, but they also create an expectation about the amount of variation. This mental impression of the routine variation is shown by a horizontal band in Figure 5.10.

When you attempt to make sense of the current values you will naturally carry this horizontal band along. Since the current values will *always* display more variation than the averages, some of the current values will routinely fall outside the band, creating the impression that some months are great, and other months are terrible.

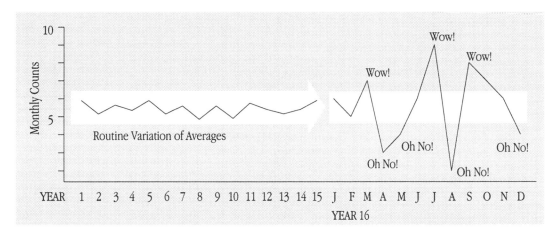

Figure 5.10: Routine Variation of Averages Used to Interpret Monthly Values

In other words, the common practice of comparing current values with the averages from the preceding years actually sets you up to make mistakes in your interpretation of the data. It inevitably leads to alternating euphoria and depression, and can result in increased sales of Prozac. In the next chapter you will learn how to separate routine variation from exceptional variation, but this only makes sense when comparing apples to apples. So, before we go on to consider one of the most powerful techniques for understanding data, you need to know better than to compare averages to individual values.

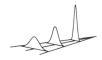

PRACTICE: The following computations will be used throughout the remainder of this book.

- Verify that the average of the data set { 3, 10, 16, 1, 5, 14, 11, 6 } is 8.25.

- Verify that the median of the data set { 3, 10, 16, 1, 5, 14, 11, 6 } is 8.0.

- Verify that the range of the data set { 3, 10, 16, 1, 5, 14, 11, 6 } is 15.

- Find the average of the data set { 10, 25, 12, 32, 26 }.

- Find the median of the data set { 10, 25, 12, 32, 26 }.

- Find the range of the data set { 10, 25, 12, 32, 26 }.

Part Two

Follow the Signals; Avoid the Noise

Chapter Six

Visualize Your Process Behavior

Flowcharts and cause-and-effect diagrams help you to visualize your process—to see it as a whole and to gain the perspective that is needed to improve your processes and systems. Bar charts allow you to make descriptive comparisons across categories. Running records allow you to see how a measure is changing over time—to spot trends and sudden changes that can be crucial to know about.

What do all of these techniques have in common? They are all graphical representations. The flowchart and cause-and-effect diagram are graphical representations of relationships. Bar charts and running records provide pictures of your data. In each case you obtain a picture that displays relationships or data in their context. In many cases these contextual displays will be sufficient (in connection with your own insight into the relationships, processes and systems represented) to suggest improvements that can be made immediately. And that is why context is the beginning of improvement. But what happens when context is not enough? What comes next? The next step is to characterize your process behavior so you can choose an appropriate improvement strategy. And to this end you will need a way of visualizing your process behavior. You will need a way of interpreting the graphs, and you will need a guide as to how to go about making improvements. This is where the *process behavior chart* comes in.

6.1 Two Types of Variation

No matter what your process, no matter what your data, all data display variation. Any measure you can think of that will be of interest to your business will vary from time period to time period. The reasons for this variation are many. There are all sorts of causes that have an impact on your process. Remember the cause-and-effect diagram? Even for the simple diagram in Figure 2.15 there were 20 causes listed for delays in delivery. Thus it is not unrealistic to think that your processes and systems will be subject to dozens, or even hundreds, of cause-and-effect relationships. And this multiplicity of causes has two consequences: it makes it easy for you to pick out an explanation for why the current value is so high, or so low; and it makes it very hard for you to know if your explanation is even close to being right.

So in your heart, you know that there is considerable uncertainty in your interpretation of the current value of any measure. But what are you going to do about this? How can you interpret the current value when the previous values are so variable? The key to understanding any time series is to make a distinction between two types of variation.

The first type of variation is routine variation. It is always present. It is unavoidable. It is inherent in the process. Because this type of variation is routine, it is also predictable. The second type of variation is exceptional variation. It is not always present. It is not routine. It comes and it goes. Because this type of variation is exceptional, it will be unpredictable.

The first benefit of this distinction is that it provides a way to know what to expect in the future, which is the essence of management.

> *While every process displays variation,*
> *some processes display predictable variation,*
> *while others display unpredictable variation.*

- A process that displays predictable variation is consistent over time. Because of this consistency we may use the past as a guide to the future.

- A process that displays unpredictable variation is changing over time. Because of these changes we cannot depend upon the past to be a reliable guide to the future.

Having made this *conceptual* distinction between predictable processes and unpredictable processes, we now need a way to do the same in *practice*. We begin by observing that while a predictable process will be the result of routine variation, an unpredictable process will possess both routine variation and exceptional variation. Thus, if we can devise a way to detect the presence of exceptional variation, we will be able to characterize our processes as being predictable or unpredictable.

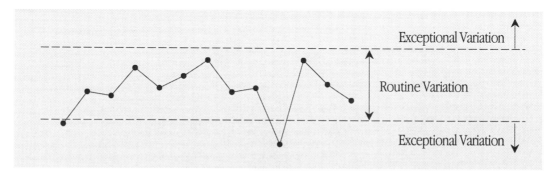

Figure 6.1: Separating Routine Variation from Exceptional Variation

In order to obtain signals of exceptional variation we will compute limits for the running record of our data. As shown in Figure 6.1, the idea is to establish limits that will allow us to distinguish between routine variation and exceptional variation.

If we compute values that place the limits too close together we will get *false alarms* (or false signals) when routine variation causes a point to fall outside the lines by chance. This is the first type of mistake we could make. We can avoid this mistake entirely by computing the limits that are far apart.

But if we have the limits too far apart we will *miss some signals* of exceptional variation. This is the second type of mistake we could make. We can minimize the occurrence of this mistake only by having the limits close together.

The trick is to strike a balance between the consequences of these two mistakes, and this is exactly what Walter Shewhart did when he created the *control chart.*[*] In his book, *Economic Control of Quality of Manufactured Product,* Shewhart came up with a way of computing limits to separate routine variation from exceptional variation so that you will have very few false alarms. Shewhart's choice of limits will bracket approximately 99% to 100% of the routine variation. As a result, whenever you have a value outside the limits you can be reasonably sure that the value is the result of exceptional variation.

6.2 Two Types of Action

So what does it mean when your current value is outside the limits and is the result of exceptional variation? How can you make use of this information? To answer this we return to the fact that every process is subject to dozens of cause-and-effect relationships.

When a process displays predictable variation, that variation may be thought of as the result of many different cause-and-effect relationships *where no one cause is dominant over the others.* While every process is subject to many different cause-and-effect relationships, predictable processes are those where the net effect of the multiple causes is a sort of static equilibrium. Deming's terminology for this condition was common cause variation.

On the other hand, when a process displays unpredictable variation, that variation must be thought of as consisting of the sum of the common cause variation plus some *additional* cause-and-effect relationships. Since the sum is unpredictable, we must conclude that the additional cause-and-effect relationships dominate the common cause variation, and therefore that it will be worth our while to identify these additional cause-and-effect relationships. For this reason Shewhart called these dominant causes assignable causes (also known as special causes).

If we characterize the routine variation of a predictable process as noise, then the exceptional variation of an unpredictable process would be like signals buried within the noise, and a process behavior chart allows us to detect these signals because it filters out the noise.

---

[*] Shewhart called routine variation "controlled variation," and exceptional variation was "uncontrolled variation." Out of this terminology Shewhart's charts came to be called control charts. However, because of the baggage associated with the word "control" this name can be quite misleading. Therefore we shall use the more descriptive name of process behavior charts to describe this versatile technique.

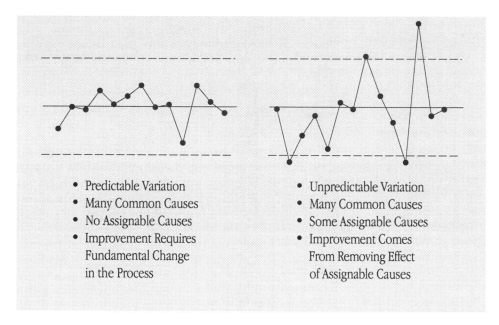

Figure 6.2: Two Types of Processes

This is how the characterization of a process as predictable or unpredictable can be the key to improving that process. If a process is predictable no one cause-and-effect relationship will stand out as the place to start. But if a process is unpredictable, the process behavior chart will allow you to detect the presence of assignable causes, so you can improve the process by working to remove the impact of these assignable causes.

Sometimes these assignable causes are external to the process—upsets due to circumstances beyond our control. At other times these assignable causes are internal to the system—former common causes that have, for whatever reason, become dominant over the other common causes.

When we identify and remove an assignable cause that was external to the process, we are, in most cases, merely returning the process to its previous condition. However, when we identify and remove the effect of an assignable cause that is internal to the process we will be improving both the process and the process outcomes. It is in the latter case that process improvement charts become the locomotive of Continual Improvement.

Thus, the path to process improvement depends upon what type of variation is present.

- If a process displays predictable variation, then the variation is the result of many common causes and it will be a waste of time to look for assignable causes. Improvement will only come by changing a major portion of the process.

- If a process displays unpredictable variation, then in addition to the common cause variation there is an extra amount of variation that is the result of one or more assignable causes. Improvement will come by finding and removing the assignable causes. Changing a major portion of the process will be premature.

Thus, the distinction between the two types of variation leads to two different routes to process improvement. When a process is unpredictable, looking for assignable causes will be a high payback strategy because the assignable causes are, by definition, dominant. On the other hand, looking for common causes of routine variation will be a low payback strategy because no single common cause is dominant. And a process behavior chart is the operational definition of an assignable cause. No guesswork is needed. Simply plot your data, compute the limits, and start to interpret the chart. Whenever points fall outside the limits, go look for the assignable causes. As you find the assignable causes, and as you take appropriate actions to remove the effects of these assignable causes from your process, you will be improving your process.

6.3 The Basic Process Behavior Chart: The *XmR* Chart

The simplest type of process behavior chart is the *chart for individual values and a moving range*. Since this is such a mouthful, we will call this chart an *XmR chart*. So how do we create this chart? The first example will use the data from the first two rows of Table 5.1, which are reproduced in Table 6.1. These values are counts of the number of yellow beads, in samples of 50 beads each, drawn from a box containing over 5000 beads.

Table 6.1: Number of Yellow Beads Out of 50 Beads

| 11 | 4 | 6 | 4 | 5 | 7 | 5 | 4 | 7 | 12 | 4 | 2 | 4 | 5 | 6 | 4 | 2 | 2 | 5 | 9 | 5 | 6 | 5 | 9 |

We begin with a running record of these 24 counts. The average of these 24 values is 5.54. We show this value as a central line for the plot. The use of a central line provides a visual reference to use in looking for trends in the values. In this case, there is no evidence of a trend in Figure 6.3.

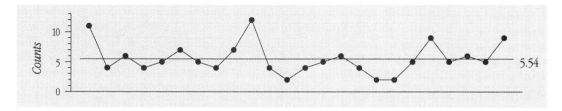

Figure 6.3: Time-Series Plot of Yellow Bead Data

In order to compute limits that are appropriate for these data—limits which will filter out the noise of the routine variation—we will need to measure the routine variation. To do this we will compute *moving ranges* for these data. The moving ranges are the differences between successive values.

Since moving ranges are used to measure variation, we do not care what the sign of the difference might be. Thus, if you get a negative value for a moving range, you change the sign and record a positive value. By convention, moving ranges are never negative. They are always taken to be positive or zero.

The first value is 11. The second value is 4. Thus, the first moving range is the difference between these two values, which is 7.

$$\begin{array}{lccc} \textit{values} & 11 & 4 & 6 \\ \textit{moving ranges} & & 7 & 2 \end{array}$$

The second count is 4. The third count is 6. The second moving range is thus 2. Continuing in this way the 23 moving ranges of Table 6.2 are found.

Table 6.2: Number of Yellow Beads Out of 50 Beads

values	11	4	6	4	5	7	5	4	7	12	4	2	4	5	6	4	2	2	5	9	5	6	5	9
moving ranges		7	2	2	1	2	2	1	3	5	8	2	2	1	1	2	2	0	3	4	4	1	1	4

These moving ranges are incorporated into the chart on a separate running record directly under the running record of the original values. The central line for this new plot will be the average of the 23 moving ranges, which is 2.61. The combined plots are shown in Figure 6.4.

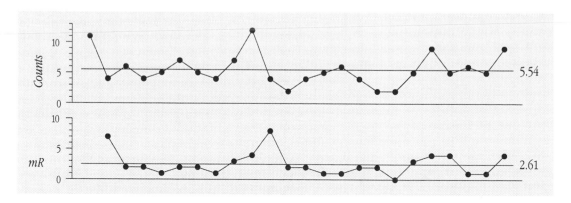

Figure 6.4: Time-Series Plots of Yellow Bead Data and Moving Ranges

The purpose of computing the moving ranges was to characterize the routine variation. The *average moving range* provides a simple summary of this routine variation, and it will be used in the computation of the limits for the two plots in Figure 6.4.

For the moving range portion of the chart (referred to as the *mR* chart), the *Upper Range Limit* will be found by multiplying the average moving range by a scaling factor of 3.27.

$$\textit{Upper Range Limit} = URL = 3.27 \times \overline{mR} = 3.27 \times 2.61 = 8.53$$

This value of 3.27 is a constant for this type of process behavior chart. This Upper Range Limit is plotted as a dashed horizontal line on the mR chart.

The limits for the individual values portion of the chart (the X chart) are called *Natural Process Limits*. They are centered on the central line. The distance from the central line to either of these limits is computed by multiplying the average moving range by a scaling factor of 2.66. The value of 2.66 is a constant for this type of process behavior chart, and is the value required to convert the average moving range into the appropriate amount of spread for the individual values. The *Upper Natural Process Limit* is found by multiplying the average moving range by 2.66, and then adding the product to the central line of the X chart. The *Lower Natural Process Limit* is found by multiplying the average moving range by 2.66, and then subtracting the product from the central line of the X chart.

$$\text{Upper Natural Process Limit} = \text{UNPL} = \overline{X} + (\,2.66 \times \overline{mR}\,) = 5.54 + (\,2.66 \times 2.61\,) = 12.48$$

$$\text{Lower Natural Process Limit} = \text{LNPL} = \overline{X} - (\,2.66 \times \overline{mR}\,) = 5.54 - (\,2.66 \times 2.61\,) = -1.40$$

Of course, since these individual values are counts, a negative *LNPL* is meaningless—counts cannot be negative. Therefore, we will have a one-sided X chart with a boundary condition on the bottom and a Natural Process Limit on the top.

The Upper Natural Process Limit is plotted as a dashed line on the individual values portion of the XmR chart. The complete XmR chart for these data is shown in Figure 6.5.

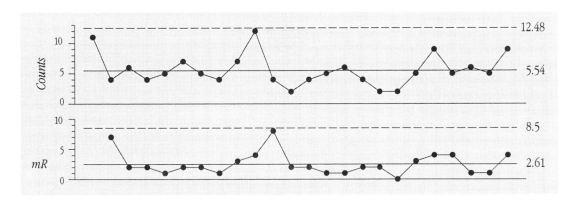

Figure 6.5: The *XmR* Chart for the Yellow Bead Data

The limits in Figure 6.5 define bands of routine variation for both the individual values and the moving ranges. As long as the counts vary between 0 and 12, and as long as the moving ranges vary between 0 and 8, there is no evidence of exceptional variation. The variation here can be explained as pure noise. There is no evidence of any signals. When a process is predictable the Natural Process Limits define what to expect in the future. From Figure 6.5 we should expect this process to continue to produce counts that cluster around 5.5, and vary from 0 to 12. The X chart for the 192 values from Table 5.1 is shown in Figure 6.6. Our prediction, based on the first 24 values, was a good prediction.

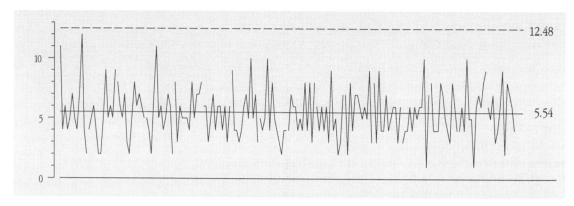

Figure 6.6: *X* Chart for 192 Counts of Yellow Beads

Thus the process behavior chart allows you to:

1. *characterize a process as predictable or unpredictable,*

2. *identify points that represent exceptional variation,*

3. *predict the average level to expect from a predictable process in the future, and*

4. *characterize the amount of routine variation to expect from a predictable process in the future.*

6.4 An *XmR* Chart for Accounts Receivable

A large company with a diversified customer base tracked their accounts receivable data on an *XmR* chart. The relevant data for one year are shown in Table 6.3, where the amounts are in millions of dollars. Since the accounts receivable vary as the sales level varies, Table 6.3 also shows the total sales for the past three months. Instead of tracking the accounts receivable in dollars, they tracked the accounts receivable as a percentage of the sales for the past three months. This adjustment of one number by another is common with all sorts of business data.

Table 6.3: Accounts Receivable for Year One

Month	A/R	Sales	A/R as % of Sales	mR	Month	A/R	Sales	A/R as % of Sales	mR
January	129.7	233.2	55.6		July	126.2	234.8	53.8	1.9
February	133.0	243.1	54.7	0.9	August	127.6	232.7	54.8	1.0
March	135.8	247.2	54.9	0.2	September	121.6	227.6	53.4	1.4
April	133.1	242.7	54.8	0.1	October	126.7	222.2	57.0	3.6
May	135.8	238.7	56.9	2.1	November	131.5	221.4	59.4	2.4
June	133.9	240.5	55.7	1.2	December	139.4	220.7	63.2	3.8

The average for the accounts receivable percentages is 56.18 percent. We use the monthly percentages to obtain the moving ranges (shown as the *mR* values in Table 6.3). The average of the 11 moving ranges is 1.69.

Using these values we compute the limits for an *XmR* chart to be:

$$UNPL = \bar{X} + 2.66\ \overline{mR} = 56.18 + (\ 2.66 \times 1.69\ ) = 60.68$$

$$LNPL = \bar{X} - 2.66\ \overline{mR} = 56.18 - (\ 2.66 \times 1.69) = 51.68$$

$$URL = 3.27\ \overline{mR} = 3.27 \times 1.69 = 5.53$$

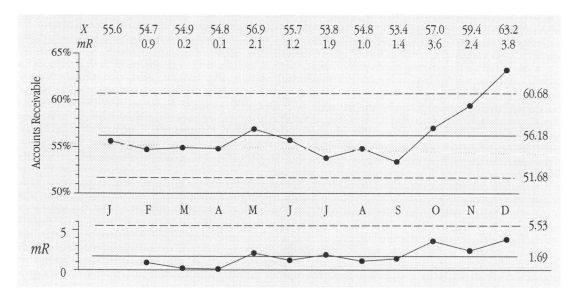

Figure 6.7: *XmR* Chart for Accounts Receivable Values

The *XmR* chart in Figure 6.7 makes three things immediately apparent:

1. The accounts receivable have averaged about 56 percent of the three-month sales values.
2. Allowing for routine variation these monthly values could climb up to 60 percent, or drop to 52 percent, *without signaling any change in the accounts receivable process.*
3. The December value of 63 percent is a signal of exceptional variation. There has been a change in the accounts receivable process, and it was a change for the worse. (While this change was *detected* in December, it could have begun to occur earlier. When trying to identify assignable causes it is often helpful to go back to the last time the running record crossed the central line. Here the change may have begun as early as October.)

Not only do you know these facts about the accounts receivable process, but you have the chart to use in communicating these facts to others. Since (in this case) a change from 56 percent to 63 percent amounts to an extra 16 million dollars being tied up in working capital each month, this was a fact worth communicating.

> *The process behavior chart allows you*
> *to separate the probable noise from the potential signals,*
> *so you can concentrate on the signals, where interesting things are happening,*
> *and can ignore the noise, where nothing much is going on.*

(This would be an appropriate time to work the exercises at the end of this chapter.)

6.5 What Do Predictable Processes Look Like?

In order to help you interpret your own process behavior charts we will characterize charts that are generated by processes that are predictable.

Table 5.1 contains the counts of the number of yellow beads in 192 samples of 50 beads each. Earlier in this chapter we used the first 24 of these values to obtain limits of 12.48 to −1.40. (Since these values are counts, and counts cannot be less than zero, the lower limit was replaced by the boundary value of zero.) If we plotted all 192 counts on an X chart, and added a histogram on the end, we would get Figure 6.8.

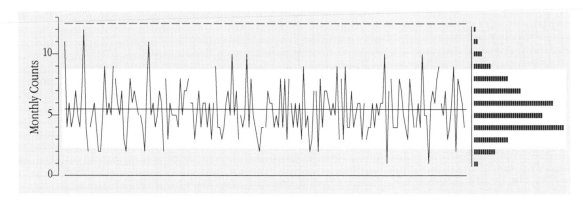

Figure 6.8: *X* Chart and Histogram for the Number of Yellow Beads in 192 Samples of 50 Beads Each

The white band shown in Figure 6.8 is symmetric about the central line. The top of this white band is half-way between the central line and the Upper Natural Process Limit. (If we had a Lower Natural Process Limit, the bottom of the band would be half-way between the central line and the *LNPL*.) Thus, the white band defines the middle 50% of the region within the limits.

Inspection of Figure 6.8 shows that the bulk of the values fall in the middle 50% of the region within the limits. Experience suggests that when the process is predictable approximately 85 percent of the values will fall within the white band. In this case 165 out of 192, or 86%, fall in this zone.

Conversely, only about 15% of the values should fall close to the upper limit or close to the lower boundary when the process is predictable. This means that when you are looking at a process behavior chart you should expect the time-series to visually *fill up the middle* portion of the regions between the limits, with only occasional values falling near the limits.

For a two-sided chart, with both upper and lower limits, there should be relatively few values in the upper 25% of the region between the limits, and relatively few values in the lower 25% of the region between the limits. With a one-sided chart, where a boundary condition falls within the computed limits, the values may pile up against the boundary, but there should still be relatively few values near the one limit.

6.6 Strong Signals and Weaker Signals

Assignable causes are *defined* by process behavior charts. Process behavior charts collect evidence of the existence of assignable causes and display that evidence for the whole world to see.

The simplest evidence of an assignable cause is a point outside the limits on either an X chart or an mR chart. Not only is this signal the simplest signal, but it is also indicates that the effect of the assignable cause is large in magnitude. Consider what it takes for a point to fall outside the limits—the assignable cause has to have an impact upon the process which is greater than the sum of all the effects of all the common causes put together. This is why it will be economically worthwhile to seek to identify the assignable causes associated with points outside the limits.

Other evidence of an assignable cause might be a sustained sequence of points on one side of the central line. While all of the points on an X chart may fall within the limits, a sequence of eight, nine, ten, or more points, all on the same side of the central line, is generally taken to be evidence of an assignable cause.

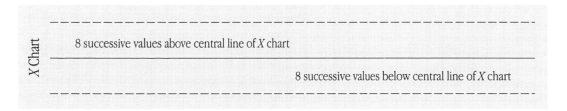

Figure 6.9: Runs Above and Below the Central Line as Signals of an Assignable Cause

Examination of the Yellow Bead data in Figure 6.10 shows that there is one run of seven, and one run of six, but no runs of eight. Since these data come from drawing beads out of a bowl, and since this process is a prototype of a predictable process, Figure 6.10 confirms that eight or more in a row on the same side of the central line is likely to represent the effect of an assignable cause.

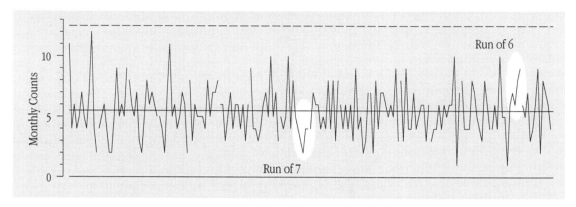

Figure 6.10: Predictable Processes Do Not Tend To Have Runs of Eight

Now if you have an assignable cause which produces a run of eight or more successive values on one side of the central line, and yet none of these points fall outside the limits, it is reasonable to conclude that (1) the assignable cause is sustained in its impact, and (2) the effect of this assignable cause is fairly small even though it is still greater than the effects of the common causes. Thus, runs of eight or more about the central line will indicate the presence of a *sustained* but *weak* assignable cause.

Another way that an assignable cause can make its presence known on an X chart is a sequence of three out of three successive values, or three out of four successive values, in the upper (or lower) 25% of the region between the limits.

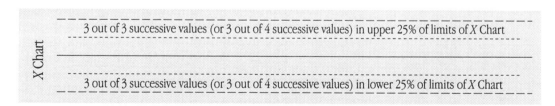

Figure 6.11: Runs Near the Limits as Signals of an Assignable Cause

While predictable processes will have *some* values which fall in the outer 25% of the region between the limits, they do not tend to show *sequences* of three or more points in these zones.

When an assignable cause results in a run of three-out-of-three or three-out-of-four points near the limits and yet none of these points are outside the limits, we can again conclude that (1) the assignable cause is sustained in its impact and (2) the effect of the assignable cause is moderate in its impact.

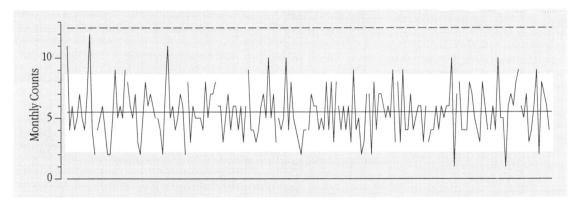

Figure 6.12: Predictable Processes Do Not Tend To Have Runs Near the Limits

Thus, we have three ways for detecting assignable causes: points outside the limits, runs near the limits, and runs about the central line.

THREE RULES FOR DETECTING ASSIGNABLE CAUSES

Detection Rule One: Points Outside the Limits

> A single point outside the computed limits will be taken as an indication of the presence of an assignable cause which has a *dominant* effect.

Detection Rule Two: Runs Near the Limits

> Three out of three, or three out of four successive values in the upper (or lower) 25% of the region between the limits will be taken as an indication of the presence of an assignable cause which has a *moderate* but sustained effect.

Detection Rule Three: Runs About the Central Line

> Eight successive values on the same side of the central line will be taken as an indication of the presence of an assignable cause which has a *weak* but sustained effect.

Detection Rules One, Two, and Three are appropriate for the X chart. For reasons which are beyond the scope of this book, Detection Rule Two and Detection Rule Three are inappropriate for the mR chart. So with the mR chart, we only look for points above the Upper Range Limit.

6.7 Why Johnnie Can't Breathe

"Teen Use Turns Upward" read the headline for a graph in the June 21, 1994 edition of *USA Today*. The data in the graph were attributed to the Institute for Social Research at the University of Michigan, and were labeled as the "percentage of high school seniors who smoke daily." The percentages for 1980 through 1993 are given in Table 6.4.

Table 6.4: Percentage of High School Seniors Who Smoke Daily

Year	'80	'81	'82	'83	'84	'85	'86	'87	'88	'89	'90	'91	'92	'93
Percentages	21.3	20.2	20.9	21.0	18.8	19.6	18.7	18.6	18.1	18.9	19.2	18.2	17.3	19.0
Moving Ranges		1.1	0.7	0.1	2.2	0.8	0.9	0.1	0.5	0.8	0.3	1.0	0.9	1.7

The article accompanying these data claimed that the jump from 17.3% in 1992 to 19.0% in 1993 was a signal that the "number of smoking 18 to 24-year-olds has leveled off, ending a downward trend that began in 1983."

What can you do to evaluate this claim? You can begin by placing these percentages on an *XmR* chart.

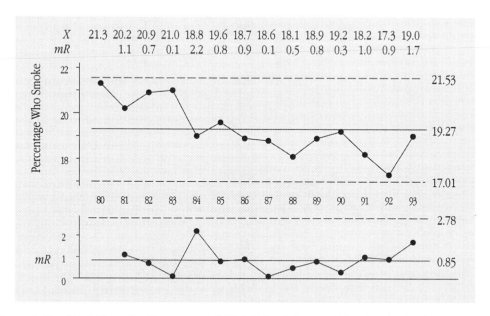

Figure 6.13: *XmR* Chart for Percentage of High School Seniors Who Smoke Daily, 1980-1993

The average of these 14 percentages is 19.27 percent. The average of the 13 moving ranges is 0.85. Using these values we obtain the following limits:

$$\textit{Upper Range Limit} \; = \; \textit{URL} \; = \; 3.27 \; \text{x} \; \overline{mR} \; = \; 3.27 \; \text{x} \; 0.85 \; = \; 2.78$$

$$\textit{Upper Natural Process Limit} \; = \; \textit{UNPL} \; = \; \overline{X} + (\, 2.66 \; \text{x} \; \overline{mR}\,) \; = \; 19.27 \; + \; (\, 2.66 \; \text{x} \; 0.85\,) \; = \; 21.53$$

$$\textit{Lower Natural Process Limit} \; = \; \textit{LNPL} \; = \; \overline{X} - (\, 2.66 \; \text{x} \; \overline{mR}\,) \; = \; 19.27 \; - \; (\, 2.66 \; \text{x} \; 0.85\,) \; = \; 17.01$$

Three of the first four values are closer to the upper limit than the central line, and the last eight values are below the central line. Thus, both Detection Rule Two and Detection Rule Three are satisfied, indicating that there has indeed been a drop in the percentage of high school seniors who smoke daily. Interpreting the X Chart in Figure 6.13 there appears to be a break between the first four years and the last 10 years. Therefore, you might decide to compute limits for each of these segments.

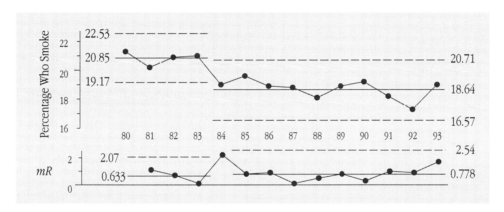

Figure 6.14: Revised *XmR* Chart for Percentage of Seniors Who Smoke Daily, 1980-1993

Figure 6.14 shows that the "downward trend" of the past 14 years could be explained by a one-time, two percent drop that occurred between 1983 and 1984. Those who are interested in preventing teenagers from smoking should try to learn what happened to the Class of '84. An understanding of this assignable cause could prove useful in anti-smoking campaigns. Many explanations of the "downward trend" may be offered. However, no matter how logical, no matter how eloquent, no matter how appealing, no explanation can be considered to have any validity unless it can account for the sudden change between '83 and '84.

But what about the "jump" from 17.3 percent in 1992 to 19 percent in 1993? The *XmR* chart in Figure 6.14 shows no evidence of any change in the teen-age use of tobacco over the ten year period from 1984 to 1993! The change from 1992 to 1993 is well within the bounds of routine variation.

So what would it take to indicate a change? A single point outside the limits on either the X Chart or the *mR* Chart would suffice. Three-out-of-three or three-out-of-four successive values in the upper 25% of the X chart would indicate an increase in the use of tobacco. Three-out-of-three or three-out-of-four successive values in the lower 25% of the X chart would indicate a drop in the use of tobacco. Eight successive values above, or below, the central line of the X chart would indicate a change in the use of tobacco. And while you are waiting for such evidence, your best estimate of the fraction of high-school seniors who smoke daily will remain 18.64 percent.

Anyone who tells you otherwise is just blowing smoke.

This ability to use the process behavior chart to gain insight, and then to use that insight to revise the chart, is part of the interactive use of process behavior charts that is the hallmark of Continual Improvement. It is the way of thinking—the learning from the process as a means of improving the process—that characterizes Continual Improvement and sets it apart from improvement programs based on wishes and hopes.

6.8 Plans, Goals, Targets, and Process Behavior Charts

Everywhere you look people are being given goals, being asked to shoot for a target, and are being evaluated on their performance relative to some plan. What do all of these plans, goals, and targets have in common? They are all, in some sense, definitions of what the customer wants (especially if we define "customer" to include our bosses). Plans, goals, budgets, and targets, help us to separate the acceptable outcomes from the unacceptable outcomes after the fact. They are the *Voice of the Customer*.

Now the Voice of the Customer will let you know when you have an unacceptable outcome, so that you can take action to remedy the situation. But it will not tell you how to avoid the unacceptable outcomes, or how to achieve the acceptable outcomes. So the Voice of the Customer will tell you *when* you are in trouble, but it will not tell you *why* you are in trouble, and it will not tell you how to get out of trouble.

Thus, plans, goals, budgets, and targets will allow you to take action on the outcomes, but they give little help in influencing those outcomes. And this is why the Voice of the Customer is often little more than wishes and hopes.

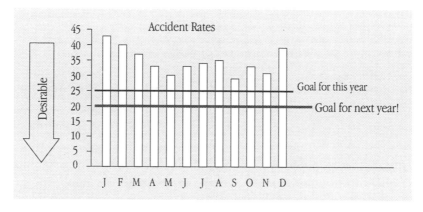

Figure 6.15: "We didn't get down to our goal this year, so we set the goal lower for next year."

Process behavior charts, on the other hand, are for taking action on the process—to look for assignable causes when they are present, with an eye toward process improvement, and to refrain from looking for assignable causes when they are absent. The process behavior chart is the *Voice of the Process*. It characterizes every process as being either predictable or unpredictable.

When a process is predictable the process behavior chart defines what you can expect in the future. The process average is likely to continue to be the same, and the future values may fall anywhere within the Natural Process Limits defined by the chart.

When a process is unpredictable the process behavior chart helps you to identify those assignable causes that are present, so that you can *take action on the process* to remove the effects of the assignable causes, and thereby improve the process.

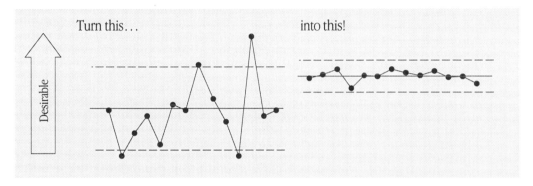

Figure 6.16: The Result of the Effective Use of Process Behavior Charts

Finally, given that we have the Voice of the Customer and the Voice of the Process, it is clearly desirable to have these two voices in alignment.

If the voices are not in alignment there are only three things you can do that will bring them into alignment: you can shift the process aim; or you can reduce the process variation; or you can change the goal. Two of these require that you have a way of taking action on your process, and the third requires you to have sophisticated political skills.

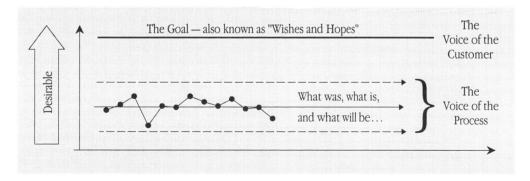

Figure 6.17: The Problem of Aligning the Two Voices

Of course, lacking an effective way of taking action on their process, and faced with unacceptable outcomes, many have resorted to the traditional approach: change the blame, distort the system, or distort the data, whatever it takes. Then they cross their fingers, claim to have fixed the problem, and hope that it will not happen again.

Thus there are three types of action that may be taken with regard to the quality of a product or a service.

1. Specifications (plans, goals, and targets) are for taking action on the outcomes—to separate the acceptable outcomes from the unacceptable outcomes after the fact. They are the *Voice of the Customer*.

2. Process behavior charts are for taking action on the process—to look for assignable causes when they are present, with an eye toward process improvement, and to refrain from looking for assignable causes when they are absent. It is the *Voice of the Process*.

3. Actions to align the two voices are appropriate. However, the lack of a well-defined voice of the process will always be an obstacle to successful alignment.

While it is easy to *say* what you want, the key question is how can you attain these wants? You may well know when the outcome does not meet your requirements, but is this shortcoming a result of the common cause variation or the result of some assignable cause? What is the voice of the process? Is the process predictable, but not capable of meeting your requirements? Or is the shortcoming a result of some breakdown either in the system or in something external to the system? If you attempt to make adjustments before you know the answers to these questions you are doomed to make mistakes.

Plans, goals, and targets have been used for many years. We have even known that we need to align the process with the plans, goals and targets. But it is the ability to listen to the voice of the process that has been missing. Process behavior charts fill this gap.

The methodology for moving toward any goal requires that you first understand where you presently are, and that is precisely where the process behavior chart comes into the picture. The process behavior chart helps you in three ways. It defines that level of performance which your process is likely to achieve when it is doing the best it can, it then gives you the information you need to move your process toward that ideal, and finally allows you to judge just how close you have come to that ideal. Collectively, these three aspects of the process behavior chart define a methodology for Continual Improvement, which is what you need to turn your wants into realities.

6.9 Exercises

EXERCISE 6.1:

For the years 1980 to 1983 it was reported that the percentages of high school seniors who smoked daily were: 21.3, 20.2, 20.9, and 21.0 respectively. Create an *XmR* chart for these data. (You may use the worksheet and the process behavior chart form on the next page.)

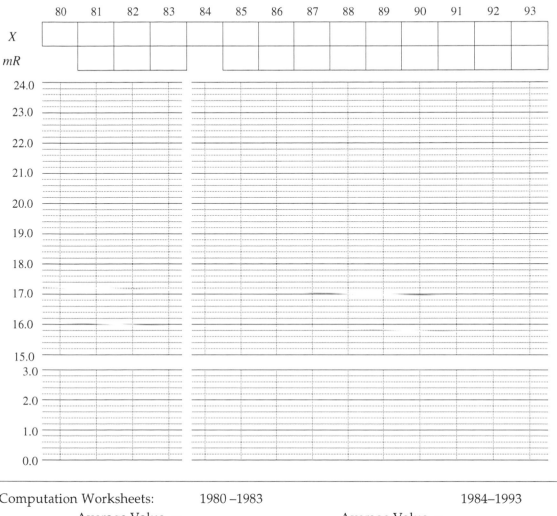

Computation Worksheets:

	1980–1983	1984–1993
Average Value =	_____	_____
Average Moving Range =	_____	_____
$2.66 \times \overline{mR}$ =	_____	_____
UNPL = $\overline{X} + 2.66\,\overline{mR}$ =	_____	_____
LNPL = $\overline{X} - 2.66\,\overline{mR}$ =	_____	_____
URL = $3.27 \times \overline{mR}$ =	_____	_____

EXERCISE 6.2:

For the years of 1984 to 1993 it was reported that the percentages of high school seniors who smoked daily were: 18.8, 19.6, 18.7, 18.6, 18.1, 18.9, 19.2, 18.2, 17.3, and 19.0 respectively. Create an *XmR* chart for these data. (Use the worksheet and form above)

EXERCISE 6.3:

A trucking company implemented a bonus plan in an effort to boost productivity at certain sites. At the end of a twelve month test period they reported the following accident rates for these sites. The values shown are the reportable injuries per million man-hours for each month. Place these values on an *XmR* chart.

Jan.	Feb.	Mar.	Apr.	May	Jun.	Jul.	Aug.	Sept.	Oct.	Nov.	Dec.
43	40	37	33	30	33	34	35	29	33	31	39

Average Value = _____   Average Moving Range = _____

2.66 x $\overline{mR}$ = _____   URL = 3.27 x $\overline{mR}$ = _____

UNPL = $\overline{X}$ + 2.66 $\overline{mR}$ = _____   LNPL = $\overline{X}$ – 2.66 $\overline{mR}$ = _____

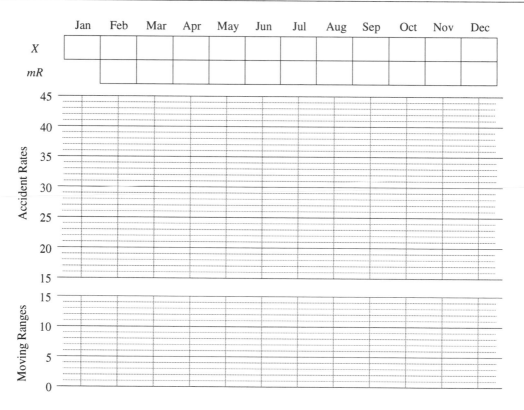

EXERCISE 6.4:

a. Interpreting the *XmR* chart above, is the "accident process" at these sites predictable?

b. If nothing is changed, what will be the average accident rate for these sites next year?

c. What range of accident rates for these sites should you expect during the next year?

d. How low would a single month's accident rate need to be to indicate a real reduction in the accident rate at these sites?

EXERCISE 6.5:

The same trucking company reported the following accident rates for those sites that did not participate in the productivity bonus plan. Once again, the values shown are the reportable injuries per million man-hours for each month. Create another *XmR* chart.

Jan.	Feb.	Mar.	Apr.	May	Jun.	Jul.	Aug.	Sept.	Oct.	Nov.	Dec.
35	37	33	32	27	29	31	22	25	30	24	19

Average Value = _____   Average Moving Range = _____

$2.66 \times \overline{mR}$ = _____ $URL = 3.27 \times \overline{mR}$ = _____

$UNPL = \overline{X} + 2.66\,\overline{mR}$ = _____ $LNPL = \overline{X} - 2.66\,\overline{mR}$ = _____

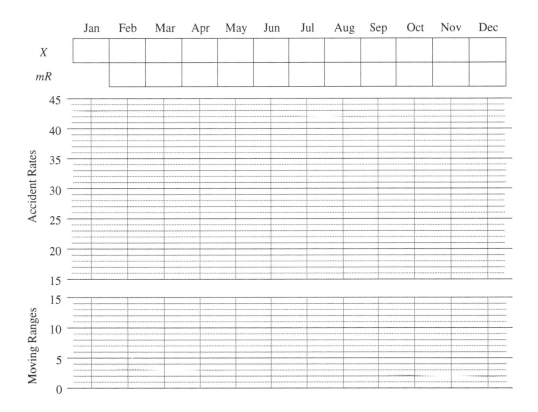

EXERCISE 6.6:

a. Interpreting the *XmR* chart above, is the "accident process" at these sites predictable?
b. If nothing is changed, what will be the average accident rate for these sites next year?
c. If nothing is changed, what range of accident rates for these sites should you expect to see during the next year?
d. How low would a single month's accident rate need to be to indicate a real reduction in the accident rate at these sites?

Chapter Seven

Using *XmR* Charts Effectively

The *XmR* chart was introduced in the previous chapter. There the computations and basic considerations were outlined. But how do you go from plotting points on a piece of paper to making process improvements? How can something this simple have an impact upon the whole organization? What is the difference between "cubicle wallpaper" and effective charts? And how can process behavior charts be the locomotive of Continual Improvement? To find the answers to these questions read about how others have done it.

7.1 Comparing Groups Using Process Behavior Charts

A trucking company decided to try to increase productivity by putting their workers on a bonus plan. Being conservative, it was decided to test the bonus plan at selected sites for a year before implementing it company wide. At the end of the year-long trial the usual measures of activity were collected and reported for two groups: Group A consisted of those sites where all of the workers were on the bonus plan; Group B consisted of those sites that did not have the bonus plan. Among the various measures reported were some accident data. Table 7.1 shows the accident rates for reportable injuries over a twelve-month period for both groups. The values are the reportable injuries per million man-hours.

Table 7.1: Accident Rates

	Jan.	Feb.	Mar.	Apr.	May	Jun.	Jul.	Aug.	Sept.	Oct.	Nov.	Dec.
Group A	43	40	37	33	30	33	34	35	29	33	31	39
Group B	35	37	33	32	27	29	31	22	25	30	24	19

I ask you, "Are these two groups different?"

You say, "Oh, yes. They clearly have different average accident rates."

I respond, "But they will always have different average accident rates—it is the nature of numerical summaries to vary from time to time and place to place. So you cannot say they are different just because they have different averages."

You say, "But I know they are different."

To which I reply, "How do you know if the difference between the average accident rates is due to a difference between the two groups or just the result of routine variation?"

"Well, I really don't."

"But don't you know how to remove routine variation?"

"You mean by putting the data on an *XmR* chart?"

"Yes."

"But how will that allow me to compare the two groups?"

"By using two charts you can characterize each group separately, and then use these characterizations to compare the groups."

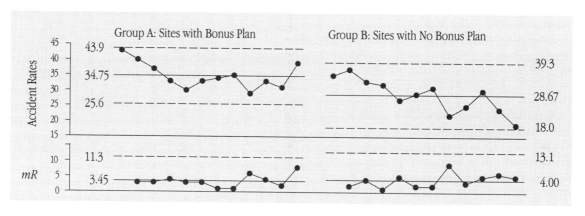

Figure 7.1: *XmR* Charts for Accident Rates

The *XmR* charts for the two groups are shown in Figure 7.1. Both groups show predictable accident rates. The sites with the bonus plan average about 35 accidents per million man-hours. Routine variation could cause this number to vary anywhere between 25.6 to 43.9 from month to month.

The sites without the bonus plan average about 29 accidents per million man-hours. Routine variation could cause this number to vary anywhere between 18.0 to 39.3 from month-to-month.

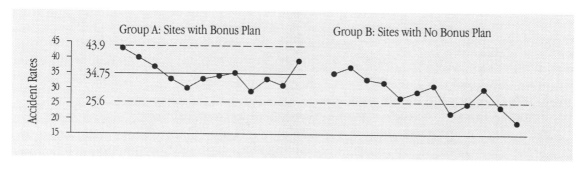

Figure 7.2: Group B Compared to Group A's Limits

So, are the two groups different? If we compare the values of one group with the limits from the other group what do we find?

In Figure 7.2 the limits for Group A are applied to the values for Group B. The four points for Group B outside the limits for Group A represent a detectable difference between the two groups.

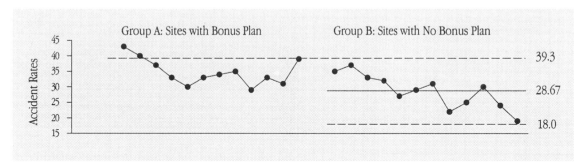

Figure 7.3: Group A Compared to Group B's Limits

In Figure 7.3 the limits for Group B are applied to the values for Group A. Again we see points outside the limits, indicating a detectable difference between the two groups. Either one of the conditions above is a license to interpret the difference between the averages as real: the sites with the bonus plan average about six more accidents per million man-hours than do the other sites.

If either Figure 7.2 or Figure 7.3 has a point outside the limits of the other group, then there is a detectable difference between the two groups, and if they are supposed to be the same, it will be worthwhile to find out why they are different. The key word here is "detectable." Two groups will always have different averages even when they are the same. It is only when the different averages represent real differences between the two groups that you will want to interpret that difference. And process behavior charts provide the simplest way to detect real differences.

7.2 The "Has a Change Occurred?" Chart

Placing high-level summaries on a process behavior chart will allow you to know when there has been a change in your system. Sometimes these changes are the intended result of actions on the part of the managers. In some cases these changes are the unintended side effects of known changes. And in other cases these changes are complete surprises. In any case, it will always be helpful to know the answer to the question "Has a change occurred?"

The following example shows how a large corporation was able to use Continual Improvement techniques to reduce their working capital by $27 million a month. In Section 6.4 we created an *XmR* chart for the accounts receivable data for Year One. This chart is

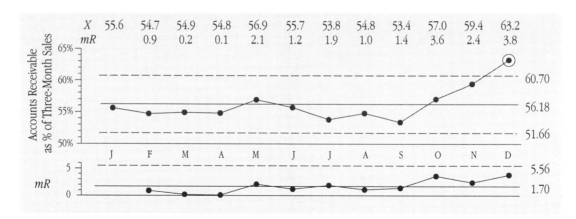

Figure 7.4: *XmR* **Chart for Accounts Receivable Values for Year One**

reproduced in Figure 7.4. There we interpreted the December value as a signal that their accounts receivable system had changed for the worse.

The explanation for the change seen in Figure 7.4 is that during the fourth quarter of Year One the accounting systems for North, South, and Central American operations were merged. Since the accounts receivable in Central and South America were slower in being collected this increase was understandable, even if it was undesirable.

Table 7.2 gives the accounts receivable data for Years One and Two in millions of dollars.

Table 7.2: Accounts Receivable for Years One and Two

Year	Month	A/R	Sales	A/R as % of Sales	Year	Month	A/R	Sales	A/R as % of Sales
One	January	129.7	233.2	55.6	Two	January	143.5	235.6	60.9
One	February	133.0	243.1	54.7	Two	February	146.2	240.8	60.7
One	March	135.8	247.2	54.9	Two	March	150.7	257.2	58.6
One	April	133.1	242.7	54.8	Two	April	145.2	253.5	57.3
One	May	135.8	238.7	56.9	Two	May	143.4	251.9	56.9
One	June	133.9	240.5	55.7	Two	June	146.6	252.3	58.1
One	July	126.2	234.8	53.8	Two	July	148.4	254.7	58.3
One	August	127.6	232.7	54.8	Two	August	132.1	259.7	50.9
One	September	121.6	227.6	53.4	Two	September	136.7	256.6	53.3
One	October	126.7	222.2	57.0	Two	October	133.4	254.3	52.5
One	November	131.5	221.4	59.4	Two	November	134.0	264.0	50.8
One	December	139.4	220.7	63.2	Two	December	142.3	268.9	52.9

Figure 7.5 shows that the increase in Accounts Receivable, which was detected in December of Year One, persisted for the first seven months of Year Two. However, because they were using the chart to track accounts receivable, and because the chart made the deficiencies in the merged system clear for all to see, they had been working during this period to improve the system.

They began by using flowcharts to visualize the systems of the three offices. Of course the three systems were different. Based on the flowcharts of these existing systems they began to create a new system that would not only create consistency between the three

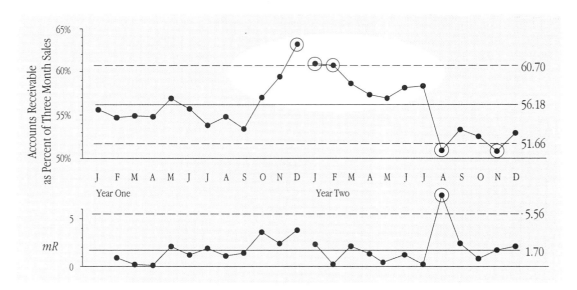

Figure 7.5: *XmR* **Chart for Accounts Receivable for Years One and Two**

offices, but would also streamline the whole system. When they had done this they created flowcharts of the new process and used these to train the employees at all three offices on how to use the new procedures.

The effect of this new system was seen in August of Year Two, when both the X chart and the *mR* chart signal that a change occurred.

The points for August and November, which fall below the limit in Figure 7.5, indicate that this process is doing better at the end of Year Two than it was at the beginning of Year One. They did not just bring the Central and South American operations into line with the North American operations, but they actually improved all three! The accounts receivable dropped from 59% of the three-month sales to 52%. This seven percent drop corresponded to an extra $17.5 million in increased liquidity each month!

So our initial limits, computed using the values for Year One, are sufficient to show three distinctly different modes of operation for the accounts receivable process during Years One and Two. Given this understanding of this process, we might wish to make these three different modes more visible by computing limits for each different mode.

For the first nine months of Year One the average is 54.97%, and the average moving range is 1.11. These values translate into limits of:

$$UNPL = \bar{X} + 2.66\,\overline{mR} = 54.97 + (2.66 \times 1.11) = 57.92$$

$$LNPL = \bar{X} - 2.66\,\overline{mR} = 54.97 - (2.66 \times 1.11) = 52.02$$

$$URL = 3.27\,\overline{mR} = 3.27 \times 1.11 = 3.63$$

For the next ten months the average is 59.04%, and the average moving range (based on the 10 values for October to July) is 1.75. These values translate into limits of:

$$UNPL = \bar{X} + 2.66\,\overline{mR} = 59.04 + (\,2.66 \times 1.75\,) = 63.70$$

$$LNPL = \bar{X} - 2.66\,\overline{mR} = 59.04 - (\,2.66 \times 1.75\,) = 54.39$$

$$URL = 3.27\,\overline{mR} = 3.27 \times 1.75 = 5.72$$

The jump from 55% to 59% corresponded to an extra $10 million being tied up in accounts receivable each month. (Sales are approximately $250 million per quarter and four percent of $250 million is $10 million).

Finally, the last five months of Year Two have an average of 52.08%, and the average moving range is, once again, 1.75. In computing this average moving range only the four values for September through December were used. The large moving range between July and August was not used because it does not represent the routine variation of the process, but rather shows the change between two modes of operation for this process. These values translate into limits of:

$$UNPL = \bar{X} + 2.66\,\overline{mR} = 52.08 + (\,2.66 \times 1.75\,) = 56.74$$

$$LNPL = \bar{X} - 2.66\,\overline{mR} = 52.08 - (\,2.66 \times 1.75\,) = 47.43$$

$$URL = 3.27\,\overline{mR} = 3.27 \times 1.75 = 5.72$$

While it was not absolutely necessary to compute three sets of limits for Years One and Two, the use of these limits helps to define the three modes of operation and to show both the deterioration and the improvement. In addition, the three central lines provide the supporting documentation for the estimates of the losses and savings associated with these changes.

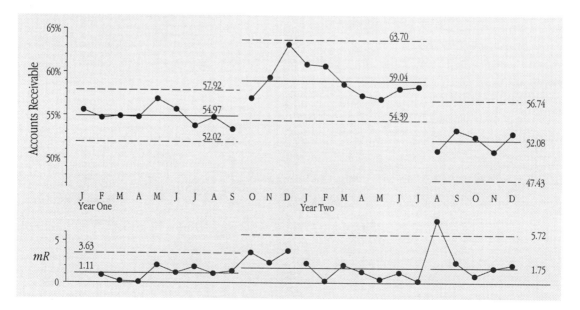

Figure 7.6: Accounts Receivable for Years One and Two

Table 7.3: Accounts Receivable for Years Three and Four

Year	Month	A/R	Sales	A/R as % of Sales	Year	Month	A/R	Sales	A/R as % of Sales
Three	January	146.4	285.7	51.3	Four	January	154.0	297.2	51.8
Three	February	148.9	279.1	53.4	Four	February	152.2	303.6	50.1
Three	March	149.9	289.1	51.8	Four	March	151.2	308.4	49.0
Three	April	154.1	285.7	53.9	Four	April	152.3	301.3	50.6
Three	May	141.6	284.6	49.7	Four	May	147.9	301.4	49.1
Three	June	145.8	281.7	51.8	Four	June	155.6	308.7	50.4
Three	July	149.5	276.1	54.2	Four	July	159.2	321.7	49.5
Three	August	145.5	287.0	50.7	Four	August	163.8	326.1	50.2
Three	September	150.1	283.9	52.9	Four	September	160.2	315.3	50.8
Three	October	142.0	277.1	51.2	Four	October	149.6	305.0	49.1
Three	November	138.1	278.1	49.7					
Three	December	150.3	279.4	53.8					

So what would you forecast for Year Three?

The limits that characterize the process at the end of Year Two are the logical limits to use in forecasting Year Three. If they do not make any further changes in the accounts receivable process, they can expect accounts receivable to average about 52% of the three-month sales. Individual months might have values as high as 56%, or as low as 48%, without being an indication of any change in the accounts receivable process.

The data for Years Three and Four are shown in Table 7.3 and are plotted against the limits from the end of Year Two in Figure 7.7.

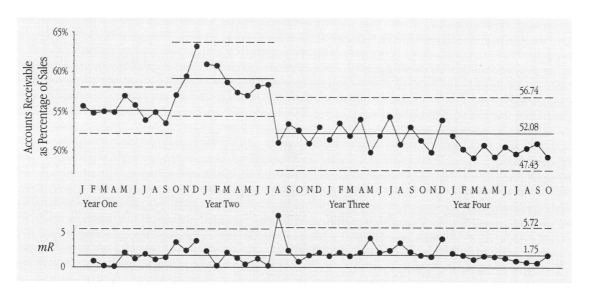

Figure 7.7: Accounts Receivable for Years One through Four

The changes made in August of Year Two resulted in a sustained reduction in the accounts receivable as a percentage of the three-month sales. Since the data for Year Three remain within the limits we do not need to revise or recompute the limits. We continue to use these limits for Year Four, where we see a long run below the central line. This run is evi-

dence that they were successful in making yet another improvement to their collection process—beginning in Year Four, they added interest charges for overdue accounts. The impact
of this change is made visible and quantifiable by the *XmR* chart.

Using the ten months of Year Four to revise the limits we get an average of 50.06% and an
average moving range of 1.32. These values yield limits of:

$$UNPL = \bar{X} + 2.66\, \overline{mR} = 50.06 + (2.66 \times 1.32) = 53.57$$

$$LNPL = \bar{X} - 2.66\, \overline{mR} = 50.06 - (2.66 \times 1.32) = 46.55$$

$$URL = 3.27\, \overline{mR} = 3.27 \times 1.32 = 4.31$$

These limits can be placed on the data for Year Four and then extended to characterize
what you expect in the future. Interpreting these limits we see that now the accounts receivable are averaging 50% of the sales for the past three months, and the variation in this figure
has been reduced. At the current sales level of $300 million per quarter this two percent
reduction in accounts receivable resulted in an additional $6 million reduction in working
capital. In all, since the beginning of Year Two, the accounts receivable percentage has been
reduced by 9 percentage points, which is currently equivalent to having an additional $27
million of increased liquidity each month.

Notice how it is the interaction between the user and the chart that makes the chart effective. One of the managers in this project said, "The charts were talking to us—telling us what
was going on in our system."

—◆—

Using process behavior charts to detect unknown changes in the process, to evaluate
planned changes in the process, and to communicate the effects of these changes to others so
that the process can be improved for the future is how the charts become the locomotive of
Continual Improvement. Here we see how changes made to an otherwise predictable process resulted first in things getting worse, and then in substantial improvements.

Another lesson of this example is to use the limits to tell the story. In both Figure 7.3 and
7.4 the limits are used to emphasize the changes made. Many beginners nervously ask,
"When do I need to revise my limits?" In computing limits the objective is not to "get the
right number," but rather to take the right action. As long as the limits provide an adequate
description of the process, they are sufficient.

"But how much data do I need before I can calculate limits?"

How much do you have? In the preceding example limits were computed at the end of
Year Two using only five values and four moving ranges, because that was all the data that
was available that was reasonable to use. In practice it is nice if you can use a dozen or even
two dozen values to compute your limits. However, we often have to work with fewer values, and useful limits may be computed using as few as five or six values.

7.3 Why Susie *Can* Breathe

People who suffer from asthma will sometimes be asked to monitor their peak exhalation rate using a device known as a peak flow meter. To use this device a person will take a deep breath and then exhale into the meter as quickly and forcefully as possible. The value recorded will be the peak flow in liters per minute. The lower the peak flow, the greater the obstruction in the airways in the lung and the more severe the asthma condition, with values below 100 being potentially life-threatening. The following is the story of how Dr. Peter Boggs and Fazel Hayati of the Asthma 2000 Group in Shreveport, Louisiana, pioneered the use of a process behavior chart in the treatment of asthma.

The patient was an 11-year-old girl with severe asthma who, prior to the beginning of this story, had been hospitalized three times in the previous year. As part of her treatment program she was asked to collect data on her peak flow rates four times each day. The data we shall use here are the peak flow rates she obtained each morning prior to taking any medication. The first 16 of these values are shown in Figure 7.8.

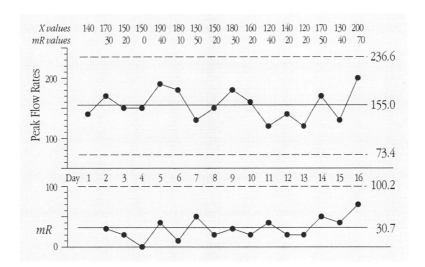

Figure 7.8: *XmR* **Chart for AM Premedication Peak Flow Rates for Days 1 to 16**

The average of these 16 values is 155. This average value is shown as a central line in Figure 7.8. This average of 155 is exactly half of this patient's predicted normal peak flow rate. In other words, without the congestion of asthma, this girl should be able to produce peak flows in the vicinity of 310. However, an average of 155 does not mean that she will get a value of 155 every day. Some days she does better, and some days she does worse. But do these swings above and below 155 represent changes in this patient's chronic condition? As we have seen in other situations, the easiest and best way of understanding variation is to use process behavior charts.

With an average of 155.0 and an average moving range of 30.7 we compute the limits:

$$UNPL = \overline{X} + 2.66\,\overline{mR} = 155.0 + (2.66 \times 30.7) = 236.6$$

$$LNPL = \overline{X} - 2.66\,\overline{mR} = 155.0 - (2.66 \times 30.7) = 73.4$$

$$URL = 3.27\,\overline{mR} = 3.27 \times 30.7 = 100.2$$

Since none of the points fall outside the limits we conclude that the variation shown by these data is common cause variation—the differences between the day-to-day values do not signal any real change in the patient's long-term status. While she experiences real physiological changes from day to day, her chronic condition is not changing during this sixteen day period. While she undoubtedly feels better when she gets a peak flow of 200 than when she has a peak flow of 120, and while she is physically doing better with scores of 200 than with scores of 120, these day-to-day changes are merely the routine variation that is part of her chronic condition. Unless this chronic condition is changed, she can expect to continue to ride this roller coaster. The Natural Process Limits of 73 to 236 suggest that good days can be interspersed with very bad days. Which is exactly what happened during the next eight days—while three days had scores above 200, one day was below 100!

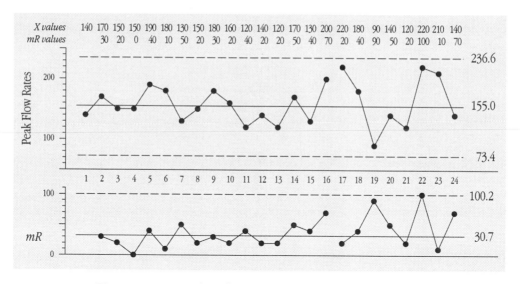

Figure 7.9: *XmR* Chart for Peak Flow Rates for Days 1 to 24

Figure 7.9 shows a process that is predictable, yet not operating at a desirable level. So how do you go about changing a predictable process? How do a physician and a patient go about changing the patient's chronic condition? This is where experience and subject matter knowledge are needed to capitalize on the information provided by the process behavior chart. The process behavior chart is the *Voice of the Process*. It tells you what type of variation is present in the process, and it can tell you when a change occurs in the process. But just how you should react to this knowledge will depend upon other information that is external to the process behavior chart. If the chart shows unpredictable variation, then you should definitely look for the assignable causes. But if the process displays predictable variation at an undesirable level, then you will have to figure out how to go about changing the process itself. *It is this interaction between the user and the chart that is the key to the effective use of process behavior charts.*

It should be noted that the process behavior chart does not supplant the physician's knowledge or judgment—but it does augment the physician's understanding of the patient's condition. With the real physiological changes that accompany the 100 unit swings shown in Figure 7.9, there will come a point where the physician should and will intervene. This intervention point will be determined by the combination of many different factors, of which the peak flow rate scores are but one element. The process behavior chart can help to evaluate the effectiveness of a course of treatment, but it is naive to assume that it could ever take the place of that synthesis of multiple physiological variables which is the core of the practice of medicine.

At this point Dr. Boggs was concerned with three main objectives. First, he wanted to increase this patient's average peak flow rate above its current level of 155 (which is only 50% of the patient's normal flow rate). Second, he wanted to change this patient's chronic condition so that the Lower Natural Process Limit would be high enough to remove the potential of severe asthma (a patient is considered to be at risk of severe asthma when Lower Natural Process Limit is below 60% of normal). Finally, he wanted to reduce the daily swings between the morning (premedication) flow rates and the evening (post medication) flow rates. (Since we are only looking at the morning values here these daily swings are not part of the record shown in Figures 7.8 and 7.9.)

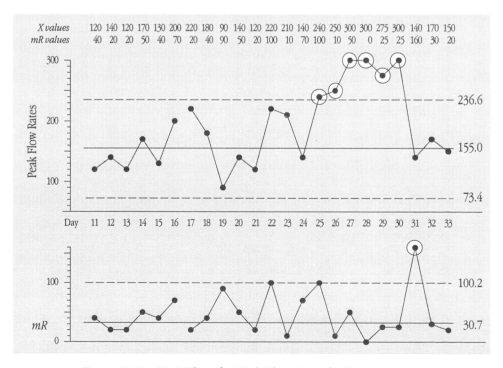

Figure 7.10: *XmR* Chart for Peak Flow Rates for Days 11 to 33

Standard allergy testing showed that this patient was allergic to dogs, house mites, and common pollens. While the patient did respond well to a more effective program of medication, she continued to show low peak flow rates in the mornings, with a large amount of variation from day to day. However, there was one notable exception.

The six points above the Upper Natural Process Limit in Figure 7.10 signal a definite and real improvement in this patient's condition. The spike on the moving range chart for Day 31 signals a sudden break—a definite change for the worse. Since the six high values corresponded to the visit to her aunt's house, and since the spike corresponded to her return home, it was clear that something in the patient's home was causing the asthma. Not only did this chart convince the physician of this, *but it also enabled the physician to convince the parents of this fact.*

Given the compelling evidence of Figure 7.10, the parents began to work to remove the allergens and irritants from the patient's environment. As they made changes at home they continued to collect the data and plot it. Figure 7.11 shows that by Day 82 they had made significant progress toward the first objective of raising the average peak flow rate. Over the period from Day 82 to Day 93 the patient had an average flow rate of 209.2 and an average moving range of 31.7. These values yield the following limits:

$$UNPL = \bar{X} + 2.66\,\overline{mR} = 209.2 + (2.66 \times 31.7) = 293.5$$

$$LNPL = \bar{X} - 2.66\,\overline{mR} = 209.2 - (2.66 \times 31.7) = 124.9$$

$$URL = 3.27\,\overline{mR} = 3.27 \times 31.7 = 103.6$$

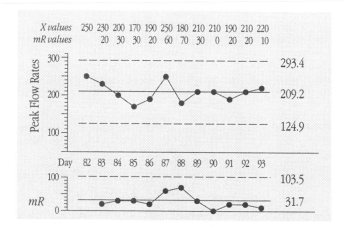

Figure 7.11: *XmR* Chart for Peak Flow Rates—Days 82 to 93

The limits from Figure 7.11 characterize an improved status for the patient. As new Peak Flow Rates were obtained they were plotted against the limits of Figure 7.11. On Figure 7.12 we see that by Day 125 they had a run of eight above the central line—evidence that is beyond a reasonable doubt—there has been further improvement in the patient's condition.

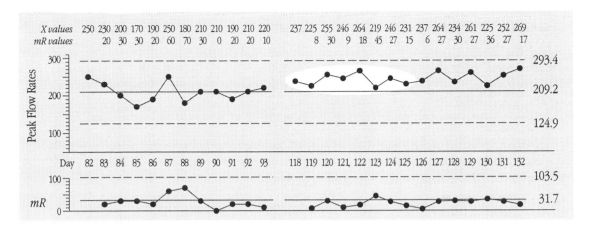

Figure 7.12: *XmR* **Chart for Peak Flow Rates—Days 82 to 93 and Days 118 to 132**

Since the objective is to use the limits to characterize the process, and since we have evidence that the process has changed, it is now appropriate to compute new limits to quantify this improvement. Between Days 118 and 132 the patient had an average peak flow rate of 244.3 with an average moving range of 24.3. These values yield the following limits:

$$UNPL = \bar{X} + 2.66\, \overline{mR} = 244.3 + (\,2.66 \times 24.3\,) = 308.9$$

$$LNPL = \bar{X} - 2.66\, \overline{mR} = 244.3 - (\,2.66 \times 24.3\,) = 179.7$$

$$URL = 3.27\, \overline{mR} = 3.27 \times 24.3 = 79.4$$

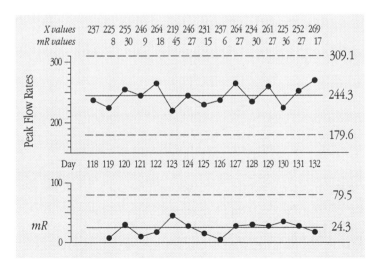

Figure 7.13: *XmR* **Chart for Peak Flow Rates—Days 118 to 132 with New Limits**

These limits show a substantial improvement compared with the baseline in Figure 7.8. Moreover, the reduced variation in these scores indicates a patient who routinely has smaller swings from one day to the next. Finally, the lower limit of 180 places this patient further away from being at risk of serious complications due to her asthma. Without some serious change in her chronic condition she is no longer liable to have episodes with scores below 180. (In contrast to this, consider the first 16 data points where 12 of the 16 values fell below 180.) The Natural Process Limits of 180 to 309 can be taken to characterize the patient's current chronic condition. She will routinely vary within these limits unless, or until, her condition is changed in some way.

The cutoff for being at risk of severe asthma is commonly taken to be a peak flow rate of less than 60 percent of normal. For this patient the cutoff is a peak flow rate of 186. So while the lower limit of 180 is still below this cutoff, the risk of severe asthma for this patient has been greatly reduced.

Continued work with this patient and her parents resulted in further improvements. Her average peak flow rate was raised to 297, which is 96 percent of her normal score. Her Lower Natural Process Limit was raised to 244, which is well above the cutoff for being at risk of severe asthma. And the variation between her morning (premedication) peak flow rates and her evening (post medication) peak flow rates was cut from over 100 points to only 34 points. This success was the result of the combination of medical knowledge, a clear way of understanding the patient's chronic condition, and the effective communication of this condition in order to obtain compliance on the part of the patient and her parents.

In this example we see how the use of the *XmR* chart allows us to separate routine variation from exceptional variation. It allows us to characterize the current status of a process, and to know when a change in that status has occurred. In short, the *XmR* charts allow us to separate the *probable noise* from the *potential signals* within our data. And this distinction is crucial to understanding and using data effectively.

7.4 What Kind of Data Belongs on an *XmR* Chart?

> *The XmR chart is intended*
> *for use with sequences of values*
> *that are logically comparable.*

In Section 7.3 the flow rates placed on the *XmR* chart were the "a.m. premedication flow rates." The patient also collected flow rates in the evening, fifteen minutes after inhaling a bronchodilator (the "p.m. postmedication flow rates"). If we use the symbol X_i to denote the a.m. premedication values, and use the symbol Y_i to denote the p.m. postmedication values, then the *time* series, in a strict sense, would consist of a string of values:

$$X_1, Y_1, X_2, Y_2, X_3, Y_3, X_4, Y_4, ..., X_i, Y_i, ...$$

While these values would be the same measure, obtained by the same instrument, on the same patient, they would be collected under *different* conditions. Dr. Boggs was interested in looking at the time series above because he wanted to know about the daily swings. So he plotted these values in the *XYXY* order. But while this arrangement of these values is a time series, it cannot be meaningfully placed on an *XmR* chart because the moving ranges would not provide the proper yardstick for setting meaningful limits. With the *XYXY* ordering above each moving range would be inflated by the effects of the medication.

So while these data may be arranged in the order *XXXX* or the order *YYYY* and then placed on an *XmR* chart, the *XYXY* ordering may only be plotted as a time series without the benefit of limits.

When values that are *known* to have come from different cause systems are mixed together on a single running record it is inappropriate to compute limits for that plot. While you can combine different measures on a running record when it makes sense to do so, and while such a running record may be interesting and informative, you cannot combine *different measures* on a single *XmR* chart. The limits of the *XmR* chart are appropriate only when the point-to-point variation can be said to characterize the routine variation present in the data. When different measures are combined in a single plot this will no longer be the case, even if the data do constitute a time series.

The *XmR* chart should not be used to compare apples and oranges.

> *The XmR chart should not be used*
> *when the moving ranges do not logically represent*
> *the routine variation of the measure being plotted on the X chart.*

Most time series are a sequence of values for a *single* measure, obtained at different points in time, under similar conditions. Such time series are usually appropriate for an *XmR* chart. Other sequences of values may also be placed on an *XmR* chart, but only when it makes sense to use the point-to-point variation as the yardstick for constructing the limits.

An example of what can happen when non-time-series data are placed on an *XmR* chart is obtained by using the Call Length Data from Table 3.1. If we divide the total connect time for each operator by the number of calls represented we would have the average call length for each operator. These averages were arranged in ascending order and are shown in Table 7.4. When the values of Table 7.4 are placed on an *XmR* chart you get Figure 7.14.

Table 7.4: Ordered Average Call Lengths by Operator

Oper.	14	7	22	17	13	2	18	6	9	20	8	10	1	11	4	3	16	19	21	12	15	5
Avg.	5.3	6.2	7.3	8.0	8.1	8.1	8.2	8.8	9.0	9.0	10.4	10.4	10.5	10.9	11.5	11.6	11.7	11.7	11.8	12.1	13.4	16.7
mR		0.9	1.1	0.7	0.1	0.0	0.1	0.6	0.2	0.0	1.4	0.0	01	0.4	0.6	0.1	0.1	0.0	0.1	0.3	1.3	3.3

The reason that the *X* chart has 15 of the 22 values outside the limits is that the limits have been artificially tightened by having the values arranged in ascending order prior to computing the moving ranges. The moving ranges of Table 7.4 do not characterize the routine variation of the average call lengths because they are based upon the *ordered values*. As a result, the moving ranges do not provide a logical yardstick to use in comparing the average call lengths, and the limits on the *X* chart in Figure 7.14 are highly artificial.

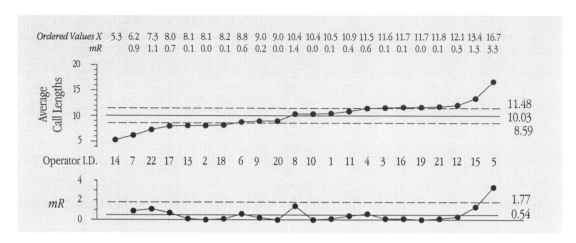

Figure 7.14: *XmR* **Chart for the Ordered Average Call Lengths**

You may place values that do not have a distinct time order on an *XmR* chart if you use an arbitrary ordering. This will be illustrated in the next section. Moreover, when arbitrary orderings are used on an *XmR* chart you are restricted to the use of Detection Rule One (a point outside the limits). Detection Rule Two (runs near the limit) and Detection Rule Three (runs about the central line) both depend heavily upon the notion of sequence—which is why they are called run tests. When the sequence is arbitrary, the use of run tests is inappropriate.

Finally, what do we learn from the moving range chart? The construction and use of the moving range chart is recommended for two reasons. First, a moving range which falls above the Upper Range Limit may be taken as an indication of a potential break in the time series—some sudden shift which is so large that it is unlikely to have occurred by chance. Second, the use of the moving range chart is a simple way to signal to others that you do know the correct way of computing the limits. Since there are many who do not know the difference between the right and wrong ways of computing limits for individual values, and since the right ways all depend upon the moving ranges, the use of an *mR* chart will differentiate you from the uninformed.

7.5   Another Way to Compute Limits for the *XmR* Chart

In the next section we will need to use an alternative method for computing the limits for an *XmR* chart. This alternative method will be based on the median moving range instead of the average moving range.

In general, the average moving range is more efficient in its use of the data than is the median moving range. However, in the presence of one or more very large ranges, the average moving range is subject to being more inflated than is the median moving range. When this happens the median moving range will frequently yield the more appropriate limits. For this reason it is worthwhile to know how to use a median moving range to compute limits for an *XmR* chart. We will illustrate use of the median moving range with the data in Table 7.5. These values are the same values as shown in Table 7.4, however now they are arranged according to the operator ID numbers.

Table 7.5: Average Call Lengths by Operator

Oper.	1	2	3	4	5	6	7	8	9	10	11	12	13	14	15	16	17	18	19	20	21	22
Avg.	10.5	8.1	11.6	11.5	16.7	8.8	6.2	10.4	9.0	10.4	10.9	12.1	8.1	5.3	13.4	11.7	8.0	8.2	11.7	9.0	11.8	7.3
mR		2.4	3.5	0.1	5.2	7.9	2.6	4.2	1.4	1.4	0.5	1.2	4.0	2.8	8.1	1.7	3.7	0.2	3.5	2.7	2.8	4.5

As usual, the average of the individual values will be used as the central line for the X chart. The average of the 22 operator average call lengths is 10.03.

To find the median moving range you must first arrange the 21 *moving ranges* in ascending order:

0.1 0.2 0.5 1.2 1.4 1.4 1.7 2.4 2.6 2.7 2.8 2.8 3.5 3.5 3.7 4.0 4.2 4.5 5.2 7.9 8.1

Because there are 21 values here, the median value will be the eleventh value from either end. In this case the median of these moving ranges is 2.8. This value will be used as the central line for the *mR* chart.

- The Upper Natural Process Limit for the X chart is found by multiplying the median moving range by the scaling factor of 3.14 and then adding the product to the average of the individual values:

$$UNPL = \bar{X} + (3.14 \times \widetilde{mR}) = 10.03 + (3.14 \times 2.8) = 18.8$$

- The Lower Natural Process Limit for the X chart is found by multiplying the median moving range by the scaling factor of 3.14 and then subtracting the product from the average of the individual values:

$$LNPL = \bar{X} - (3.14 \times \widetilde{mR}) = 10.03 - (3.14 \times 2.8) = 1.2$$

- The Upper Range Limit for the *mR* chart is found by multiplying the median moving range by the scaling factor of 3.86:

$$URL = 3.86 \times \widetilde{mR} = 3.86 \times 2.8 = 10.8$$

The scaling factors of 3.14 and 3.86 used in the preceding calculations are specific constants developed for computing limits for an *XmR* chart using a median moving range. They are the appropriate values to convert the median moving range into the values needed to filter out the routine variation.

The *XmR* chart in Figure 7.15 shows no evidence of detectable differences in average call lengths for these 22 operators. Therefore, given these data, it would be inappropriate to reprimand Operator 5 or to congratulate Operator 14. Using these data you cannot meaningfully differentiate between these operators on the basis of their average call lengths.

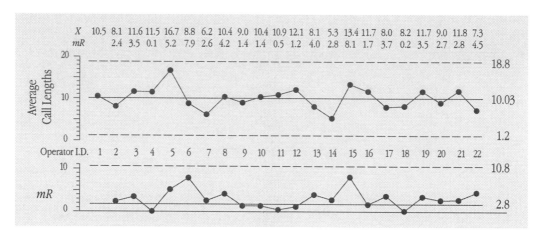

Figure 7.15: *XmR* **Chart for Operator Average Call Lengths**

Why does Figure 7.15 work when Figure 7.14 did not work? In Figure 7.15 the ordering of the values was an arbitrary ordering *which did not depend upon the values themselves.* Instead of using the operator ID numbers, we could have used operator names. Any arbitrary ordering that does not depend upon the X values will result in moving ranges that can be considered to represent the background variation. While logical orderings are preferred to arbitrary ones, there are times when arbitrary orderings are all that are available.

7.6 Charting Profits and Losses

This example shows a report-card chart for an unpredictable process, illustrates a situation where the median moving range is the preferred method of computing limits, and outlines a process of investigation that uses the charts to determine how much uncertainty should be attached to forecast values.

One company always began its monthly report with a sentence like:

"January's pretax earnings of $2.5 million were $4.4 million better than our forecast."

While these numbers sound good, it takes the perspective of context and time to fully comprehend just what they mean. And the simplest way to gain this perspective is to use an *XmR* chart. The actual earnings for this company for one year are given in Table 7.6.

Table 7.6: Actual Earnings

Month	J	F	M	A	M	J	J	A	S	O	N	D
Actual Earnings	2.5	2.3	16.3	6.3	7.6	16.3	7.1	7.8	7.8	9.9	10.5	- 4.8
Moving Ranges		0.2	14.0	10.0	1.3	8.7	9.2	0.7	0.0	2.1	0.6	15.3

Simply reading over these numbers is enough to give you a sense that this company's earnings are fairly erratic. Also the moving ranges are either small or large, indicating big swings in the earnings. If we look at a stem-and-leaf plot of these moving ranges we get:

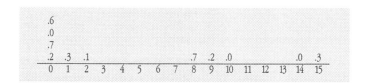

Figure 7.16: Stem-and-Leaf Plot of Moving Ranges from Table 7.6

The average moving range is 5.64, while the median moving range is 2.1. The stem-and-leaf plot in Figure 7.16 is very disjointed. There are no values anywhere near the average value of 5.64. Also the average and the median are quite different. When taken together, these two facts suggest that the average moving range has been inflated. Therefore, we shall use the median moving range to compute limits for the *XmR* chart.

Using the median moving range we get the following limits:

$$UNPL = \bar{X} + 3.14\ m\tilde{R} = 7.47 + (\ 3.14 \times 2.1\ ) = 14.07$$

$$LNPL = \bar{X} - 3.14\ m\tilde{R} = 7.47 - (\ 3.14 \times 2.1\ ) = 0.87$$

$$URL = 3.86\ m\tilde{R} = 3.86 \times 2.1 = 8.12$$

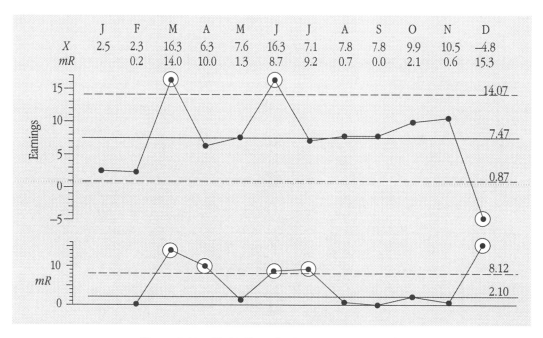

Figure 7.17: *XmR* Chart for Earnings Per Month

The chart in Figure 7.17 shows that the earnings for this company are erratic and changing from month to month. Their sales levels and expenses are changing to such an extent that even this high level summary does not fall within the computed limits. Here the computed limits do not predict the future earnings. The earnings for this company simply do not display that long-term consistency which is the essence of a predictable process.

Therefore, rather than using the past earnings as a guide to predict future earnings, they will have to use their knowledge about the current conditions to guess (estimate or forecast) what their earnings will be each month. Evidently this was done, because they have a forecast value for the earnings each month. These forecasts are shown in Table 7.7.

Of course, the next logical question is how accurate are their forecasts? This can be determined by subtracting the forecast earnings from the actual earnings and plotting the difference on an *XmR* chart.

Table 7.7: Forecast Earnings and Actual Earnings

Month	J	F	M	A	M	J	J	A	S	O	N	D
Actual Earnings	2.5	2.3	16.3	6.3	76	16.3	7.1	7.8	7.8	9.9	10.5	−4.8
Forecast Earnings	−1.9	2.8	12.7	3.9	5.6	9.9	6.7	4.7	5.6	7.0	8.9	−0.4
Actual − Forecast	4.4	−0.5	3.6	2.4	2.0	6.4	0.4	3.1	2.2	2.9	1.6	−4.4

The average of these differences is 2.01, and the average moving range is 2.96. (Since the median moving range of 2.7 is close to the average moving range we do not see the discrepancy observed on the previous page. Therefore, we shall use the average moving range to compute the limits for this *XmR* chart.)

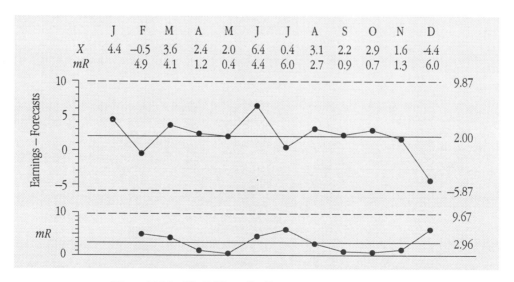

Figure 7.18: *XmR* **Chart for Earnings Minus Forecasts**

Figure 7.18 tells us several things about this company's earnings forecasts. First of all, the central line for the X chart shows that their earnings average about $2.0 million better than their forecasts. In other words, the best estimate of their earnings will be the published forecast plus two million. Whether this is deliberate or unconscious, there is a two million dollar bias in the forecast values, and the chart documents this bias.

Second, since all of the points fall within the limits, their earnings vary around this average in a predictable manner.

Third, the interpretation of the limits on the X chart would suggest that for any given published forecast you could predict that the earnings would be in the interval:

$$[\text{ forecast} + \$10 \text{ million }] \text{ to } [\text{ forecast} - \$6 \text{ million }]$$

That is, their earnings could exceed their published forecasts by as much as $10 million, or they could fall short by as much as $6 million.

"Such limits are far too wide to be useful." Are they? It is not the limits that are at fault but rather the noise in the data. The limits in Figure 7.18 are based upon the data given. *These limits are wide simply because these data are full of noise.* The process behavior chart limits are the Voice of the Process. Whether or not you like the Voice of the Process does not matter to the process.

"But the uncertainty in the forecasts indicated by these limits is greater than their average earnings. Figure 7.17 shows their average earnings for this year to be around $7.5 million per month, while the uncertainty in Figure 7.18 is plus or minus $8 million. How can they use numbers that are this uncertain?"

The answer is that they must use these numbers very carefully. If they do not know how weak their forecasts are, they will be tempted to interpret them as being more precise than they actually are, and thereby confuse noise with signals. No matter what method or technique you may use to obtain a forecast, it is the noise in the data that will limit how good that forecast can possibly be. The number you use may be the best number available, but it can still be overwhelmed by noise. You cannot begin to use a number properly until you know its limitations. Process behavior charts explicitly show those limitations. Other techniques hide these limitations by sweeping them under the rug.

7.7 How Do You Use These Charts for Continual Improvement?

Process behavior charts provide an objective way of separating routine variation (probable noise) from exceptional variation (potential signals). The importance of this distinction is made every time you turn on a radio—we have yet to see someone deliberately tune in and listen to static.

Once you and your co-workers have a way to separate potential signals from probable noise, you will find it much easier to agree on what constitutes a signal and therefore what deserves attention. At the same time, you and everyone else will spend less time chasing noise, dreaming up explanations of routine, common cause variation, and generally spinning your wheels.

Thus, the real secret of the effective use of process behavior charts is in the follow-through. It is how you use the charts to discover what your process can do, or can be made to do. It is how you interact with the chart to understand the behavior of your process. It is how you communicate your process knowledge to others in a way that they can comprehend quickly and easily.

In short, the secret of the effective use of process behavior charts is the way of thinking that goes with them. And you only get this through sound teaching and much practice.

The alternative is described in Chapter Nine.

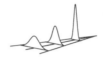

7.8 Exercises

EXERCISE 7.1:

The moving ranges in Table 7.5 are, respectively:

2.4, 3.5, 0.1, 5.2, 7.9, 2.6, 4.2, 1.4, 1.4, 0.5, 1.2, 4.0, 2.8, 8.1, 1.7, 3.7, 0.2, 3.5, 2.7, 2.8, and 4.5

The average is 10.03. Find the average moving range.
Compute limits for an *XmR* chart using the average moving range.
Compare these limits with those shown in Figure 7.15. Is there any practical difference?

Computation Worksheets:	EXERCISE 7.1	EXERCISE 7.2
Average Value = _____		Average Value = _____
Average Moving Range = _____		Median Moving Range = _____
$2.66 \times \overline{mR}$ = _____		$3.14 \times \widetilde{mR}$ = _____
$UNPL = \overline{X} + 2.66\,\overline{mR}$ = _____		$UNPL = \overline{X} + 3.14\,\widetilde{mR}$ = _____
$LNPL = \overline{X} - 2.66\,\overline{mR}$ = _____		$LNPL = \overline{X} - 3.14\,\widetilde{mR}$ = _____
$URL = 3.27 \times \overline{mR}$ = _____		$URL = 3.86 \times \widetilde{mR}$ = _____

EXERCISE 7.2:

The percentages of high school seniors who smoked daily for the years 1984 to 1993 are: 18.8, 19.6, 18.7, 18.6, 18.1, 18.9, 19.2, 18.2, 17.3, and 19.0 respectively. The moving ranges for these values are:

$$0.8, \ 0.9, \ 0.1, \ 0.5, \ 0.8, \ 0.3, \ 1.0, \ 0.9, \text{ and } 1.7.$$

Find limits for an *XmR* chart using the median moving range.
Compare these limits with those in the latter portion of Figure 6.14.
Is there any practical difference?

EXERCISE 7.3:

Verify the limits shown in Figure 7.18.

Computation Worksheets:	EXERCISE 7.3	EXERCISE 7.4
Average Value = _____		Average Value = _____
Average Moving Range = _____		Median Moving Range = _____
$2.66 \times \overline{mR}$ = _____		$3.14 \times \widetilde{mR}$ = _____
$UNPL = \bar{X} + 2.66\,\overline{mR}$ = _____		$UNPL = \bar{X} + 3.14\,\widetilde{mR}$ = _____
$LNPL = \bar{X} - 2.66\,\overline{mR}$ = _____		$LNPL = \bar{X} - 3.14\,\widetilde{mR}$ = _____
$URL = 3.27 \times \overline{mR}$ = _____		$URL = 3.86 \times \widetilde{mR}$ = _____

EXERCISE 7.4:

Compute limits for the data in Figure 7.18 using the median moving range.

Chapter Eight

What Makes the *XmR* Chart Work?

This chapter may not be of immediate interest to the beginner. It is included here because there are many questions which inevitably arise when people start using process behavior charts. When these questions arise, it is helpful to have access to some explanation of what makes the charts work. The purpose of this chapter is to provide these explanations. Therefore, the time to read the following sections is when you have questions about the background of the process behavior chart technique. So treat the following sections like selections in a cafeteria line to be picked up or skipped over as appropriate.

8.1 The Logic Behind Process Behavior Charts

The logic behind process behavior charts is shown in Figure 8.1. In order to justify the use of summary statistics to compute the limits, we begin with the tentative assumption that the process is predictable.

Next, based upon the summary statistics, a prediction is made concerning how the process should behave. In particular, this prediction comes in the form of calculated limits which define the expected amount of routine variation for the data.

Finally, the observed values are compared with the predicted limits. There are two possible outcomes for this comparison:

1. If the observations are consistent with the predictions, then the process may be predictable. At least there is no solid evidence to contradict the assumption of predictability for the process.

2. If the observations are inconsistent with the predictions, the process is unpredictable. This is due to the nature of the way the limits were computed. The inconsistency between the observations and the predictions is almost surely due to an incorrect assumption of predictability rather than a violation of the principles behind the calculation of the limits.

Thus, evidence of unpredictability is strong evidence which can safely be used as the basis for action. The absence of such evidence is not as conclusive, but since no action is required, the process should be left alone until such a time when the process behavior charts indicate that the process has changed.

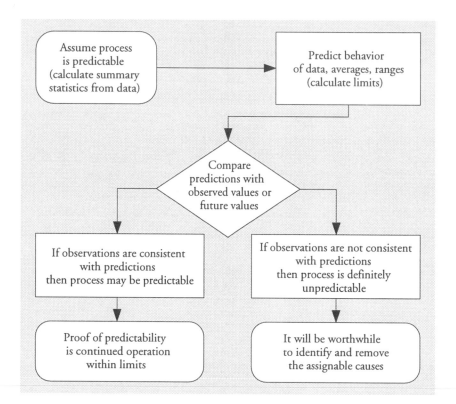

Figure 8.1: The Logic Behind Process Behavior Charts

It will always be a mistake to look for an assignable cause prior to detecting a change in the process. No matter how eloquent the explanation, action taken in the absence of a detectable signal from the data is essentially based upon nothing more than wishes and hopes. This is why it is imperative to learn how to separate potential signals from probable noise. Process behavior charts are the primary tool for filtering out the probable noise which is present in every data set.

8.2 Why Three-Sigma Limits?

Shewhart chose to draw the line between routine variation and exceptional variation according to the formula:

$$\text{Average} \pm 3\,\text{Sigma}$$

which is why the Natural Process Limits for the individual values, the Upper Range Limit, and those limits which we will encounter later may all be referred to as *three-sigma limits*. They are all specific applications of the generic formula above. But why did Shewhart decide to use this formula instead of some other? To find Shewhart's rationale we have to go to his first book, *Economic Control of Quality of Manufactured Product*. Some excerpts which explain his thinking follow:

> "Hence we must use limits such that through their use we will not waste too much time looking unnecessarily for trouble."

We do not want to have an undue number of false alarms—that is, we do not want values to fall outside the limits by accident. Since you are supposed to look for an assignable cause whenever a point falls outside the limits, an excessive number of false alarms would undermine your credibility and discredit the technique.

> "The method of attack is to establish limits of variability...such that, when [an observation] is found outside these limits, looking for an assignable cause is worth while."

We do not want to detect each and every little change in the process, but only those changes that are large enough to dominate the common cause variation. It is just those assignable causes, whose impact is great enough to justify the time and expense of investigation, that we are interested in detecting and removing. We want to detect the strong signals.

> "If more than one statistic is used, then the limits on all the statistics should be chosen so that the probability of looking for trouble when any one of the chosen statistics falls outside its own limits is economic."

Multiple statistics generate multiple opportunities for false alarms, so we need to be very conservative in what we call a potential signal.

> "...we usually choose a symmetrical range characterized by [t-sigma] limits"

A symmetric interval is generic and safely conservative. The term *sigma* denotes a standard unit of dispersion.

> "Experience indicates that $t = 3$ seems to be an acceptable economic value."

Theory suggests that three-sigma limits should filter out virtually all of the probable noise, and experience indicates that three-sigma limits are sufficiently conservative for practice.

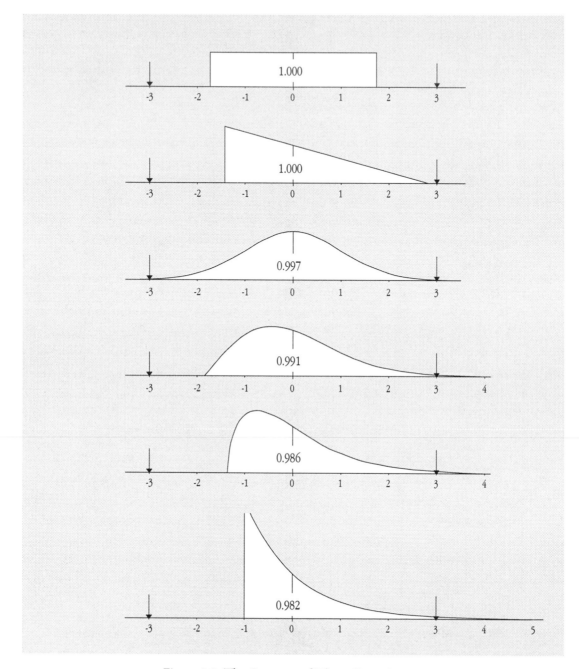

Figure 8.2: The Coverage of Three-Sigma Limits

"Hence the method of establishing allowable limits of variation in a statistic depends upon theory to furnish the expected value and the standard deviation of the statistic, and upon empirical evidence to justify the choice of [three-sigma] limits."

Three-sigma limits are not used because they correspond to some theoretical probability. They are used because they are consistent with theory and have been thoroughly proven in practice to be sufficiently conservative. However, since it is hard to draw pictures to convey the weight of the empirical evidence, we shall have to resort to the use of theory to show just how conservative and effective three-sigma limits happen to be. To this end, Figure 8.2 shows six curves, each of which represents a theoretical probability distribution function. These six curves were selected to represent a broad range of shapes. The three-sigma limits are shown in each case, and the proportion of the area that falls within the three-sigma limits is shown on each curve.

The first remarkable thing we can learn from Figure 8.2 is that, in each case, the three-sigma limits cover virtually all of the common cause variation. This means that we do not have to have a "well-behaved" process in order for the limits to work. They are completely general, and work with all types of process behaviors. When a process is predictable, no matter what the shape of the histogram, virtually all of the routine values will fall within the interval defined by the formula: Average ± 3 Sigma. This is why process behavior charts, with their three-sigma limits, will yield very few false alarms.

The second thing we can learn from Figure 8.2 is what it tells us about points that fall outside the three-sigma limits—they are much more likely to be due to a dominant assignable cause than to any common cause. So when a point falls outside the limits you will be justified in looking for an assignable cause.

The third thing we can learn from Figure 8.2 is what happens with very skewed distributions. The three lower curves have lower limits that look like they will be very ineffective. A process with such a skewed histogram would have to move by a huge amount to show any values below the lower limit. While this is a fair interpretation of the three bottom curves shown in Figure 8.2, the reality is somewhat different. In practice, skewed distributions occur when the data pile up against a boundary or barrier. This barrier would be on the left in Figure 8.2. Such a barrier precludes any substantial shift toward the lower limit, and effectively makes the lower limit irrelevant. The chart will be a one-sided chart, with the only real potential for change being a shift to the right. And it is the long right-hand tails that get covered by the three-sigma limits in these cases. So with skewed data the chart places the protection just where you need it. (Of course, three-sigma limits work equally well when the data are skewed to the left.)

The fourth thing we can learn from Figure 8.2 is that we do not need to be overly concerned about the exactness of our computations. We do not have to get the exact three-sigma limits—anywhere in the vicinity will suffice. In those extreme situations where the curves go all the way out to the three-sigma limits, they are very flat when they get there. If our calculations should err a little bit, and we end up with 2.5 sigma limits, or 3.5 sigma limits, we will still be filtering out virtually all of the noise, and anything we detect will be a potential signal.

Figure 8.3 shows the 192 counts from Table 5.1. These counts were used in groups of 24 values at a time to compute limits, resulting in the eight sets of limits shown above. While the limits vary, the message remains the same: this process is predictable. Three-sigma limits

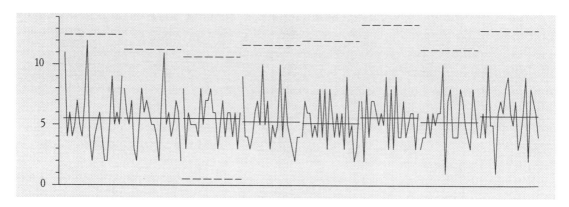

Figure 8.3: Computed Three-Sigma Limits Filter Out Routine Variation

filter out the probable noise.

Figure 8.4 shows 600 values obtained from a chemical process. After every 100 batches they would recompute the limits. No matter which segment you pick there are points outside the limits and the interpretation of the chart remains the same: this process is unpredictable. Thus, three-sigma limits allow you to detect the potential signals, even when the limits are computed using the data from the unpredictable process.

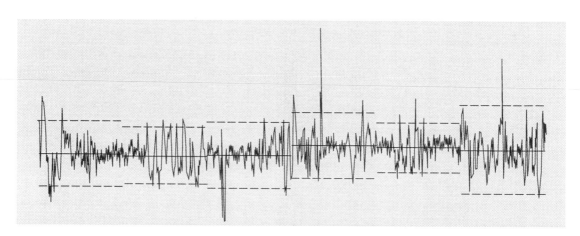

Figure 8.4: Computed Three-Sigma Limits Detect Potential Signals

When we compute three-sigma limits from our data we do not have to worry about whether or not we found the "right" value. Anywhere in the ballpark will suffice. The objective is not to find the right number, but rather to take the right action.

Three-sigma limits are not used because they correspond to some theoretical probability. They are used because they are consistent with theory and have been thoroughly proven in practice to be sufficiently conservative. They filter out the probable noise and reveal the potential signals. Three-sigma limits work. Accept no substitutes.

8.3 Where Does the Value of 2.66 Come From?

In Figure 8.1 the first box says "calculate summary statistics from data," while the second box says "calculate limits." In practice this is just what we do: we leap from the summary statistics to the limits in a single step by the use of the scaling factors such as 2.66, etc. The reason for this is simple—process behavior charts were first used in a day when there were no hand-held calculators, no desk-top computers, and no spreadsheet programs. When people were doing the computations by hand all short-cuts were appreciated. And that is exactly what values like 2.66 are: computational short-cuts. These values accomplish two operations in one computation.

The first operation is to convert the summary statistic for dispersion into a measure of dispersion that is appropriate for the data. That is, we need to convert, say, the average moving range into a measure of dispersion for the individual values. If we denote the individual values by the symbol, X, then we could denote this measure of dispersion for the X values as *Sigma(X)*. The formula for this conversion is:[*]

$$Sigma(X) \ = \ \frac{\overline{mR}}{d_2}$$

When working with moving ranges the effective subgroup size is $n = 2$. (This is because each moving range is a two-point moving range, based on pairs of successive values.) With an effective subgroup size of two, the value for d_2 is 1.128 (see Table 1 in the Appendix).

The second operation is to compute the three-sigma distance. Thus we get:

$$3 \ Sigma(X) \ = \ 3 \ \frac{\overline{mR}}{1.128} \ = \ \frac{3 \ \overline{mR}}{1.128} \ = \ 2.660 \ \overline{mR}$$

So when you use the scaling factors, such as 2.660, you are computing the appropriate three-sigma limits. It is automatic. The scaling factors incorporate the multiplier of 3.0 along with the appropriate adjustment terms to convert the raw statistic into the desired limit. While the derivation of some of the other constants is more complex than that shown above, the basic operations are the same. We need a variety of scaling factors because there are different dispersion statistics which need to be converted into the appropriate measure of dispersion.

8.4 But How Can We Get Good Limits From Bad Data?

In order for the process behavior chart approach to work it has to be able to *detect* the presence of assignable causes even though the limits may be computed from data which are *affected* by the assignable causes. In other words, we have to be able to get good limits from

---

[*] See footnote on Table One of the Appendix for a more complete explanation of *Sigma(X)*.

bad data. This requirement places some constraints on how we perform our computations.

In order to get good limits from bad data with an *XmR* chart you will have to use the moving ranges to characterize dispersion. The moving ranges measure the short-term, point-to-point variation and then the computations use this short-term variation to place limits on the long-term variability. This is why limits for an *XmR* chart *must* be computed using either the average moving range or the median moving range. You cannot use any other measure of dispersion to compute limits for an *X* chart.

Specifically, you cannot use global measures of dispersion, such as the standard deviation statistic computed on a single pass through all of the data to compute limits. Whenever the data are affected by assignable causes a global measure of dispersion will always be severely inflated, resulting in limits that will be too wide and a process behavior chart that will be misleading.

So do not attempt to use any do-it-yourself formulas. Use the formulas and the scaling factors shown in the next section, and if a stranger, or even a friend, offers you another way of computing limits, just say no!

8.5 So Which Way Should You Compute Limits?

When data occur one value at a time it will usually be logical to place them on an *XmR* chart. The two-point moving range will be used to measure the routine variation, and this variation will be summarized using either the average moving range or a median moving range.

When using the average moving range the formulas for the central lines and limits of an *XmR* chart are:

$$UNPL_X = \bar{X} + 2.660\ \overline{mR}$$
$$CL_X = \bar{X}$$
$$LNPL_X = \bar{X} - 2.660\ \overline{mR}$$
$$URL_R = 3.268\ \overline{mR}$$
$$CL_R = \overline{mR}$$

When using a median moving range the formulas for the central lines and limits of an *XmR* chart are:

$$UNPL_X = \bar{X} + 3.145\ \widetilde{mR}$$
$$CL_X = \bar{X}$$
$$LNPL_X = \bar{X} - 3.145\ \widetilde{mR}$$
$$URL_R = 3.865\ \widetilde{mR}$$
$$CL_R = \widetilde{mR}$$

While the limits above are sometimes referred to as the *control limits for X* and the *upper control limit for R*, we have chosen to call them Natural Process Limits and the Upper Range Limit in the interest of clarity.

Of course, because of the nature of the scaling factors, you cannot "mix and match" them. You have to use the scaling factors that are specific to your summary measure of dispersion. If you use an average moving range to compute limits, you have to use the factors 2.660 and 3.268. If you use a median moving range to compute limits, you have to use the factors 3.145 and 3.865. As was shown in the previous chapters, rounding these scaling factors off to 2.66, 3.27, 3.14, and 3.86 is acceptable.

But how can you choose between these two computational approaches? Both are right. In the end it comes down to a matter of judgment and personal choice. The objective of the computations is to obtain values that will bracket approximately 99 percent to 100 percent of the common cause variation, and both approaches will do this.

The average moving range will generally be easier for people to use because they already know how to find an average. To use the median moving range you will have to know how to find a median. While this is not hard, it is new to many and therefore creates an extra barrier to the use of the charts.

The average moving range is more efficient in its use of the data than is the median moving range. However, in the presence of one or more very large ranges the average moving range is subject to being more inflated than the median moving range. When this happens the median moving range will frequently yield the more appropriate limits.

The limits based upon an average moving range will begin to "solidify" when 17 or more values are used in the computation. Limits based upon a median moving range will begin to "solidify" when 23 or more values are used in the computation. Fewer data may be used with either approach, but the limits will be progressively "softer" as the amount of data used decreases.

So you may choose to always use an average moving range, or you may choose to always use a median moving range, or you may choose to switch between them depending upon the characteristics of the data. Take your choice.

8.6 Chunky Data

Most problems with process behavior charts are fail-safe. That is, the charts will err in the direction of hiding a signal rather than causing a false alarm. Because of this feature, when you get a signal, you can trust the chart to be guiding you in the right direction.

There is only one exception to this fail-safe feature of the process behavior charts, and that is chunky data. Data are said to be chunky when the distance between the possible values becomes too large. Measuring a person's height to the nearest yard would result in chunky data—an increment of one yard is so large that it will obscure the variation from person to person. Excessive round-off is one way to create chunky data. Using measurement units that are too large is another way.

Table 8.1: **Fifty Values from a Fairly Predictable Process**

214.0	214.3	213.7	213.4	213.5	213.8	214.3	214.3	214.5	214.6
213.9	213.4	214.7	214.8	214.9	214.3	214.1	213.7	213.8	214.0
214.2	214.2	214.5	213.5	213.6	213.6	214.4	214.3	213.6	213.7
214.2	214.7	213.7	214.2	213.8	214.3	213.7	214.5	213.7	213.8
214.1	214.2	214.7	214.0	214.0	214.2	213.7	213.4	214.0	213.2

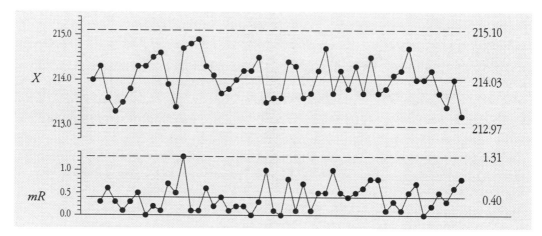

Figure 8.5: *XmR* Chart for Fifty Values from a Fairly Predictable Process

The effect of chunky data upon a process behavior chart will be illustrated by starting with a set of values that are fairly predictable, and then rounding these values off to make them chunky. The *XmR* chart for the values in Table 8.1 is given in Figure 8.5. (The values in Tables 8.1 and 8.2 should be read row by row.) In Table 8.2 the values from Table 8.1 were rounded off and then used to create the *XmR* chart in Figure 8.6.

None of the values in Figure 8.5 fall outside the limits. Yet in Figure 8.6 ten individual values and one moving range fall outside the limits. The only difference between these two charts is the size of the increments for the values. The points outside the limits in Figure 8.6 have nothing to do with the behavior of the underlying process. They are the result of chunky data.

> *Chunky data can result in points that fall outside the limits*
> *even when the underlying process is predictable.*

Fortunately, when this problem exists, it is easy to identify. The way to identify chunky data begins with an inspection of the values to determine the size of the increment present. You want to determine just how close together two of the values could be—what is the measurement unit used. You may do this by examining the values or the moving ranges since they will both display the same sized increments. In Table 8.1 the values are recorded

Table 8.2: Fifty Values from a Fairly Predictable Process Rounded to Whole Numbers

214	214	214	213	214	214	214	214	214	215
214	213	215	215	215	214	214	214	214	214
214	214	214	214	214	214	214	214	214	214
214	215	214	214	214	214	214	214	214	214
214	214	215	214	214	214	214	213	214	213

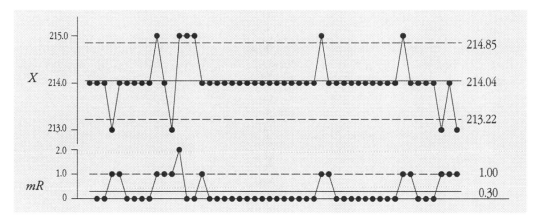

Figure 8.6: *XmR* Chart for Fifty Rounded Values from a Fairly Predictable Process

to one decimal place. In Table 8.2 the values are given to the nearest whole number.

Next you will need to determine how many possible range values there are between zero and the Upper Range Limit. Since the ranges will display the same sized increments as the individual values, you can begin with zero and count by increments until you get a value above the *URL*. If the number of possible range values, including zero, within the limits is three or less, then you have chunky data.

In Figure 8.5 the *mR* chart has an *URL* of 1.31. With an increment of 0.1, there are a total of 14 possible values for the ranges below the limit. In Figure 8.6 the *URL* is 1.00. With an increment of 1.0, there are only two possible values (namely 0 and 1) within the limits of this *mR* chart.

> *For the XmR chart, your data can be said to be chunky if there are three or fewer possible values below the Upper Range Limit. When this happens the limits for the X chart will be distorted. In order to be safe from the distorting effects and artificial signals created by chunky data, you need to have a minimum of four possible values below the Upper Range Limit.*

Thus Figure 8.5 is free of the effects of chunky data, while Figure 8.6 suffers the effects of chunky data. We therefore cannot safely interpret the signals on Figure 8.6 as being due to assignable causes in the process—the points outside the limits are a consequence of using chunky data to construct the chart.

The procedure for checking for chunky data consists of three steps:

1. Determine the increment displayed by the individual values.
2. Determine the Upper Range Limit.
3. Determine the number of possible values for the ranges within the limits. If this number is below the threshold your data are chunky.

For average and range charts (see Chapter 12) with subgroups of size n > 2, the data will be said to be chunky when the range chart has four or fewer possible values within the limits.

For average and range charts with subgroups of size n = 2, the data will be said to be chunky when the range chart has three or fewer possible values below the Upper Range Limit.

When you have chunky data the remedy is to use smaller increments in the values. If you cannot do this then you will not be able to compute appropriate limits for your process behavior chart—you are effectively limited to using a running record.[*]

8.7 Exercises

EXERCISE 8.1:
Another formula for $Sigma(X)$ is: [†]

$$Sigma(X) = \frac{m\widetilde{R}}{d_4}$$

For moving ranges the effective subgroup size is $n = 2$, and for $n = 2$ the value for d_4 is 0.954. Verify that the scaling factor to convert the median two-point moving range into an estimate of $3\ Sigma(X)$ should be 3.145.

EXERCISE 8.2:
Figure 8.5 was characterized as a fairly predictable process.
What potential signal exists in Figure 8.5?
Is this a strong signal?

---

[*] For a more complete explanation of this problem see *Understanding Statistical Process Control, Second Edition*, by Wheeler and Chambers, Section 9.1.

[†] See footnote on Table One of the Appendix for a more complete explanation of *Sigma(X)*.

Chapter Nine

Avoiding Man-Made Chaos

9.1 Creating Man-Made Chaos

Today in countless organizations around the world, individuals will be given pages of numbers and told to analyze the data and prepare a report. Perhaps you have been given this job. What did you do? What do you think most of these people will do? In our experience, most people simply look up what was done last time—and then repeat it. Only the details and the data are updated—the format for the report is the same from month to month, quarter to quarter, and year to year.

As an illustration, we will use the quarterly sales data for six regions. The report for the Fourth Quarter of Year Four might consist of a list of the sales figures, along with such interpretative guides as the percentage change from the previous quarter and the percentage change from the same quarter last year.

Table 9.1: Quarterly Sales Volumes for Fourth Quarter of Year Four

	Sales Volumes	Percent Change from Last Quarter		Percent Change from Same Quarter Last Year		Performance Index
Region F	670	21.6%	very good	65.4%	very good	+ + + +
Region D	802	14.4%	good	25.3%	very good	+ + +
Region E	462	27.3%	very good	8.5%	good	+ + +
Region C	1,196	–18.4%	very bad	5.6%	good	–
Region B	878	–11.9%	bad	–12.1%	bad	– –
Region A	952	–8.3%	bad	–26.5%	very bad	– – –

Once these values have been collected and the comparison percentages computed, the question is what to do next. Since the regions are different sizes it is inappropriate to rank them according to sales amounts. But the percentages might be compared.

We could rank these regions according to the percent changes from the previous quarter. This approach would yield the ranking E, F, D, A, B, C. The winner would be Region E, with its 27.3 percent gain, and the loser would be Region C with its 18.4 percent drop.

But we could also rank the regions using the percent changes from the same quarter last year, which would result in the ordering F, D, E, C, B, A. Clearly Region F with its 65.4 percent gain should be singled out for special praise, while Region A with its 26.5 percent drop should be closely examined.

But which ordering should they use? In order to solve the dilemma this company created a performance index. The performance index combined the two percentages for each region by characterizing each percentage as very good (++), good (+), bad (−), or very bad (− −), and then adding up the pluses and minuses and using the results to rank the regions. The ranking in Table 9.1 is based upon this performance index as shown in the last column.

Clearly Regions F, D and E won the esteem sweepstakes this quarter. For their "superior performance" these three regions were awarded plaques to place on their office walls. Regions A and B received reprimands. And the manager for Region C kept his head down and stayed quiet. Since this was the way it had always been, everyone accepted that this was the way it should be. You learned to "take your beatings like a man" or else you got out of sales.

Three months later this whole game was played out again.

Table 9.2: Quarterly Sales Volumes for First Quarter of Year Five

	Sales	Percent Change from Last Quarter		Percent Change from Same Quarter Last Year		Performance Index
Region A	1041	9.3%	good	36.1%	very good	+ + +
Region B	939	6.9%	good	6.4%	good	+ +
Region C	1330	11.2%	very good	−1.6%	bad	+
Region D	749	−6.6%	bad	8.3%	good	0
Region F	588	−12.3%	very bad	26.2%	very good	0
Region E	420	−9.1%	bad	−5.7%	bad	− −

Obviously Regions A and B took their reprimands to heart! They moved from the cellar to the top of the list for the next quarter. While Regions A and B got commendations, Region E received the only reprimand handed out this quarter.

Table 9.3: Quarterly Sales Volumes for Second Quarter of Year Five

	Sales	Percent Change from Last Quarter		Percent Change from Same Quarter Last Year		Performance Index
Region F	699	18.9%	very good	30.4%	very good	+ + + +
Region D	762	1.7%	good	5.4%	good	+ +
Region E	454	8.1%	good	−0.2%	bad	0
Region A	1020	−2.0%	bad	1.2%	good	0
Region B	834	−11.2%	very bad	−2.0%	bad	− − −
Region C	1003	−24.6%	very bad	−25.9%	very bad	− − − −

For the Second Quarter of Year Five, Region E moved up in rankings, while Region F took the honors. Regions B and C received reprimands. After all, management's job is to assign blame, isn't it?

Table 9.4: Quarterly Sales Volumes for Third Quarter of Year Five

	Sales	Percent Change from Last Quarter		Percent Change from Same Quarter Last Year		Performance Index
Region F	743	6.2%	good	34.8%	very good	+ + +
Region D	807	5.9%	good	15.1%	good	+ +
Region E	447	–1.5%	bad	23.1%	very good	+
Region C	1197	19.4%	very good	–18.3%	very bad	0
Region A	976	–4.3%	bad	–5.9%	bad	– –
Region B	688	–17.5%	very bad	–31.0%	very bad	– – – –

For the Third Quarter of Year Five, Region C moved up in the rankings, but Region B fell to the bottom. So while Region A was reprimanded, Region B was threatened. Regions F and D were commended, while regions E and C tried to avoid attention.

Table 9.5: Quarterly Sales Volume for Fourth Quarter of Year Five

	Sales	Percent Change from Last Quarter		Percent Change from Same Quarter Last Year		Performance Index
Region A	1,148	17.6%	very good	20.6%	very good	+ + + +
Region C	1,337	11.7%	good	11.8%	very good	+ + +
Region B	806	17.2%	very good	–8.2%	bad	+
Region F	702	–5.5%	bad	4.7%	good	0
Region D	781	–3.2%	bad	–2.6%	bad	– –
Region E	359	–19.7%	very bad	–22.3%	very bad	– – – –

The report for the last quarter of Year Five is shown in Table 9.5. Regions A and C received commendations, while Regions D and E were reprimanded. And so the cycle continues—"win some, lose some, and some get rained out."

Consider the net effect of all of this "data analysis." Table 9.6 summarizes the actions taken.

Table 9.6: Summary of Management Actions Based On Sales Figures

Table	Quarter	Commended	Reprimanded
9.1	IV, Yr 4	F, D, E	A, B
9.2	I, Yr 5	A, B	E
9.3	II, Yr 5	F, D	B, C
9.4	III, Yr 5	F, D	A, B
9.5	IV, Yr 5	A, C	D, E

Over the course of these five quarters all six regions have received one or more commendation plaques to place on the office wall. Yet, in the same period of time, all the regions except Region F have managed to receive one or more reprimands.

This kind of management amounts to nothing more than the use of "carrots and sticks." Yet that is all that this type of "data analysis" will permit. When the analysis is flawed, the actions will, of necessity, also be flawed.

Notice what has happened here.

- Data were used to create a quarterly report.
- These quarterly reports were full of descriptive and comparative values.
- Not knowing what else to do, these values were used to generate a ranking.
- The ranking was used to define "winners" and "losers."
- The winners celebrated and the losers commiserated.
- After the hangovers disappeared, the whole cycle began again.

And the result is *man-made chaos*.

9.2 Description Is Not Analysis

The conflicting messages of the commendations and reprimands described in the previous section constitute man-made chaos. This chaos is the result of the faulty interpretation of numbers. It is based upon the idea that "two numbers which are not the same are different." This concept is simple, straightforward, and wrong. In fact, it is wrong on several levels.

First of all, there is the distinction between the measure itself and the thing measured. If we measured the same thing repeatedly, with sufficient precision, we would commonly obtain different values. Even in the realm of accounting this is true because every accounting figure is dependent upon the assumptions or categorizations that were required for the computation. Change the assumptions and categorizations in rational and reasonable ways, and the figures will change. Thus, in practice, there is a certain amount of variation in every measure.

Next, there is the problem of measuring something at different points in time. Over time, not only may the assumptions and categorizations change, but the raw inputs will definitely change. The people doing the work may change. Even the rules of how to compute the measure may change. Thus, in practice, there is a certain amount of variation *over time* in every measure.

Finally, there is the problem of comparing measures of different things. When different regions are compared using common measures there is the problem of whether or not the measures were collected and computed the same way. If the assumptions and decisions necessary to collect the raw data and to compute the measures are not all exactly the same, then it is unrealistic to assume that the measures for the different regions are comparable. Even if the two regions performed exactly the same, they would not necessarily get the same values on a given measure. Thus, in practice, there is a certain amount of variation from *place to place* in every measure.

Given these multiple sources of variation in our measures, we should always make a distinction between the numbers themselves and the properties which the numbers represent. Of course, this is precisely what is not done when numbers are used to create rankings. The rank ordering of the values is transferred over to the items represented by those values, regardless of whether or not the items being ranked actually differ. No allowance is made for variation.

Yet we see rankings everywhere. For example, U.S. cities are scored on various extrinsic features and then these scores are ranked and the winners and losers are announced. Some cities are identified as "most livable," and others are listed as "least livable." Such rankings are usually the result of not knowing what else to do with the numbers. This syndrome may be characterized by, "What can we do with our numbers?—Well, we can place them in order. Maybe that will show us something."

Whenever actions are taken based upon the assumption that any numerical difference is a real difference, those actions will ultimately be arbitrary and capricious. This is an inevitable consequence of the fact that the above assumption ignores the effects of variation. Variation is random and miscellaneous, and it undermines all simple and naive attempts to interpret numbers. And yet our lives are governed by such interpretations of numbers. Any time the value of some measure changes, people are required to identify the source of that change, and then to take steps to keep it from happening again. We hear calls for accountability, the explanation of all "variances," and tighter control. The result is man-made chaos.

Descriptive summaries may be interesting, but they should never be mistaken for analysis. Analysis focuses on the question of why there are differences. Just because two numbers are different, however, does not mean that they represent things which are different. This discrepancy between the numbers and those things which the numbers represent is the essence of the uncertainty of interpreting data. Even when nothing else changes, the numbers will. This is why descriptive summaries are inadequate, by themselves, to provide the insight needed for a meaningful analysis. They may be used as part of an analysis, but you cannot interpret the descriptive summaries at face value.

Any effective analysis must separate that variation which is due to noise from that which may be attributed to signals. Variation due to common causes must be filtered out before we can identify that variation which may be due to assignable causes.

In this language, the problem with the typical "analysis" shown in Tables 9.1 to 9.5 is a failure to make any allowance for noise. All differences are interpreted as signals, with the consequence that reprimands and commendations are handed out at random each quarter.

In the next section we will examine each region using *XmR* charts.

9.3 Charts for Each Region

Region E

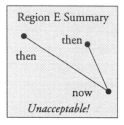

Region E was ranked at the bottom of the list for the Fourth Quarter of Year Five, as shown in Table 9.5. Their sales had dropped 19.7% from the previous quarter and were down 22.3% from the same quarter last year. Needless to say, Region E received a reprimand for the Fourth Quarter of Year Five.

But this executive summary does not tell the full story, as we can see by placing the sales values for Region E on an X chart.

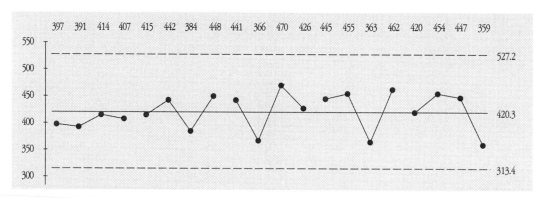

Figure 9.1: Quarterly Sales for Region E

First of all, there is no evidence that sales in Region E are growing, and there is no evidence that the sales are dropping. Even though the sales for the last quarter were down, this is within the bounds of what can be expected. Each of the previous three years has had comparable low quarters. Basically, the sales for Region E appear to be highly variable from quarter to quarter, and this variation dominates this time series. The limits in Figure 9.1 show that routine variation can amount to as much as 107 units on either side of the average of 420.

So what about the 19.7% drop in sales from the previous quarter? What about the 22.3% drop in sales from the same quarter last year? What insights do these percentages provide? While it is never good to hear that sales have dropped, the question remains as to whether or not this drop represents a change to the system. Since the sales value of 359 is within the limits, it is within the realm of routine variation. While the sales were down, they are not low enough to indicate a change to the system.

What should we forecast for the First Quarter of Year Six? The central line value of 420 will be the best forecast. Unless the system changes, and it has not shown any evidence of change during the past five years, the best forecast for *each* quarter of Year Six will be 420.

Region D

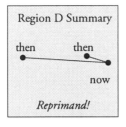

Region D was ranked next to the bottom of the list in Table 9.5. Their sales had dropped 3.2% from the previous quarter and were down 2.6% from the same quarter last year. Because of these disappointing results, Region D received a reprimand for the Fourth Quarter of Year Five.

But this executive summary is wrong, as we can see when we place the sales values for Region D on an *X* chart.

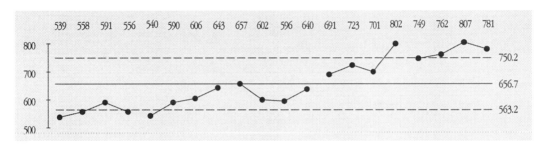

Figure 9.2: Quarterly Sales for Region D

The *X* chart for the sales for Region D shows a definite upward trend. While the horizontal limits of Figure 9.2 make the trend clear, they do not adequately characterize this process. Here is a case where we need trended limits. To fit such limits to these data we begin by finding a trend line.

To establish a trend line for Region D we divide the data into two halves and compute the averages: the first ten quarters have an average of 588.2, while the last ten quarters have an average of 725.2. The first of these half-averages is plotted at the mid-point of the first ten quarters—time period 5.5 (see "plus mark" on Figure 9.3). The second of these half-averages is plotted at the mid-point of the last ten quarters—time period 15.5 (the second plus mark). Then these two points are connected to form a trend line, as shown in Figure 9.3.

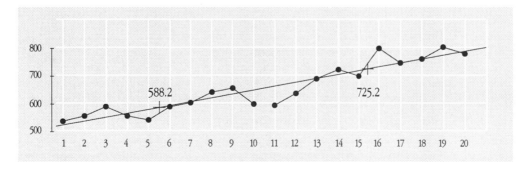

Figure 9.3: Trend Line for Quarterly Sales for Region D

From these two half-averages we can estimate the trend. The difference between the two half-averages, divided by the number of time periods between them, will be the estimated increment per time period:

$$\text{Trend per quarter} \ = \ \frac{725.2 - 588.2}{10 \text{ quarters}} \ = \ 13.7 \text{ units per quarter}$$

Since the limits in Figure 9.2 are 93.5 units on either side of the central line, we place trended limits 93.5 units on either side of the half-average points to get the chart shown in Figure 9.4.

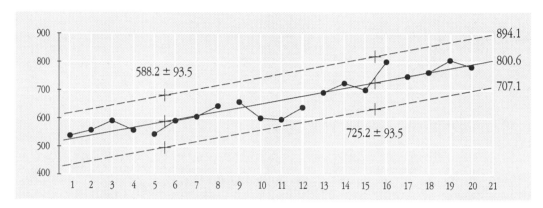

Figure 9.4: Trended Limits for *X* Chart for Quarterly Sales for Region D

Recall that Region D received a reprimand for their performance during the Fourth Quarter of Year Five. And just what was the basis for this reprimand? Looking at Figure 9.4 you have to wonder. The sales in the Fourth Quarter of Year Five were right on the trend line, and sales throughout Year Five had been progressing according to the estimated trend.

The reason for the reprimand was a drop in the percent differences. These percent differences were low for the Fourth Quarter of Year Five because sales were up in both the Fourth Quarter of Year Four and the Third Quarter of Year Five. Thus, Region D earned their reprimand not because the last quarter was bad, but because they had had two good quarters in the past! So what insight is gained by comparing this quarter's sales with the sales in previous quarters? What do such descriptive percentages accomplish? They only serve to confuse the numerically illiterate.

The trend line value for the First Quarter of Year Six (time period 21) is computed to be the average value at time period 15.5 plus 5.5 periods at 13.7 units per period:

$$725.2 \ + \ (5.5 \times 13.7) \ = \ 800.6$$

This would be a reasonable forecast value for Region D. The trended limits place bounds on this forecast. Sales of 894 (800.6 + 93.5) or above in the First Quarter of Year Six would be exceptional. Sales of 707 (800.6 − 93.5) or below would also be exceptional. Sales levels in between would be unremarkable except to verify the continuation of the historical trend. Forecast values for the following quarters would increase by 13.7 units each quarter.

Region B

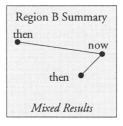

Region B Summary

then

now

then

Mixed Results

Region B was not singled out for attention in Table 9.5. While their sales had increased 17.2% from the previous quarter, earning them a "very good," their sales were down 8.2% from the same quarter last year, earning them a "bad." Because of this mixed performance, Region B did not receive either a reprimand nor a commendation for the Fourth Quarter of Year Five.

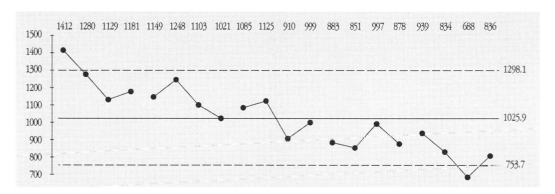

Figure 9.5: *X* **Chart for Quarterly Sales for Region B**

However, the X chart shows that the quarterly sales for Region B are definitely declining, and have been doing so for the past five years. So while the executive summary did give Region B a break from the beatings, it did not reveal the nature of the problem with the sales in this region.

To fit a trend line we once again split the data into halves. The first ten quarters have an average of 1173.3, while the last ten quarters have an average of 878.5. This gives an estimated trend of:

$$\text{Trend per quarter} = \frac{878.5 - 1173.3}{10 \text{ quarters}} = -29.48 \text{ units per quarter}$$

The limits are 272.2 units on either side of the central line in Figure 9.5. Setting limits the same distance on either side of the half-averages yields the chart in Figure 9.6.

Visually, the graph in Figure 9.6 shows that we should forecast the sales for Region B to be about 700 units next quarter. The wide limits indicate that there is a lot of noise in these sales values. Sales could be as good as 972 units, or as low as 428 units, without indicating that the downward trend has changed. Of course, the main questions are why there is this trend, and can anything be done about it? If not, get ready to close Region B.

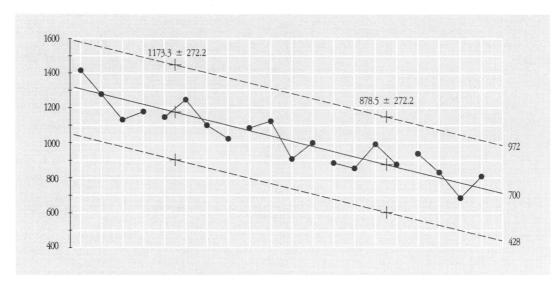

Figure 9.6: Trended Limits for *X* Chart for Quarterly Sales for Region B

In the past two examples we have not made any adjustment in the width of the limits when we placed them around a trend line. Shouldn't we make some adjustment for the trend? In most cases there will not be enough of a change to warrant the effort. For example, we estimated that the sales for Region B were dropping by almost 30 units per quarter. This trend would affect the moving ranges in the following manner: every time the sales go down from one quarter to the next this trend would increase the size of the moving range by 30 units; but every time the sales go up from one quarter to the next this trend would decrease the size of the moving range by 30 units. In this case, eleven moving ranges would be 30 units too large, and 8 moving ranges would be 30 units too small. If we adjusted each moving range by adding or subtracting the appropriate amount, and then recomputed the average moving range, the result would be 97.7 instead of 102.3. This adjustment would result in limits that are 5% narrower than those shown in Figure 9.6. While slightly narrower limits might increase the sensitivity of the chart in Figure 9.6, they will not remedy the situation, and if the trend is not changed, the width of the limits will be a moot point. The objective is insight, with an eye toward improvement, rather than calculating the "right" numbers. Therefore, we recommend placing limits on either side of the trend line using the factors given in the previous chapters: 2.660 times the average moving range, or 3.145 times the median moving range.

Region C

Region C was ranked next-to-the-top in Table 9.5. Their sales had increased 11.7% from the previous quarter and were up 11.8% from the same quarter last year. As a result of this "superior performance" Region C received a commendation plaque for this quarter.

We shall begin by looking at the first four years of data for Region C. The X chart shown in Figure 9.7 has limits based upon the median moving range of 84.

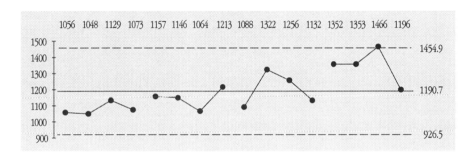

Figure 9.7: X Chart for Quarterly Sales for Region C, Years One to Four

Overall, Figure 9.7 suggests a trend. The first seven values are below the central line. Six of the last seven values are above the central line. And one point falls above the upper limit. Given these multiple indications we might decide to estimate a trend line for these data.

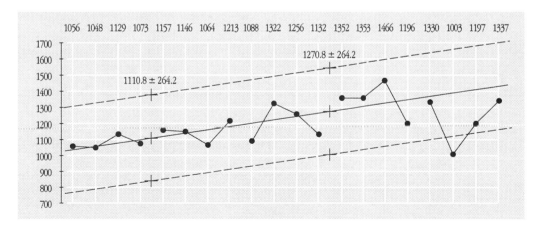

Figure 9.8: Trended Limits for X Chart for Quarterly Sales for Region C

Using the first four years to determine the trend, the first eight quarters have an average of 1110.8, while the last eight quarters have an average of 1270.6. The mid point of the first eight quarters is time period 4.5. The mid-point of the last eight quarters is time period 12.5. Plotting 1110.8 at time period 4.5, and plotting 1270.6 at time period 12.5 yields a trend line which has an estimated trend of:

$$\text{Trend per quarter} \; = \; \frac{1270.6 - 1110.8}{8 \text{ quarters}} \; = \; 19.98 \text{ units per quarter}$$

Placing the limits ± 264.2 on either side of this trend yields the trended chart in Figure 9.8.

So while the sales for Region C had been increasing about 20 units per quarter, that is no longer the case. We detect a change for the worse in the Second Quarter of Year Five. The change could have begun as early as the last quarter of Year Four. Furthermore, while sales have bounced back the last two quarters, they are still below the trend line. Horizontal limits will be more appropriate for the near future for Region C. So while Region C got a plaque for "superior performance," their sales have flattened out and show no sign of returning to the former trend. Once more, the executive summary got the story wrong.

Region A

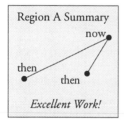

Region A Summary

now

then

then

Excellent Work!

Region A was the top-ranked region in Table 9.5. Their sales had increased 17.6% from the previous quarter and were up 20.6% from the same quarter last year. As a result of this "superior performance" Region A received a commendation plaque for this quarter.

But once again, a longer-term perspective tells a different story.

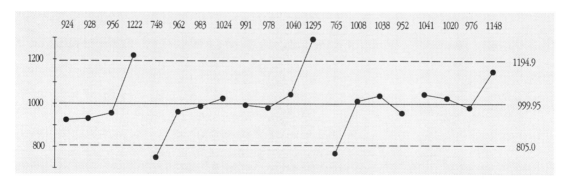

924 928 956 1222 748 962 983 1024 991 978 1040 1295 765 1008 1038 952 1041 1020 976 1148

1200 .... 1194.9

1000 ——————————————————————————— 999.95

800 .... 805.0

Figure 9.9: *X* Chart for Quarterly Sales for Region A

The *X* chart for Region A shows several interesting things. While the overall level of sales for Region A has not changed during the past five years, the values outside the limits signal changes in the system that generated the sales. Back in Year One there was pressure to make the year look good. In response to this pressure, salesmen got their customers to buy ahead and stockpile the product. And it worked. Year one looked good. Unfortunately, the sales in the First Quarter of Year Two were so low that merely returning to normal looked like a dramatic improvement. At the end of Year Three this whole sorry episode was repeated, with the same result. Now, at the end of Year Five, this biannual disaster is happening once again. The only remarkable thing about the Fourth Quarter of Year Five is that they failed to go above the upper limit. You should not look for a strong First Quarter for Year Six. In fact, a good forecast would probably be about 800. If history repeats itself, the remaining three quarters of Year Six should average about 1000.

So what is the value of the knowledge that the sales for Region A increased 17.6% from the previous quarter and 20.6% from the same quarter last year? Even though these numbers appear to be very good news, properly interpreted, they are harbingers of doom to come. Once more the local, limited comparisons mislead rather than inform.

Region F

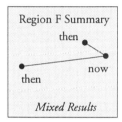

Region F Summary

then

now

then

Mixed Results

Region F was ranked fourth in the list shown in Table 9.5. Their sales had dropped 5.5% from the previous quarter, but were up 4.7% from the same quarter last year. This mixed performance left Region F in the middle of the list, where it did not receive any special attention following the Fourth Quarter of Year Five.

Once again the X chart tells a different story.

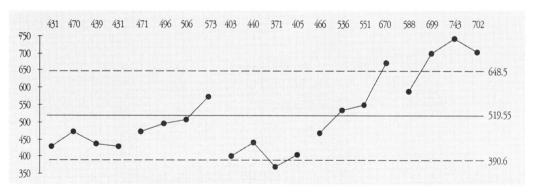

Figure 9.10: *X* Chart for Quarterly Sales for Region F

The limits in Figure 9.10 were based upon the median moving range value of 41. Clearly there is a trend in these data, so we should think about trended limits. But how shall we compute a trend line? If we use all five years and split the data into two groups of ten quarters each like we have done with other regions, then we would get half-averages of 466.0 and 573.1, which would result in a trend of:

$$\text{Trend per quarter} = \frac{573.1 - 466.0}{10 \text{ quarters}} = 10.7 \text{ units per quarter}$$

However, the graph shows that Year Three was a complete disaster, and nowhere near this trend.

A second way of computing a trend line would be to use only the last three year's data. The first six quarters of this three-year period have a half-average of 436.8 while the last six quarters have a half-average of 658.8. These values result in a trend of:

$$\text{Trend per quarter} = \frac{658.8 - 436.8}{6 \text{ quarters}} = 37.0 \text{ units per quarter}$$

While such a trend would indeed be nice, it may be a bit optimistic to assume that this rate of growth will continue in the future.

A third way of computing a trend line for these data would be to use selected years as the basis for the trend. For example, we could use Year One and Year Five to construct a trend. The average for Year One is 442.8. This value would be plotted at the mid-point of year one (time period 2.5). The average for Year Five is 683.0. This value would be plotted at the mid-point of Year Five (time period 18.5). Since these two values are separated by 16 quarters, the trend would be:

$$\text{Trend per quarter} = \frac{683.0 - 442.8}{16 \text{ quarters}} = 15.0 \text{ units per quarter}$$

This third estimate of a trend line avoids the depressing effect of the drop from Year Two to Year Three. At the same time it avoids the excessive optimism of using only the last three years. Which is why it is used in Figure 9.11. If the sales in Region F do better than this, the chart will tell us and we can then revise our trend line. There is always an element of judgment required to use process behavior charts.

Using the trend line in Figure 9.11, our forecast for the sales in Region F for the next

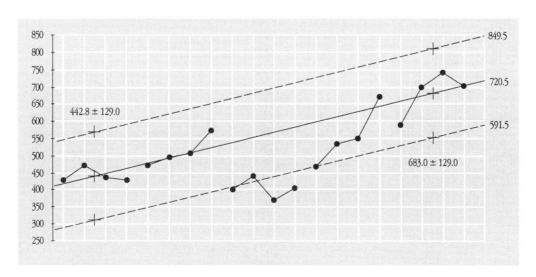

Figure 9.11: Trended Limits for *X* Chart for Quarterly Sales for Region F

quarter would be 720.5. They could go as high as 850, or as low as 590 without indicating any deviation from this trend line.

9.4 So What If We Combined All Six Regions?

Figure 9.2 shows the quarterly sales for Region D to be unpredictable during the past five years. Figure 9.5 shows the quarterly sales for Region B to be unpredictable during the past five years. Figure 9.7 shows the quarterly sales for Region C to be unpredictable during the past five years. Figure 9.9 shows the quarterly sales for Region A to be unpredictable during the past five years. And Figure 9.10 shows the quarterly sales for Region F to be unpredictable during the past five years.

So what should we expect when we place the total sales for each quarter on an *XmR* chart? This *X* chart is shown in Figure 9.12, with limits based upon the average moving range of 221.7. No point is even close to falling outside the limits even though five of the six regions had one or more points outside the limits on their *X* charts.

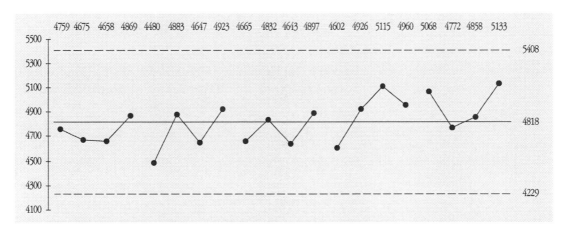

Figure 9.12: *X* Chart for Quarterly Sales for All Six Regions Combined

Time series which consist of the sum of many different components will tend to be more predictable than their components—the whole is more predictable than the parts. As the individual components of a time series are accumulated the noise also accumulates. With each additional component there is more room for the values to average out, leaving a time series that is globally predictable even though the individual components are unpredictable. That this happens should not be surprising. The signals present in the individual component series are added in with nonsignals before they are plotted on the aggregate chart. This dilution of the signals is the reason that Figure 9.12 does not have points outside the limits or long runs about the central line. The chart in Figure 9.12 correctly indicates that the aggregate sales are predictable, and the wide limits do indicate the amount of noise contained in these values. So if you encounter wide limits do not be dismayed. They simply mean that your data contain a lot of noise, which is to be expected with highly aggregated time series.

With such highly aggregated time series the decision to use a trend line will be a matter of judgment. Figure 9.13 shows the results of fitting a trend to the data of Figure 9.12. The half-averages are 4739 and 4897, giving an estimated trend of approximately 16 units per quarter.

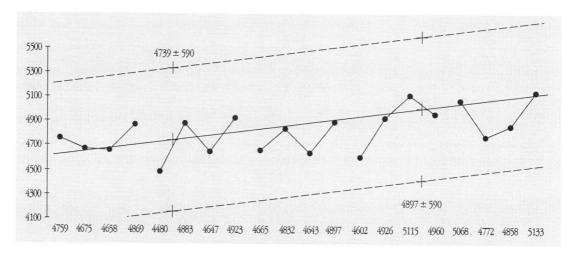

Figure 9.13: Trended Limits for *X* Chart for Quarterly Sales for All Six Regions Combined

9.5 Avoiding Man-Made Chaos

As seen above, description is not analysis. Description may allow you to make comparisons, some of which may even be meaningful, but it will not provide the needed insight into the system that produced the descriptive values. In fact, descriptive measures tend to make the underlying system invisible. This is why description will not provide a basis for prediction. It only deals with what is past, without providing any clue to what may happen in the future.

Yet the essence of management is prediction, and while prediction requires knowledge, explanation does not. Description may be the basis of explanation, but analysis is required for knowledge. Which is why a new approach to presenting and interpreting data is needed. The old ways simply do not do the job.

The use of process behavior charts for presenting and interpreting data represents a new paradigm in data analysis. While the technique is simple, the revolution in thinking is profound. Therefore, you must begin by practicing the technique in order to learn the new way of thinking.

While it may be interesting to compare the sales volumes for different regions, such a comparison is mere description, not analysis. Differences between the values for the different regions may be informative, just as it is sometimes informative to compare apples and oranges, but the limitations of such comparisons must be respected. Because the regions are different it is unrealistic to expect the measures from different regions to be the same. The sales volumes for one region simply do not provide the proper context for interpreting the sales volumes for another region. When it comes to analysis, the only meaningful comparisons are comparisons of a measure with itself over time.

No data have any meaning apart from their context.

In order to properly use any number, you must understand the limitations of that number. Among these limitations are:
- the qualifications which apply to the collection of the raw data,
- the inconsistencies that occur in the way the data are collected, and
- the assumptions made when the raw data are transformed into the number reported.

Without an appreciation of these limitations you are likely to think that numbers are more objective than they truly are.

This tendency to think that numbers have some magic objectivity begins with the subliminal suggestions of elementary school—the multiplication table is very straightforward. Therefore, anything which may be expressed with numbers must also be very straightforward. Unfortunately, this is not the case. Not only are there the issues of just how certain values should be classified (Does this belong in inventory or supplies?), but also the very quality of the numbers may be questionable. This is especially true when data are obtained from multiple sources.

When data have been collected for one purpose, it is very hard to use those data for a different purpose. Data that are routinely collected may be little more than someone's best guess, based upon a cursory examination of the present, a knowledge of the past, and skewed by unstated assumptions. In order to have good data for a given purpose you will usually have to collect the data for that specific purpose. And even then there will always be noise present in the values.

While all data contain noise,
some data contain signals.
Before you can detect a signal within any data set
you must first filter out the noise.

Process behavior charts provide us with a way to filter out the noise that is present in all data. They help us to separate the variation that is due to common causes from that which is due to assignable causes. Since our actions will be different for these two types of variation, this distinction is critical for every analysis.

> *You have to detect a difference*
> *before you can estimate that difference,*
> *and only then can you assess*
> *the practical importance of that difference.*

Regions are different. No data are needed to support this claim. It is self evident. Data may be used to describe the differences, but not all the differences in the numbers are due to differences between the regions. Since cross-region comparisons are essentially "apples to oranges," it is difficult to determine how to filter out the noise in such descriptive uses of data. However, when a measure is compared with itself over time, process behavior charts provide a way to separate the routine variation from the signals we need to know.

The old approach to data analysis consisted of the accumulation of descriptive measures, the construction of descriptive graphs, and the ranking of regions based upon the descriptive numbers. The result was a pile of bar graphs and pie charts.

The conventional approach to improvement has been to tinker with your good processes and to replace or redesign your bad processes. In contrast to this, process behavior charts provide the insight you need to improve both good and bad processes. When a process is unpredictable it will be worthwhile to eliminate assignable causes of excessive variation. When a process is predictable any improvements will require fundamental changes in the process. While this is directly contrary to much conventional wisdom, it has been proven to work time and time again, in all types of endeavors, all over the world.

It is this paradigm shift provided by process behavior charts that is the foundation of Continual Improvement. When managers do not understand the how to listen to the Voice of the Process, their efforts for improvement will be misdirected, resulting in increased costs, wasted effort, lower morale, and loss of business.

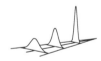

9.7 Exercises

EXERCISE 9.1:

The sales values for Region E for the first ten quarters were:

397,   391,   414,   407,   415,   442,   384,   448,   441,   366

The sales values for Region E for the next ten quarters were:

470,   426,   445,   455,   363,   462,   420,   454,   447,   359

(a) Plot the sales values on the X chart.

Exercise 9.1 (continued)

(b) Compute the half-averages and plot the trend line on the X chart.

(c) Compute the 19 moving ranges and find the average moving range.

(d) Find the Upper Range Limit.

(e) Multiply the average moving range by 2.66, and use this value with the half averages to obtain trended limits for the X chart.

(f) What single value would you use as a forecast for time period 21?

(g) What range of possible values would you expect for time period 21?

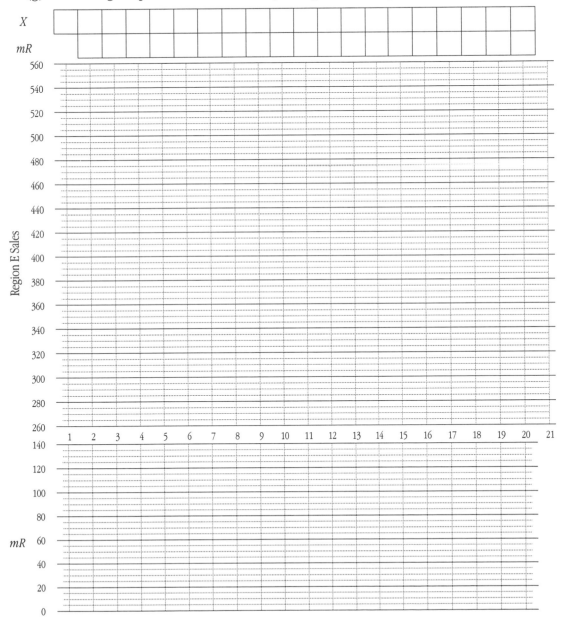

EXERCISE 9.2:

The percentages of "high school seniors who smoke daily" are shown below for the years 1980 through 1993.

Year	80	81	82	83	84	85	86	87	88	89	90	91	92	93
Percentages	21.3	20.2	20.9	21.0	18.8	19.6	18.7	18.6	18.1	18.9	19.2	18.2	17.3	19.0
Moving Ranges		1.1	0.7	0.1	2.2	0.8	0.9	0.1	0.5	0.8	0.3	1.0	0.9	1.7

The article accompanying these data claimed that the jump from 17.3% to 19.0% was a signal that the "number of smoking 18 to 24-year-olds has leveled off, ending a downward trend that began in 1983." We will examine this last statement by computing a trend line for these data and placing limits on either side of the trend line.

(a) Plot the percentages and moving ranges on the following page.

(b) Compute the average percentage for the six years 1980, 1981, 1982, 1983, 1984, and 1985, and plot this half-average at the mid point of this six-year period (halfway between 82 and 83).

(c) Compute the average percentage for the six years 1987, 1988, 1989, 1990, 1991, and 1992, and plot this half-average at the mid point of this six-year period (halfway between 89 and 90).

(d) Draw a trend line connecting the half-averages.

(e) Use all thirteen values to compute the average moving range and then multiply by 3.268 to find the Upper Range Limit. Plot this limit and the central line on the mR chart.

(f) To construct trended limits compute values that are ± 2.66 times the average moving range on either side of the half-averages, plot these points, and connect them to get Upper and Lower Trended Natural Process Limits.

(g) In order for the 1993 value to signal the end of a downward trend it would have to fall outside the trended limits. Does the value for 1993 fall outside the limits?

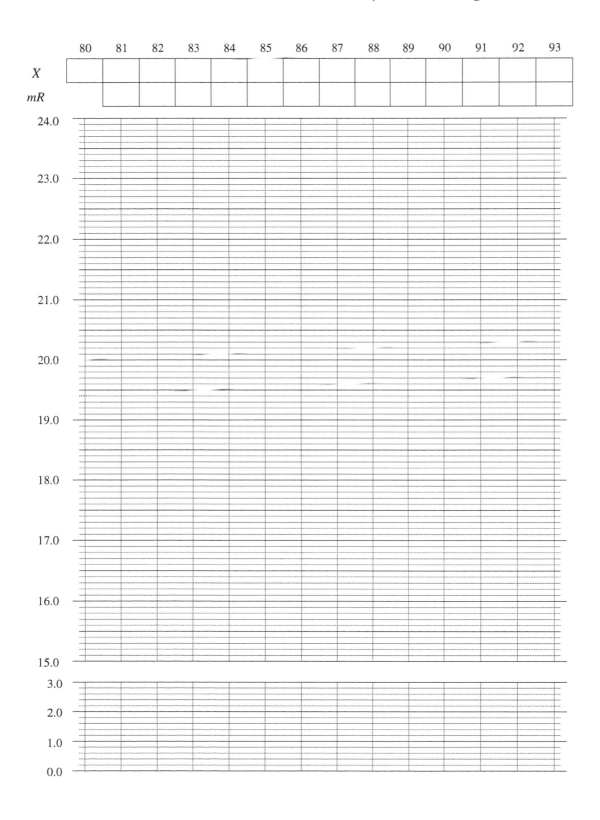

Chapter Ten

Charts for Count Data

10.1 Counts and Measurements

Traditional charting techniques make a distinction between data which are based upon measurements and data which are based upon counts. With measurement data you choose the number of decimal places recorded. With counts there are no decimal places recorded—you will be using the counting numbers { 0, 1, 2, 3, 4, ...}. Throughout this book the term "measures" is used as a generic reference to "some general characteristic of a process." A measure may consist of either a *count* or a *measurement*.

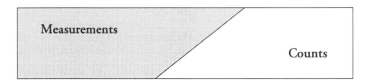

Figure 10.1: Two Types of Measures

The main reason for making a distinction between measurements and counts is that counts are slippery. Anyone with fingers and toes knows how to count, and yet this apparent simplicity can get you into trouble. Obtaining the count is only half the job. In addition to the count, you also need to know the *area of opportunity* for that count. In fact, it is the area of opportunity that *defines* the count.

And what is the area of opportunity for a count? It is the region within which the counts occur. It has to do with what is being counted, how it is being counted, and what possible restrictions there might be upon the count. Until you know the area of opportunity for a count you do not know how to interpret that count.

But before we consider areas of opportunity for counts, it might be advisable to characterize some measures that are being used today. The list on the next page consists of counts, measurements, and ratios of the two. This list is based upon a list appearing in Peter Scholtes' book, *The Leader's Handbook*.

TYPE OF MEASURE	MEASURE
count	• Number of complaints (by type or category)
measurement	• Sales volume in dollars
count	• Number of employees leaving
measurement	• Hours per quarter spent in training
count	• Absences (by type, by area)
measurement	• Overtime
count	• Number of orders coming from a particular advertising medium
measurement	• Cycle time (order to delivery)
count	• Grievances (by type, by area)
measurement	• Cycle time for special requests
count	• Accidents (by type, by area)
measurement	• Time between policy changes
count	• Number of suggestions made
measurement	• Dollar volume of transactions this week
count	• Number of transactions per week
measurement	• Time spent performing rework
count	• Number of transactions requiring rework/special processing
measurement	• Inventory levels (in dollars)
count	• Errors in order fulfillment
measurement	• Direct cost of errors in order fulfillment
count	• Sales volume in units
measurement	• Earnings (by type, location, and sector)
count	• Payroll errors (by type, by area)
measurement	• Cash flow
ratio of counts	• Proportion of customers who are repeat customers
ratio of counts	• Proportion of customers who were referred to you by other customers
ratio of counts	• Proportion of browsers who purchase something
ratio of counts	• Proportion of suggestions implemented
ratio of counts	• Proportion of transactions completed on time
ratio of counts	• Proportion of transactions requiring rework
ratio of measurements	• Proportion of time spent in rework
ratio of measurements	• Proportion of sales coming from a particular sector
ratio of measurements	• Percent over budget or under budget
measurement	• Forecast sales
measurement	• Actual sales
measurement	• Actual sales minus forecast sales
measurement	• Expenses (by type)
measurement	• Cycle time for filling job vacancies (by type, by area)
measurement	• Accounts receivable
ratio of measurements	• Accounts receivable as percentage of sales
count / measurement	• Transactions per teller-hour

10.2 Areas of Opportunity

There are two different types of count data; counts of items and counts of events. The difference between these two types of counts is mainly a difference in the areas of opportunity.

Counts of Items

When you are characterizing each item in a set of **n** items according to whether or not that item possesses some attribute, and counting the number of items with that attribute, your measure will be a *count of items*.

Counts of items have a finite counting number, **n**, as their area of opportunity—the value you obtain may be any counting number from 0 to **n**. You may count those items having the attribute or you may count those items not having the attribute, but in the end, each item either does or does not count.

Examples of this type of counts are:

Number of orders generated by a particular advertisement

Number of employees retiring

Absences (by type, by area)

Number of transactions requiring rework/special processing

Number of orders filled incorrectly

Number of incorrect payroll checks

Notice that for each count listed above, you can count the items with the attribute listed, or you can count the items *not* having the attribute listed. In other words, you could insert the word "not" into each description above and still have a meaningful statement.

Counts of items are actually "counts of items having some attribute," and we can change the definition of the attribute at our discretion. This is not the case with counts of events.

Counts of Events

Since you cannot have half of an event, events are countable—you must use the counting numbers to keep track of events. The area of opportunity for a *count of events* is the region within which the events occurred. This region might be a finite region of space and time, or a finite region of product, or a finite number of manhours worked.

Examples of counts of events are:

Number of complaints (by type)

Grievances (by type, by area)

Number of suggestions made

Accidents (by type, by area)

Number of transactions per week

Sales volume in units

Notice that for a count of events you cannot count the *nonevents*. We cannot count the number of noncomplaints, or the number of nonsuggestions made, or the number of nonaccidents. This is the easiest way to tell the difference between counts of events and counts of items having some attribute.

When working with counts of events the definition of the area of opportunity can be vague. In fact, for a given count, it may be defined in different ways. The area of opportunity for the number of transactions might be the number of hours the business was open, or it might be the number of manhours worked. Either could serve as the area of opportunity for this count. The key to defining the area of opportunity for counting events is that it must be some finite region of space, or time, or production, or activity, which serves to define the region within which the events occur.

Counts of Items or Events

Some counts could be either a count of items or a count of events depending on how you define the count and the area of opportunity. Errors in order fulfillment could belong to either category. If you count all types of errors, so that a single order could have more than one error, then this might be considered a count of events. However, if you count the number of orders with errors, you have a count of items.

If you count the number of sales per week, you are counting events. If you count the number of visitors to the store who made a purchase, you are counting items.

Finally, we can occasionally treat counts of items as if they are counts of events. This happens when the counts are small relative to **n**, so that **n** does not actually place a practical upper bound on the values for the counts. An example of this might be the number of absences for a given company on a given day. The actual number of absences will (usually) be so much smaller than the possible number that it will not matter much whether we consider this count to be a count of items or a count of events.

When working with counts it is critical to know the size of the area of opportunity for each count. The distinction between counts of items and counts of events is important only to the extent that it will help you to carefully define your areas of opportunity.

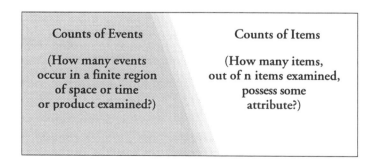

Counts of Events	Counts of Items
(How many events occur in a finite region of space or time or product examined?)	(How many items, out of n items examined, possess some attribute?)

Figure 10.2: Two Types of Counts

Now why does all this matter? Why should you be concerned about areas of opportunity and whether a count is a count of items or a count of events? This all becomes important when the area of opportunity varies from time-period to time-period. As long as the area of opportunity stays approximately the same from period to period, we can compare the counts directly. However, when the size of the area of opportunity for a count changes appreciably from period to period, we can no longer compare the counts—we have to compare the *rates*. And a rate is obtained by dividing a count by its area of opportunity.

For example, consider comparing the number of transactions on successive days of the week. The number of transactions per day might vary considerably while the number of transactions per visitor to the store might be comparable from day to day. In other words, the variation of the count might be due to the variation in the area of opportunity. This type of variation is not what we want to track, for if it was, we would be directly measuring the area of opportunity as a variable of interest.

So, in order to use count data effectively, you need to ask the following questions:
- What is being counted?
- What is the area of opportunity for these counts?
- Are the areas of opportunity approximately the same for successive counts?

Failure to consider these questions may result in useless data. Consider the problem of tracking complaints. How do you count complaints? Do you count the number of complaints you receive each month? Or do you count the number of customers who complained? What do you do when one customer complains six times—give him the phone number of your competition? Careful instruction, careful distinctions, and clear communication of those distinctions will be needed before you can begin to collect useful count data.

A pediatrics unit reported the number of "concerns per month." Their data are shown in Table 10.1.

Table 10.1: Number of Concerns Each Month for a Pediatric Unit

J	F	M	A	M	J	J	A	S	O	N	D	J	F	M	A	M	J	J	A	S
20	22	9	12	13	20	8	23	16	11	14	9	11	3	5	7	3	2	1	7	6

Questions about these data might be:
- What is a "concern?" How is it defined? Are these complaints? Or are these internally generated counts? Where is the border between a concern and a nonconcern?
- Why does the number of concerns drop? Did they get better? Or did half the physicians (those considered to be "troublemakers") leave the practice?
- The hospital administrator is using these numbers to challenge the orthopedics unit to improve—is that valid?

For our purposes, let us assume that "concerns" is just an antiseptic term for complaints. We could characterize the area of opportunity for the count of complaints in several ways. We could consider the area of opportunity to be the number of office visits. Or we could consider the area of opportunity to be the number of procedures performed, or the number of manhours worked by primary care-givers. Which should we use? You get to choose. Any will work, but you need to plan in advance, and this information needs to be reported along with the data.

Then there is the matter of what constitutes a complaint. Does a complaint about a chilly reception room count? What you count, and how you count it, are matters of choice, but they are choices you need to make before you begin to collect the data! Your choice of the area of opportunity will determine the ways that you can use the counts to understand your process.

We did not put the data of Table 10.1 on a graph because we do not know the context for these counts. Without context we are unable to make sense of the numbers, no matter what type of graph we may choose to use. Without a knowledge of the areas of opportunity we do not even know if the counts can be directly compared.

10.3 Collecting Good Count Data

Do not despair. You can collect useful count data. But it is never quite as easy as it sounds. The essence of the problem of count data is two-fold: what should be included in your count and what is the area of opportunity that you might use to adjust the counts to make them comparable?

So you should begin with a written description of what is to be included in your count and the threshold for being included. Give examples. Be as specific as possible.

Next, you should consider what area of opportunity is appropriate for your count. This area of opportunity must be something that can be measured or counted, and which bears some clear relationship to the count. The test here is rationality. There must be some logical connection between the size of the area of opportunity and the size of the count. For any one count there may be several different possible ways to characterize the area of opportunity, and for this reason alone, the choice must be made initially. Of course, as time grants you more insight, you may need to change the area of opportunity for a given count, but that is no excuse for overlooking this important step at the beginning. If you do not choose an appropriate area of opportunity for your count, then you will almost certainly have people collect data in different, and inconsistent, ways.

Do you count the on-the-job accidents (a count of events) or the injured persons (a count of items)? Either would probably work, but these two counts are basically different in their structure.

Say that you track the ways your customers heard about you. You might count the number of customers referred to you by other customers. What should be the area of opportunity? The total number of customers in your customer base, or the number of customers who made a purchase this month? Either would work, but one will be much easier to obtain. In fact, to get useful data you might have to shift from counting customers to counting transactions as an approximate area of opportunity.

You might track the sales generated through your website. The number of website orders divided by the number of website visits would be a proportion based upon counts.

But the proportion of your sales that came from these website orders would be a ratio of measurements.

There is no simple, cut-and-dried formula for obtaining good count data. The process is a mixture of planning and common sense, with some thought given to how to adjust for variable areas of opportunity.

If you do not know the area of opportunity for a count,
you do not know how to interpret that count.

10.4 Charts for Counts

When a sequence of counts,

$X_1, X_2, X_3, ...,$

has areas of opportunity denoted by

$a_1, a_2, a_3, ...,$

and when these areas of opportunity are all approximately the same size,

you may place the counts directly on an

XmR chart.

When the areas of opportunity are approximately the same size the counts may be compared directly, and the X chart will enable us to make these comparisons regardless of whether we have counts of items or counts of events. At the same time the mR chart will directly measure the dispersion present in the data and allow us to compute empirical limits that are appropriate for these counts.

As long as the average count is greater than 1.0 the XmR chart will provide a satisfactory way of placing count data on a process behavior chart. When the average count falls to the region of 1.0 or below, the XmR chart for counts will display the problem identified in Chapter Eight as chunky data. This problem undermines your ability to use the moving range to compute the limits for the counts. When you have an average count of 1.0 or less you are working with rare events or rare attributes, and you may wish to consider the alternative ways of charting rare events and rare attributes shown in Section 11.7.

—◆—

The supervisor of a telephone order service center audits 60 orders each day. Each order is characterized by whether or not it contains an error. The numbers of orders found to have one or more errors in the daily audits for 21 working days are shown on the XmR chart in Figure 10.3. The average of these 21 counts is 19.2. The median moving range is 4.0.

Figure 10.3 shows one value above the Upper Natural Process Limit and a run of 11 successive values below the central line. These are both indications that this process is not predictable. Moreover, with an average of 19 out of 60, the error rate is far too high. Thus, the chart tells us that this process is unpredictable and unacceptable. The fact that it is unacceptable means that we should want to change this process. The fact that it is unpredictable means that there is hope that this error rate can be reduced.

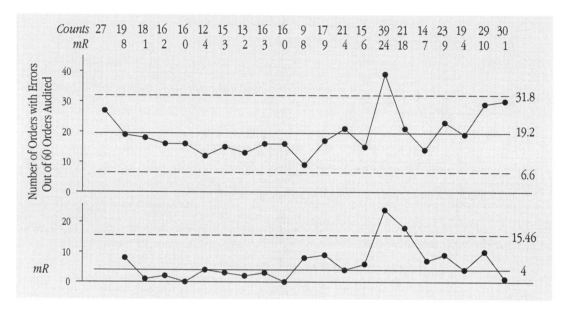

Figure 10.3: *XmR* Chart for Number of Orders with Errors

The fact that each sample consisted of 60 orders is what made it possible to place the counts directly on the *XmR* chart in this example. In general, whenever the areas of opportunity are approximately the same, you can make direct comparisons between the counts. Traditionally, areas of opportunity are considered to be approximately the same when the largest area is no greater than 1.5 times the smallest area.

Alternatively, if the ratio:

$$\frac{\text{Minimum Area of Opportunity}}{\text{Average Area of Opportunity}}$$

is 80 percent or greater, and the ratio:

$$\frac{\text{Maximum Area of Opportunity}}{\text{Average Area of Opportunity}}$$

is 120 percent or smaller, then the areas of opportunity are approximately the same.

10.5 Charts for Rates Based On Counts

When a sequence of counts,

$$X_1, X_2, X_3, ...,$$

has areas of opportunity denoted by

$$a_1, a_2, a_3, ...,$$

and when these areas of opportunity are different in size,

the rates $\dfrac{X_1}{a_1}$, $\dfrac{X_2}{a_2}$, $\dfrac{X_3}{a_3}$, *... will be directly comparable,*

and these rates may be placed on an XmR chart .

Counts which have differently sized areas of opportunity are not directly comparable. Therefore, when your counts have different sized areas of opportunity you have to convert the counts into rates before making comparisons. A count is converted into a rate by dividing the count by its own area of opportunity.

An example of rates on an *XmR* chart was given in Figure 6.14. There, for any given year, the percentage of high school seniors who smoke daily is based upon the ratio of the number who smoke to the number questioned. The number questioned is the area of opportunity, and since this number varied from year to year, the counts were converted into proportions prior to making comparisons. When it does not make sense to compare the counts, we compare the rates instead.

Another example is given by the data obtained when a manager tracked the number of orders requiring premium freight. Each day she noted how many orders were made, **n**, and how many of these were shipped by premium freight, X. The proportions, *p*, are the number of expedited orders for a day divided by the total number of orders for that day. The data are shown in Table 10.2 and the *p* values are plotted on an *XmR* chart in Figure 10.4. The average of the proportions is 0.245, and the average moving range is 0.033.

Figure 10.4 shows a predictable process in which about 25 percent of the transactions are expedited. On any given day it could go as high as 33 percent or dip as low as 16 percent without indicating any process change.

Table 10.2: The Proportion of Orders Shipped by Premium Freight

Date	X	n	p	mR	Date	X	n	p	mR	Date	X	n	p	mR	Date	X	n	p	mR
1	27	102	.265	—	8	28	99	.283	.037	15	19	101	.188	.036	22	21	94	.223	.020
2	31	146	.212	.053	9	37	143	.259	.024	16	33	140	.236	.048	23	32	139	.230	.007
3	70	280	.250	.038	10	47	235	.200	.059	17	68	292	.233	.003	24	65	229	.284	.054
4	54	207	.261	.011	11	46	185	.249	.049	18	44	207	.213	.020	25	46	170	.271	.013
5	69	322	.214	.047	12	70	271	.258	.009	19	74	257	.288	.075	26	75	290	.259	.012
6	101	410	.246	.032	13	105	469	.224	.034	20	124	511	.243	.045	27	117	407	.287	.028

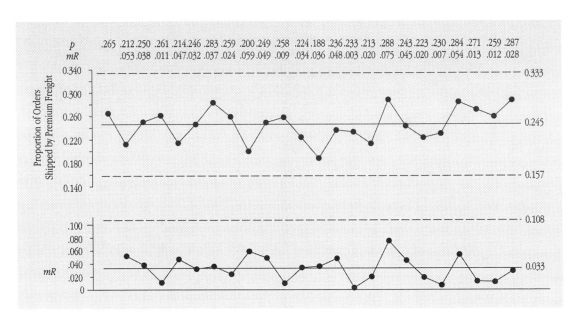

Figure 10.4: *XmR* **Chart for Proportion of Orders Shipped by Premium Freight**

When we place counts or rates on an *XmR* chart we still have to satisfy the requirements of rational subgrouping. This means that the counts or rates must come from a system or process where it makes sense to use the moving range to measure dispersion.

Moreover, when *rates* based on counts are placed on an *XmR* chart, you will still need to have an average *count* that is greater than 1.0 in order for the moving ranges to yield appropriate limits. As noted earlier, the computations for the *XmR* chart will break down when the average count falls below 1.0.

10.6 Some Cautions About Ratios Involving Counts

We work with the counts themselves whenever the areas of opportunity are approximately the same size because it is simpler to do so. When the areas of opportunity are appreciably different from period to period we convert the counts into rates. But ratios are more complex than simple measures and present their own difficulties.

When a ratio contains a count in the numerator that ratio will only be able to take on certain values:

$$\frac{0}{a}, \frac{1}{a}, \frac{2}{a}, \frac{3}{a}, \frac{4}{a}, \frac{5}{a}, \ldots$$

So while you may compute these ratios to any number of decimal places, they are not really numbers from a continuum. Instead they possess a certain discreteness which is obscured by the computation of the ratio.

When a ratio contains counts in *both* the numerator and the denominator, the distance between the discrete values for the ratio will be determined by the count in the denominator.

$$\frac{0}{n}, \frac{1}{n}, \frac{2}{n}, \frac{3}{n}, \frac{4}{n}, \frac{5}{n}, \cdots$$

Say for example, you are counting the success rates for a particular procedure at four local hospitals. You could count the number of times in the past year each hospital has performed the procedure, and you could count the number of successful procedures (if you are careful to define what constitutes a success). Then you divide the latter number by the former to obtain the success rate for each hospital. The four hospitals have success rates of 100%, 86%, 80%, and 60%. So who is best?

Hospital One (100%) performed this procedure 1 time during the past year.

Hospital Two (86%) performed this procedure 7 times during the past year.

Hospital Three (80%) performed this procedure 50 times during the past year.

Hospital Four (60%) performed this procedure 5 times during the past year.

If you had to undergo this procedure, where would you want to go?

When we express a ratio as a percentage it is natural to think "by the hundred." In fact that is exactly what *per centum* means in Latin. So when you report a percentage you are essentially reporting a rate in "parts per hundred." While this makes sense when your denominator is a count that is at least 40 or greater, it can be misleading when the area of opportunity is a small count.

To understand this, consider what would happen to the percentages above if each hospital had one fewer successful procedures during the past year. Hospital One would go from 100% to 0%. This is the minimum change for Hospital One. Clearly, we do not know the success "percentage" for Hospital One to the parts-per-hundred level. Hospital Two would go from 86% to 71%, a 15% change. So while the percentages lull you into thinking in terms of parts per hundred, your minimum change here is 15%. Hospital Three would go from 80% to 78%, while Hospital Four would go from 60% to 40%. Thus, it is only with Hospital Three that we know the success rate to anything like the parts-per-hundred level.

Expressing numbers in percentages, or ratios, implies to your reader that a certain amount of continuity exists. When the ratio involves small counts this implied property is absent.

When you have to work with ratios where the denominators are small counts you should report *both* the numerator and denominator values along with each ratio (similar to what was done in Table 10.2). When the data are displayed directly on the chart these values should also be on the chart. This is the only approach that has any integrity. Failure to do this invites your readers to over-interpret the ratios.

So there are two problems with ratios involving counts.

- *Counts in the numerator create a discreteness for the possible values.*
- *Counts in the denominator limit how close together these possible values can be.*

When all of the counts in the denominator are sufficiently large (say 40 or more), the possible values will be fairly close together, and the discreteness of the ratios can be ignored in practice. But when some of the counts in the denominator are small (say 20 or less), the ratios (commonly computed to at least two decimal places) will be much more discrete than they look. We shall refer to this problem of small counts in the denominator as *chunky ratios*.

Count data with unequal areas of opportunity will result in chunky ratios when all three of the following conditions exist:

- The counts are counts of items.
- The areas of opportunity, n_i, vary by more than $\pm 20\%$ from the average, $\bar{n}$.
- Some of the areas of opportunity, n_i, are counts that are smaller than 20.

When you attempt to place chunky ratios on a process behavior chart you will have wide limits. This is simply a manifestation of the fact that chunky ratios contain little information. The small areas of opportunity which create the chunky ratios will also result in process behavior charts that are very insensitive. This insensitivity will make you want to avoid working with chunky ratios if at all possible.

10.7 Summary

When working with count data you will need to know the areas of opportunity for the counts in order to make sense of the data. For completeness these areas of opportunity must be reported along with the counts.

When the areas of opportunity are approximately the same size from period to period you may place the counts directly on an *XmR* chart.

When the areas of opportunity vary more than $\pm 20\%$ from the average size of the areas of opportunity you should convert the counts into rates before plotting them on a process behavior chart. This is done by dividing each count by its own area of opportunity. These rates may then be placed on an *XmR* chart.

The one real restriction on the use of the *XmR* chart with data based on counts is the restriction of chunky data. This problem is seen with data based on counts whenever the average count falls to 1.0 or below. But then, when the average count falls below 1.0 you have rare events or rare attributes, and it will generally be more satisfactory to measure the area of opportunity between rare events than to try to count the rare events themselves.

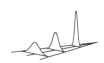

10.8 Exercises

EXERCISE 10.1:

Using the values shown for the average and the median moving range, verify the limits shown in Figure 10.3.

EXERCISE 10.2:

Using the values shown for the average and the average moving range, verify the limits shown in Figure 10.4.

Part II: Follow the Signals; Avoid the Noise

Chapter Eleven

Traditional Charts for Count Data

Count data have traditionally been placed on special process behavior charts. This chapter will explain these special charts and outline when they may be used. Since all of the charts in this chapter may be considered to be special cases of the X chart, and since the XmR chart provides a universal way of placing count data on a process behavior chart, it is not necessary for the beginner to work through this chapter. While this chapter is included here for completeness, in practice it may be skipped over. If you already know about the charts described in this chapter, you may find the comparisons between the XmR chart and the traditional charts of interest.

11.1 Charts for Binomial Counts: the np-Chart

The np-chart is a chart for individual counts where those individual counts satisfy two special conditions:

Binomial Condition 1: The count is a count of items. That is, each count is the count of the number of items, out of **n** items, that possess some attribute.

Binomial Condition 2: Let **p** denote the probability that a single item possesses the attribute. *The value of* **p** *must remain constant* for each of the **n** items in a single sample. (Among other things, this means that the items possessing the attribute do not cluster or clump together. Also, whether or not one item possesses the attribute will not affect the likelihood that the next item will possess the attribute.)

When these two conditions are met, the counts can be said to be characterized by the binomial probability model, and this model may be used to compute the limits for the counts according to special formulas. However, if the second condition does not hold, then the use of the binomial probability model will be incorrect.

Counts which satisfy the two conditions above, and which have areas of opportunity that are approximately constant, can be placed on an np-chart.

- The plot for the *np*-chart will be the running record of counts.

- The central line for the *np*-chart will be the average count, which can be denoted as either:

$$CL_{np} = \bar{X} \quad \text{or} \quad n\bar{p}$$

where the average proportion of items with the attribute is defined by:

$$\bar{p} = \frac{\text{total number of items in baseline samples with attribute}}{\text{total number of items examined in baseline samples}}$$

- Since the binomial model establishes a relationship between location and dispersion we do not compute moving ranges, or any other measure of dispersion for an *np*-chart. Instead we use $\bar{p}$ to compute our three-sigma distance according to the formula:

$$\text{Estimated three-sigma distance for binomial counts} = 3\sqrt{n\bar{p}(1-\bar{p})}$$

- So our Upper Control Limit for the *np*-chart will be:

$$UCL_{np} = n\bar{p} + 3\sqrt{n\bar{p}(1-\bar{p})}$$

- And our Lower Control Limit for the *np*-chart will be:

$$LCL_{np} = n\bar{p} - 3\sqrt{n\bar{p}(1-\bar{p})}$$

- The upper limit will be meaningful only when it is less than the area of opportunity, **n**. If the computed upper limit exceeds **n**, then there is no upper limit. Likewise, when the computed lower limit is less than 0 there will be no lower limit.

Table 11.1: Number of Orders with Errors Out of 60 Orders Audited

X	27	19	18	16	16	12	15	13	16	16	9	17	21	15	39	21	14	23	19	29	30

The supervisor of a telephone order service center audits 60 orders each day. Each order is characterized by whether or not it contains an error. The numbers of orders found to have one or more errors in the daily audits for 21 working days are shown in Table 11.1. These counts were also shown on the *XmR* chart in Figure 10.3.

Do the data of Table 11.1 satisfy the binomial conditions? They are counts of items (orders with errors), and in the absence of any more specific knowledge about the service center or the auditing process, it seems reasonable to assume that each order audited has the same chance of having an error. So we might put these counts on an *np*-chart.

The total number of errors found in these 21 samples was 404. The total number of orders examined was 21 times 60 = 1260. Thus,

$$\bar{p} \;=\; \frac{404}{1260} \;=\; 0.3206$$

so that the central line will be:

$$CL_{np} \;=\; \mathbf{n}\,\bar{p} \;=\; (60)\,(0.3206) \;=\; 19.2$$

and the estimated three-sigma distance will be:

$$3\sqrt{\mathbf{n}\,\bar{p}\,(1-\bar{p})} \;=\; 3\sqrt{19.2\,(0.6794)} \;=\; 10.8$$

so that the control limits will be:

$$UCL_{np} \;=\; \mathbf{n}\,\bar{p} \;+\; 3\sqrt{\mathbf{n}\,\bar{p}\,(1-\bar{p})} \;=\; 19.2 + 10.8 = 30.0$$

$$LCL_{np} \;=\; \mathbf{n}\,\bar{p} \;-\; 3\sqrt{\mathbf{n}\,\bar{p}\,(1-\bar{p})} \;=\; 19.2 - 10.8 = 8.4$$

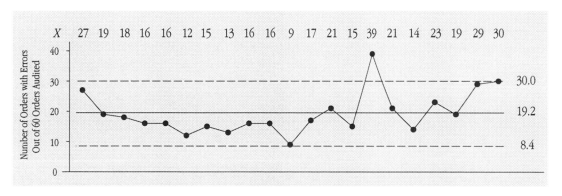

Figure 11.1: *np*-Chart for Number of Orders with Errors

If you compare the *np*-chart in Figure 11.1 with the X chart in Figure 10.3 you will see that there is no practical difference. Even though the limits are slightly different (31.8 and 6.6 instead of 30.0 and 8.4) the two charts tell the same story.

Note also that the *np*-chart is a chart for individual values. The points plotted are the individual counts for each sample. This is why there is such a strong degree of similarity between the *np*-chart and the X chart. They both use the same plot, and they both have the same central line. They only differ in the way they compute the three-sigma distance.

11.2 Charts for Binomial Proportions: the *p*-Chart

The *p*-chart is appropriate when you have *rates* based on counts which satisfy the two binomial conditions in the preceding section. The *p*-chart is a chart for binomial proportions.

If a set of counts satisfy the two binomial conditions given in the preceding section, and if the smallest of their areas of opportunity is greater than 80% of the average size of their areas of opportunity and the largest of their areas of opportunity is less than 120% of the average size of their areas of opportunity, then it is acceptable to consider the *counts* to be roughly comparable. Such counts may be charted directly using either an *XmR* chart or an *np*-chart, or they may be converted into *rates* and placed on a *p*-chart.

If a set of counts satisfy the two binomial conditions given in the preceding section, and if their areas of opportunity vary by *more* than ± 20 percent from the average size of the areas, then we must convert the counts into rates prior to placing them on any chart. As noted earlier, counts are converted into rates by dividing each count by its own area of opportunity.

When working with counts that satisfy the two binomial conditions we will denote the area of opportunity for the ith count, X_i, by the symbol:

$$n_i$$

The ratio of the ith count, X_i, to its area of opportunity, n_i, will be a *proportion*, and will be denoted by:

$$p_i = \frac{X_i}{n_i}$$

- The *p*-chart will be based upon a plot of the p_i values. The central line will be defined by the average proportion of items having the attribute, $\bar{p}$.

$$\bar{p} = \frac{\text{total number of items in baseline samples with attribute}}{\text{total number of items examined in baseline samples}}$$

- For the ith sample the three-sigma distance will be estimated by:

Estimated three-sigma distance for binomial proportions $= 3\sqrt{\dfrac{\bar{p}(1-\bar{p})}{n_i}}$

- So the limits for a *p*-chart will be computed to be:

$$\bar{p} \pm 3\sqrt{\frac{\bar{p}(1-\bar{p})}{n_i}}$$

- If the computed value for the upper limit exceeds 1.0, then there is no upper limit. If the computed value for the lower limit falls below 0.0, then there is no lower limit.[*]

Table 11.2: The Proportion of Orders Shipped by Premium Freight

Date	X	n	p	Date	X	n	p	Date	X	n	p	Date	X	n	p
1	27	102	.265	8	28	99	.283	15	19	101	.188	22	21	94	.223
2	31	146	.212	9	37	143	.259	16	33	140	.236	23	32	139	.230
3	70	280	.250	10	47	235	.200	17	68	292	.233	24	65	229	.284
4	54	207	.261	11	46	185	.249	18	44	207	.213	25	46	170	.271
5	69	322	.214	12	70	271	.258	19	74	257	.288	26	75	290	.259
6	101	410	.246	13	105	469	.224	20	124	511	.243	27	117	407	.287

The data of Table 10.2 are repeated in Table 11.2. The counts satisfy the two binomial conditions and the areas of opportunity vary considerably, so the proportions, p, will be placed on a p-chart. The total number of orders shipped by premium freight during this period was 1403. The total number of orders was 5706. Thus, the average proportion of orders shipped by premium freight is:

$$\bar{p} = \frac{1403}{5706} = 0.246$$

The estimated three-sigma distance for a p-chart depends upon the value of **n**. This means that the limits for the p-chart for Table 11.2 have to be computed for each point—a total of 24 times in all. The result is shown in Figure 11.2.

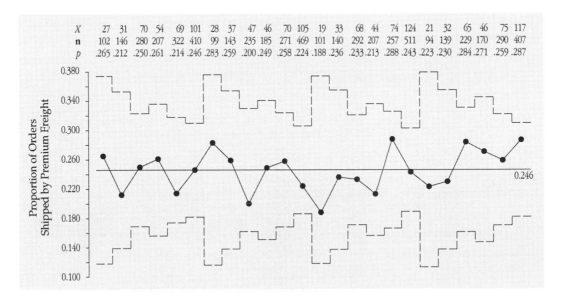

Figure 11.2: p-Chart for Proportion of Orders Shipped by Premium Freight

---

[*] These formulas apply to *proportions*. They are not appropriate when *proportions* are converted into *percentages*.

Just as in Figure 10.2, these data reveal a predictable process. Unlike Figure 10.2, this chart was a lot of work to create. With a *p*-chart you effectively have to compute your limits every time you plot a point. Because of this complexity, people have been using simplified versions of the *p*-chart for years.

One traditional modification consists of using an average value of **n** in the computations. For the data of Table 11.2, this average value of **n** is 238. Using this value for **n** yields limits of 0.330 and 0.162. These are the narrower of the two sets of limits shown in Figure 11.3. The wider set of limits are those from the *X* chart in Figure 10.2. (The offset in the two central lines occurs because the *X* chart uses a simple average of the proportions while the *p*-chart uses a weighted average.)

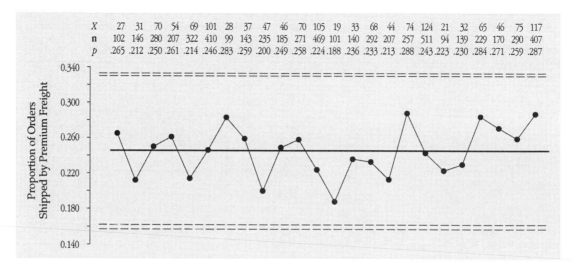

X	27	31	70	54	69	101	28	37	47	46	70	105	19	33	68	44	74	124	21	32	65	46	75	117
n	102	146	280	207	322	410	99	143	235	185	271	469	101	140	292	207	257	511	94	139	229	170	290	407
p	.265	.212	.250	.261	.214	.246	.283	.259	.200	.249	.258	.224	.188	.236	.233	.213	.288	.243	.223	.230	.284	.271	.259	.287

Figure 11.3: Limits for *X* Chart and Limits for *p*-Chart Based on Average Value for n

The *p*-chart is a chart for individual values. This is why it tells essentially the same story as the *X* chart. So what is the difference between the *XmR* chart and the *np*-chart and the *p*-chart? The main difference is in the way these charts estimate the three-sigma distance. The *XmR* chart empirically measures the variation present in the data (using the moving ranges). The *np*-chart and the *p*-chart assume that a binomial probability model is appropriate for the data—and the binomial model requires the variation to be a function of the location (and the area of opportunity). Thus, the *p*- and *np*-charts use a theoretical value for the three-sigma distance. If the theory is right, then the theoretical value is right, and the empirical value will mimic the theoretical value. But if the theory is wrong, then the theoretical value will be wrong, yet the empirical value will still be correct. Think it over….

11.3 Charts for Poisson Counts: the *c*-Chart

The *c*-chart is a chart for individual counts where those counts satisfy two special conditions:

Poisson Condition 1: The count is a count of events.

Poisson Condition 2: The events occur independently of each other, and the likelihood of an event is *proportional* to the size of area of opportunity. (This means that the likelihood of an event is not affected by *which* portion of the continuum of space or time or product is selected as the area of opportunity—there is a uniform likelihood of an event throughout each sample.)

There are many counts that satisfy the first of these conditions but fail to satisfy the second condition. Such data cannot be said to follow the Poisson probability model.

Counts which satisfy the two conditions above, and which have areas of opportunity that are approximately constant, can be placed on an *c*-chart.

- The plot for the *c*-chart will be the time-series of count values.

- The central line for the *c*-chart will be the average count, which can be denoted as either:

$$\bar{X} \quad \text{or} \quad \bar{c}$$

where the average count of events is defined by:

$$\bar{c} = \frac{\text{total number of events observed in baseline samples}}{\text{total number of baseline samples}}$$

- Since the Poisson model establishes a relationship between location and dispersion we do not compute moving ranges for a *c*-chart. Instead we use $\bar{c}$ to compute our three-sigma distance according to the formula:

$$\text{Estimated Three-Sigma Distance for Poisson Counts} = 3\sqrt{\bar{c}}$$

- So the control limits for the *c*-chart will be:

$$\bar{c} \pm 3\sqrt{\bar{c}}$$

- When the value computed for the lower limit is negative there will be no lower limit.

The Poisson probability model has been the standard model for accident data since its first use in characterizing the number of Prussian troops injured by Prussian mules. The data in Figure 11.4 are the number of lost-time accidents for one plant. There were 49 accidents in the past 31 months, giving an average count of 1.58 accidents per month. Since the areas of opportunity for these counts (the number of man-hours worked each month) are approximately the same we can consider these counts to be comparable and place them on a c-chart. With an average count of 1.58 accidents per month, the upper control limit will be:

$$UCL_c = 1.58 + 3\sqrt{1.58} = 5.35$$

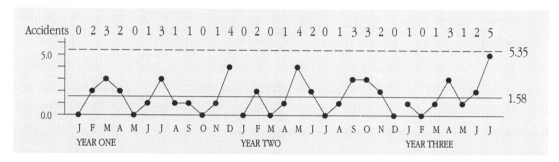

Figure 11.4: c-Chart for Lost Time Accidents

11.4 Charts for Poisson Rates: the u-Chart

The u-chart is appropriate when you have *rates* based on counts which satisfy the two Poisson conditions in the preceding section. The u-chart is a chart for individual rates.

If a set of counts satisfy the two Poisson conditions given in the preceding section, and if their areas of opportunity vary by *less* than ± 20 percent, then it is acceptable to consider the counts to be roughly comparable. Such counts may be charted directly using either an XmR chart or a c-chart.

If a set of counts satisfy the two Poisson conditions given in the preceding section, and if their areas of opportunity vary by *more* than ± 20 percent, then we shall convert the counts into rates prior to placing them on a chart. As noted earlier, counts are converted into rates by dividing the each count by its own area of opportunity.

When working with counts that satisfy the two Poisson conditions we will denote the area of opportunity for the ith count, X_i, by the symbol:

$$a_i$$

The ratio of the ith count to its area of opportunity will be a rate, and will be denoted by:

$$u_i = \frac{X_i}{a_i}$$

- The u-chart will be based upon a plot of the u_i values. The central line will be defined by the average rate $\bar{u}$.

$$\bar{u} = \frac{\text{total number of events observed in baseline period}}{\text{sum of the areas of opportunity in baseline period}}$$

- For the ith sample the three-sigma distance will be estimated by:

$$\text{Estimated Three Sigma Distance for Poisson Rates} = 3\sqrt{\frac{\bar{u}}{a_i}}$$

- So the limits for a u-chart will be computed to be:

$$\bar{u} \pm 3\sqrt{\frac{\bar{u}}{a_i}}$$

- If the value computed for a lower limit falls below 0.0, then there is no lower limit for that sample.

As an example of the use of rates based upon Poisson counts we will use the data for the number of hospital days per month for a small health-care plan. The data are given in Table 11.4. Each month the total number of days which members of the health plan spent in the hospital is reported. Since the number of members is changing from month to month, the area of opportunity for this count is taken to be the membership on the first day of the month times the number of days in that month. When the counts are divided by the number of member days a very small ratio is obtained. To turn these small numbers into numbers that are easy to use they are multiplied by 1,000,000. The resulting rate is the hospitalization days per million member days (hosp. days/mmd).

For this two-year period, the total number of hospital days was 17,690 while the total number of member days was 85,392,513. This gives an average rate of 0.0002072 which, when multiplied by one million is:

$$\bar{u} = \frac{\text{total number of hospital days in baseline period}}{\text{total number of million member days in baseline period}} = \frac{17\,690}{85.392\,513} = 207.2$$

As with the p-chart, the u-chart requires that the limits be computed for each point. The u-chart for Table 11.3 is shown in Figure 11.5. At the beginning of this chart there is one point above the upper limit and a run of four points near the upper limit. At the end of this two-year period there is a run of ten successive values below the central line. Of course the health plan administrators were happy to see this evidence of a downward trend.

Table 11.3: Hospital Days Per Million Member Days

Month	No. of Hosp. Days	No. of Member Days	Hosp. Rate/ mmd	Month	No. of Hosp. Days	No. of Member Days	Hosp. Rate/ mmd
Jan.	656	2,864,648	229.0	Jan.	762	3,589,304	212.3
Feb.	620	2,725,604	227.5	Feb.	735	3,371,676	218.0
Mar.	681	2,972,063	229.1	Mar.	780	3,833,863	203.5
Apr.	681	3,000,390	227.0	Apr.	737	3,667,800	200.9
May	660	3,102,449	212.7	May	770	3,917,966	196.5
Jun.	731	3,125,700	233.9	Jun.	727	3,773,580	192.7
Jul.	694	3,366,972	206.1	Jul.	784	4,006,316	195.7
Aug.	695	3,381,294	205.5	Aug.	839	4,121,853	203.5
Sept.	683	3,362,310	203.1	Sept.	779	3,978,360	195.8
Oct.	729	3,406,373	214.0	Oct.	853	4,182,985	203.9
Nov.	715	3,480,510	205.4	Nov.	804	4,137,480	194.3
Dec.	743	3,657,287	203.2	Dec.	832	4,365,730	190.6

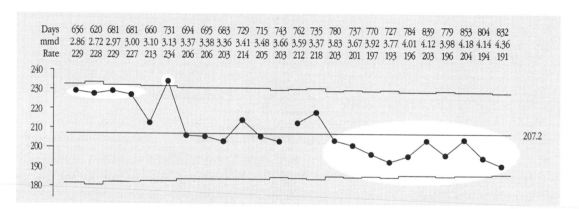

Figure 11.5: *u*-Chart for Hospital Days per Million Member Days

Of course there is little difference between the *u*-chart and the X chart for the same data, which is shown in Figure 11.6.

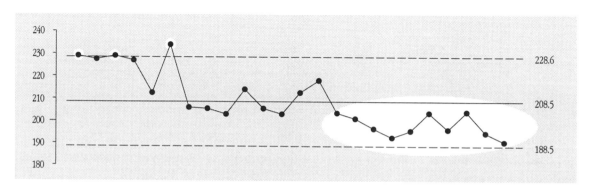

Figure 11.6: X Chart for Hospital Days per Million Member Days

For the X chart the average of the rates is 208.5, and the average moving range is 7.54, giving Natural Process Limits of 228.6 and 188.5. Both the u-chart and the X chart tell the same story. These rates show a definite downward trend over this two-year period.

11.5 So How Should You Chart Count Data?

The XmR chart gives limits that are *empirical*—they are based upon the variation that is present in the data (as measured by the moving ranges). The np-chart, the p-chart, the c-chart, and the u-chart all use a specific probability model to construct *theoretical* limits. These theoretical limits all use an estimate of the three-sigma distance that is based upon the value for the central line.

- If the theoretical model correctly describes the data, then the theoretical limits will be appropriate.

- If the theoretical model correctly describes the data, then the empirical limits will mimic the theoretical limits, and will also be appropriate.

- If the theoretical model does not correctly describe the data, then the theoretical limits will be incorrect, while the empirical limits will still be appropriate.

So if you are sophisticated enough to judge when the different probability models apply, by all means use the theoretical approach. But if you are not sure about when to use a particular probability model, then you may still use the empirical approach of the XmR chart. Remember, the objective is to take the right action, rather than to find the "right" number.

Data Characterized by Binomial Model		Data Characterized by Poisson Model		Other Data Based On Counts	
Area of Opportunity = **n**		Area of Opportunity = **a**		Area of Opportunity	
constant **n**	variable **n**	constant **a**	variable **a**	constant	variable
np-chart or *XmR* for Counts	*p*-chart or *XmR* for Rates	*c*-chart or *XmR* for Counts	*u*-chart or *XmR* for Rates	*XmR* for Counts	*XmR* for Rates

Figure 11.7: Charts for Count Data

The only instance of count data which cannot be reasonably placed on an XmR chart is that of very rare items or very rare events: data for which the average count per sample falls below 1.0. The problem with trying to put such data on an XmR chart is the problem of chunky data, which was described in Chapter Eight.

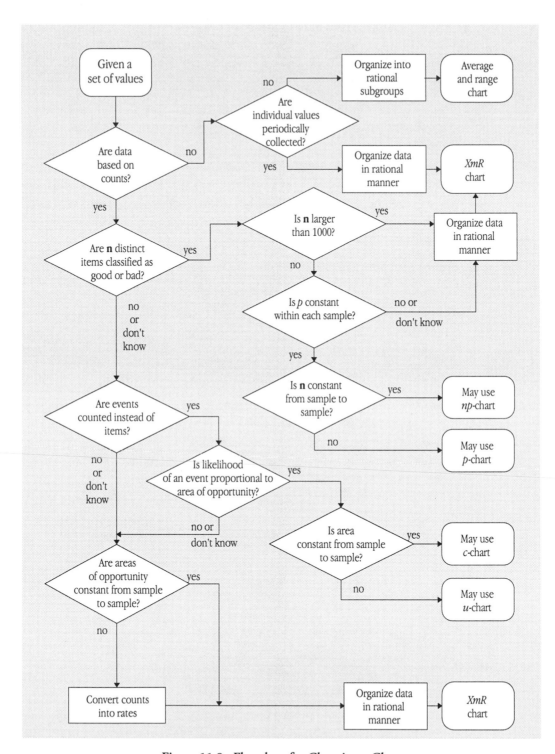

Figure 11.8: Flowchart for Choosing a Chart

11.6 *XmR* Charts for Chunky Ratios

The *p*-chart allows for the discreteness that is inherent in chunky ratios. Some who have gotten used to the complexity of the *p*-chart are not satisfied with using the constant-width limits of the ordinary *XmR* chart when the data consists of chunky ratios. They fear that they will miss signals and get an excessive number of false alarms when using an *XmR* chart for chunky ratios.

Both experience and research have shown that the ordinary *XmR* chart will still have an acceptable false alarm rate of 1 percent or less even when used with chunky ratios. However, if you wish, you may adjust the limits on the X chart to allow for the different sized areas of opportunity of the chunky ratios. The qualification and the procedure are given below.

The following modification of the standard *XmR* chart is appropriate when:

- you are working with counts of items,
- the areas of opportunity, n_i, vary by more than $\pm 20\%$ from the average, $\bar{n}$, and
- some of the areas of opportunity are less than 20.

When these three conditions exist you will be working with chunky ratios, and you might wish to adjust the limits on the X chart to allow for this chunkiness.

To adjust the limits for chunky ratios you begin by computing the average size for the areas of opportunity in the baseline samples:

$$\bar{n} = \text{average size of the areas of opportunity for baseline ratios}$$

Next you compute the chunkiness scaling factor w_i for the ith ratio:

$$w_i = \sqrt{\frac{\bar{n}}{n_i}}$$

where n_i is the area of opportunity for the ith ratio. The limits for the ith ratio on the X chart are calculated according to the formula:

$$\bar{X} + 2.660 \; w_i \; \overline{mR} \quad or \quad \bar{X} \pm 3.145 \; w_i \; \widetilde{mR}$$

The data of Table 11.2 are repeated in Table 11.4. The average area of opportunity is:

$$\bar{n} = 238.$$

The smallest area of opportunity is 94, which is 39% of 238. The maximum area of opportunity is 511, which is 215% of 238. So the areas of opportunity vary –61% and +115% from the average size of 238.

Table 11.4: The Proportion of Orders Shipped by Premium Freight

Date	X	n	p	mR	w	Date	X	n	p	mR	w
1	27	102	.265		1.53	15	19	101	.188	.036	1.54
2	31	146	.212	.053	1.28	16	33	140	.236	.048	1.30
3	70	280	.250	.038	0.92	17	68	292	.233	.003	0.90
4	54	207	.261	.011	1.07	18	44	207	.213	.020	1.07
5	69	322	.214	.047	0.86	19	74	257	.288	.075	0.96
6	101	410	.246	.032	0.76	20	124	511	.243	.045	0.68
8	28	99	.283	.037	1.55	22	21	94	.223	.020	1.59
9	37	143	.259	.024	1.29	23	32	139	.230	.007	1.31
10	47	235	.200	.059	1.01	24	65	229	.284	.054	1.02
11	46	185	.249	.049	1.13	25	46	170	.271	.013	1.18
12	70	271	.258	.009	0.94	26	75	290	.259	.012	0.91
13	105	469	.224	.034	0.71	27	117	407	.287	.028	0.76

Thus the counts of Table 11.4 are (1) counts of items where (2) the areas of opportunity vary by more than ± 20 percent. Since none of the values for **n** are less than 20, these data do not satisfy the third condition for chunky ratios. However, since the computations are the same regardless of the size of the n_i values, we will use the data of Table 11.4 to illustrate the computation of variable width limits for the X chart.

To place the proportions of Table 11.4 on an *XmR* chart with variable limits we will need to compute the moving ranges using the proportions. We will also have to compute the chunkiness scaling factors, w_i, for each sample. These values are shown in Table 11.4. The average of these proportions is 0.245, and the average moving range is 0.033. The limits are computed for each point according to the formulas given earlier in this section, and are plotted as shown in Figure 11.9.

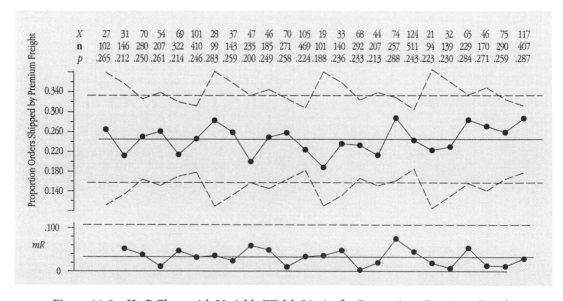

Figure 11.9: *XmR* Chart with Variable Width Limits for Proportions Premium Freight

The straight limits in Figure 11.9 are those from the ordinary *XmR* chart given in Figure 10.4. Points that would be outside the variable width limits would also be close to, or outside, the straight limits. On the other hand, some points that would be outside the straight limits could still be within the variable width limits. This means that using the straight line limits with chunky ratios would result in slightly more false alarms, but relatively few missed signals.

Figure 11.10 compares the variable width limits on the *X* chart with those of the *p*-chart. The *p*-chart limits are shown stairstep style. While the two sets of limits are not identical, they are sufficiently close that there will be no practical difference in using one over the other. However, as noted earlier, the *p*-chart limits are based on a theoretical model, and are appropriate only when the data satisfy the binomial conditions. The *X* chart limits are empirical, and will work without reference to any particular probability model.

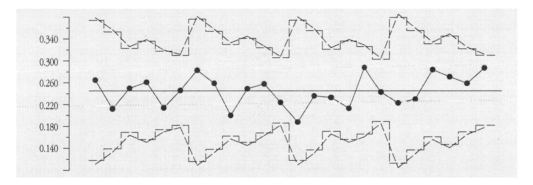

Figure 11.10: Variable Width Limits for *X* Chart Compared to *p*-Chart Limits (Premium Freight Data)

Table 11.5: Hospital Days Per Million Member Days

Month	No. of Hosp. Days	No. of Member Days	Hosp. Rate/ mmd	mR	w	Month	No. of Hosp. Days	No. of Member Days	Hosp. Rate/ mmd	mR	w
Jan.	656	2,864,648	229.0		1.11	Jan.	762	3,589,304	212.3	9.1	1.00
Feb.	620	2,725,604	227.5	1.5	1.14	Feb.	735	3,371,676	218.0	5.7	1.03
Mar.	681	2,972,063	229.1	1.6	1.09	Mar.	780	3,833,863	203.5	14.5	0.96
Apr.	681	3,000,390	227.0	2.1	1.09	Apr.	737	3,667,800	200.9	2.6	0.98
May	660	3,102,449	212.7	14.3	1.07	May	770	3,917,966	196.5	4.4	0.95
June	731	3,125,700	233.9	21.2	1.07	June	727	3,773,580	192.7	3.8	0.97
July	694	3,366,972	206.1	27.8	1.03	July	784	4,006,316	195.7	3.0	0.94
Aug.	695	3,381,294	205.5	0.6	1.03	Aug.	839	4,121,853	203.5	7.8	0.93
Sept.	683	3,362,310	203.1	2.4	1.03	Sept.	779	3,978,360	195.8	7.7	0.95
Oct.	729	3,406,373	214.0	10.9	1.02	Oct.	853	4,182,985	203.9	8.1	0.92
Nov.	715	3,480,510	205.4	8.6	1.01	Nov.	804	4,137,480	194.3	9.6	0.93
Dec.	743	3,657,287	203.2	2.2	0.99	Dec.	832	4,365,730	190.6	3.7	0.90

The variable limit *XmR* chart may also be used with ratios based on counts of events. The chunkiness scaling factor would be defined as the square root of the ratio of the average area of opportunity to the area of opportunity for a particular period. The data of Table 11.3 are repeated in Table 11.5, along with the moving ranges for the hospitalization rates and the chunkiness weighting factors, w_i. The average is 207.6, the average moving range is 7.53, and the average number of member days is 3.558 million.

The variable limit *XmR* chart for these data is shown in Figure 11.11. The *u*-chart limits are shown stairstep style on the same graph. In this instance the *u*-chart limits fall outside the variable width limits for the *X* chart. As before, there is no practical difference between these two charting techniques.

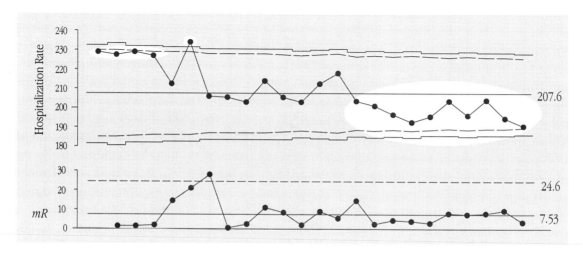

Figure 11.11: Variable Limit *XmR* Chart Compared to *u*-Chart Limits

So, for those who are sophisticated enough to judge when a particular probability model should apply to a given set of count data, there are the traditional, model-specific, charts—the *np*-chart, the *p*-chart, the *c*-chart, and the *u*-chart. These charts use a probability model to justify the computation of the three-sigma distance based upon the value for the central line—that is, they use a measure of location to also characterize dispersion. When the probability model does approximate the behavior of the counts this practice is sound. If the probability model does not approximate the behavior of the counts then the formulas for the traditional, model-specific, charts will be incorrect.

If you do not feel sophisticated enough to judge the appropriateness of various probability models, you may place your count based data on an *XmR* chart. The empirical limits of the *XmR* chart will always be appropriate.

11.7 Process Behavior Charts for Rare Events

There is a limitation on the use of the *XmR* chart with count data. Just as with measurement data, the process behavior chart limits will be corrupted when the measurement increment becomes too large to properly reflect the variation of the data. When the round-off obscures the process variation the process behavior limits will be artificially constricted, and the chart becomes unreliable (see Section 8.6). This also can happen with count data. Typically, count data can be said to be chunky when the average count falls below 1.0 per sample. When the average count falls below 1.0 per sample, the only charts available are the *np*-, *p*-, *c*-, and *u*-charts. However, since these charts become very insensitive when the average count falls below 1.0 per sample, there is very little to be gained by charting the counts of rare events. The following example illustrates this problem and outlines a solution.

Chemical plants are required to track spills. While spills are not desirable, and while everything possible is done to prevent them, there are occasional spills. Over the past few years one plant has averaged one spill every eight months. Of course, if the plant averages one spill every eight months, then in those months in which they have a spill their spill rate is *700 percent above average.* When dealing with very small numbers, such as the counts of rare events, a one unit change can result in a huge percentage difference. The usual process behavior chart for these data would be the *c*-chart, and the basic statistic for a *c*-chart is the average count. During the first four years there were a total of six spills. Six spills in 48 months gives an average of:

$$\bar{c} = \frac{6 \text{ spills}}{48 \text{ months}} = 0.125 \text{ spills per month}$$

This average will be the central line for the *c*-chart, and the upper control limit will be computed to be:

$$UCL_c = \bar{c} + 3\sqrt{\bar{c}} = 0.125 + 3\sqrt{0.125} = 1.186$$

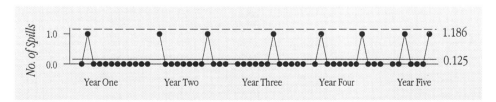

Figure 11.12: *c*-Chart for Spills

The *c*-chart is shown in Figure 11.12. In spite of the fact that a single spill is 700 percent above the average, the *c*-chart does not show any points outside the limits. It would take two spills in a single month to make this chart signal a change. This is not a problem with the charts, but rather a problem with the data themselves. (When you are averaging one spill every eight months, a month with two spills will be a remarkable event whether or not one is using a process behavior chart!) Counts of rare events are inherently insensitive and weak. No matter how these *counts* are analyzed there is nothing to discover on this chart.

CAUTION: The sequences of zeroes in Figure 11.12 do not constitute runs below the central line. In the first place you have to make allowance for the chunkiness of the values. Zero is as close to the central line as these values can be, and therefore should not be interpreted as being either above or below the central line. Secondly, when working with counts, a count of zero means that nothing was found, which is a negative type of information, rather than a positive signal of anything.

Yet there are other ways to characterize rare events. Instead of *counting* the number of spills each year (counting events), you could instead *measure* the number of days between the spills (measure the area of opportunity). For the first four years the time intervals between the spills are computed as follows.

Table 11.6: Dates of Spills

Date of Spill	2/23/01	1/11/02	9/15/02	7/6/03	2/19/04	9/29/04	3/20/05	7/13/05
Day of Year	54	11	258	188	50	272	79	194
Days Between Spills		322	247	295	227	222	172	115

One spill in 322 days converts into a spill rate of:

$$\frac{1 \text{ spill}}{322 \text{ days}} = 0.0031 \text{ spills per day}$$

Multiplying the daily spill rate by 365 gives a yearly spill rate.

(0.0031 spills per day) x (365 days per year) = 1.13 spills per year.

Table 11.7: Instantaneous Spill Rates

Days Between Spills		322	247	295	227	222
Spills per Day		0.0031	0.0040	0.0034	0.0044	0.0045
Spills per Year	X	1.13	1.48	1.24	1.61	1.64
Moving Ranges	mR		0.35	0.24	0.37	0.03

Thus, the interval between the first and second spills is equivalent to having 1.13 spills per year. Continuing in this manner, the intervals between the first six spills are converted into five instantaneous spill rates (in spills per year). These five spill rates and the accompanying moving ranges are shown in Table 11.7.

The average spill rate during the first four years is 1.42 spills per year. The average moving range is 0.2475. Using these values we obtain the *XmR* chart shown in Figure 11.13.

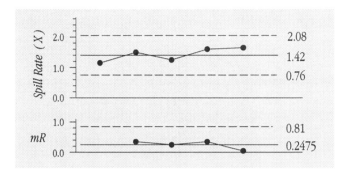

Figure 11.13: *XmR* Chart for Spill Rates

The two spills in the current year had intervals of 172 days and 115 days respectively. These intervals convert into spill rates of 2.12 spills per year and 3.17 spills per year. When these values are added to the *XmR* chart the result is Figure 11.14.

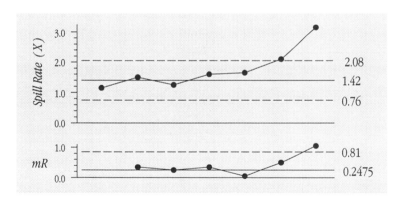

Figure 11.14: Complete *XmR* Chart for Spill Rates

Since the limits shown in Figures 11.13 and 11.14 are based on four moving ranges they must be interpreted as being very soft. (The greater the number of moving ranges used the more solid the limits become—they are constrained to be closer to the theoretical values. The limits are said to be soft when fewer than 17 moving ranges are used.) While the first spill in the current year is outside the limit, it is barely outside. Given the softness of limits based on four moving ranges, it is difficult to say if the first spill in the current year is a definite signal or not. However, the second spill is far enough outside the limits to be safely interpreted as a definite signal—there has been an increase in the spill rate during the current year.

One should also note that while the chart in Figure 11.14 has both upper and lower limits, it is possible that rare events will result in *XmR* charts which only have an upper limit. In such a case, both the times between events and the instantaneous rates are likely to have a highly skewed distribution like the one on the bottom of Figure 8.2. When this happens, and you want to detect a deterioration in the process, the instantaneous rates will be the values to plot on an *XmR* chart (above the upper limit is equivalent to an increased rate of occurrence). On the other hand, if you are trying to detect improvement, such as in the question of whether or not a prevention program has been effective in reducing lost-time accidents, then the *times between events* will be the values to plot on an *XmR* chart (here a large value corresponds to a long time between events).

In general, *counts are weaker than measurements.* Counts of rare events are no exception. When possible, it will always be more satisfactory to *measure the activity* than to merely *count events*.

CAUTION: The use of the time between events, as outlined in this section, makes sense only as long as the events themselves come from a single system of causes. Measuring the time between events when one event comes from one cause system and the other event comes from another cause system does not make sense. For example, a single plant may have an environmental permit that requires notification for any one of a dozen different types of events. If every notification event is tracked, and if the time between notifications is used as suggested in this section, then just what does it mean when a point goes above the upper limit on the X-chart? Generally, such a point will denote the *concurrency* of events from separate and independent systems. This will not produce any insight into how to improve the process. Moreover, a chart which combines events coming from separate cause systems will not even be useful as a report card since points above the upper limit will indicate concurrency rather than a change in the system. Such a chart will not allow one to learn from an analysis of the past.

11.8 Summary

When dealing with count data you may choose to use a theoretical approach or an empirical one. With the theoretical approach you will, of necessity, have to be concerned with the appropriateness of the assumptions required by the theory. When you have a strong belief in the appropriateness of the assumptions, the use of the theoretical approach will allow you to detect departures from the theoretical model. David S. Chambers' famous example of personnel reporting fictitious data which is given in *Out of the Crisis*, page 265, and in *Understanding Statistical Process Control, Second Edition*, page 283, will serve to illustrate this point. There the failure of the data to behave as they ought to behave, given the conditions under which they were supposed to have been collected, was a clear indication that the data were artificially restricted in range. They were never allowed to get too high, nor were they allowed to get too low. The *XmR* chart for these data does not show this problem as clearly as the *p*-chart. So there are occasional instances where the theoretical model provides additional insight beyond what can be obtained from the *XmR* chart. Yet, for most who have to use process behavior charts, the verification of the assumptions required for the use of the theoretical model is the greatest hurdle in the charting of count data. Experts may tread here; others need to be very careful.

Another bonus of the theoretical approach is the elegance of the equations—only one statistic is needed, and no scaling factors are required—yet this elegance can be accessed only after the assumptions have been verified. The complexity of the latter will generally more than offset the advantage of simple computations.

- When a theoretical model is appropriate both the theoretical approach and the empirical approach will yield limits that are quite similar.

- When the theoretical model used is inappropriate the theoretical approach will yield incorrect limits, while the empirical approach will still yield appropriate limits.

- Which is why you can't go far wrong using an *XmR* chart with count data.

Chapter Twelve

Average and Range Charts

The previous six chapters have discussed the individual value and moving range chart (XmR chart). In this chapter we introduce another type of chart: the average and range chart (also known as the X-bar and R chart). While average and range charts are somewhat more specialized than XmR charts they do have certain advantages which make them particularly well-suited for specific applications. At the same time, their greater specialization imposes certain restrictions upon their use. The advantages, restrictions, and issues surrounding average and range charts are the topics of this chapter.

Administrative applications of the average and range chart will be discussed and illustrated in this and the next chapter. However, in the introduction of this technique, we will use a simple production example.

12.1 Shewhart's Average and Range Charts

In Shewhart's book, *Economic Control of Quality of Manufactured Product*, the basic chart is the average and range chart. The reason for this is seen in the title above—Shewhart was focused on manufacturing problems, which was natural since he worked with Western Electric and Bell Laboratories.

When you are making widgets you usually have the option of collecting multiple measurements within a short period of time. When this happens it is logical to arrange these data—which are collected under essentially the same conditions—together into a group. Since there will be many of these small groups it is customary to call them *subgroups*, and the act of arranging the data into these subgroups is called *subgrouping*.

When you have data arranged in subgroups you can characterize the location of the process using the subgroup averages, and you can characterize the dispersion of the process using the subgroup ranges.

Imagine that you operate a small winery and that your bottling operation consists of a simple, single-head filler. You can fill about 300 bottles per hour, and you wish to monitor the filling operation by actually checking the fill weights of five bottles each hour. A timer is used to select one bottle every twelve minutes, and the five bottles from each hour are arranged together in a single subgroup. The fill weights are measured in milliliters (ml), and the label fill weight is 750 ml. The fill weights for the first hour are:

$$751 \text{ ml}, \ 754 \text{ ml}, \ 756 \text{ ml}, \ 754 \text{ ml}, \ \text{and} \ 753 \text{ ml}$$

These five values comprise the first subgroup.

The subgroup average is 753.6 ml.

The subgroup range is 5 ml, which is the difference between the maximum value of 756 ml and the minimum value of 751 ml.

These five measurements, along with their average and range, are placed on the average and range chart, and the subgroup average and subgroup range are plotted as shown in Figure 12.1:

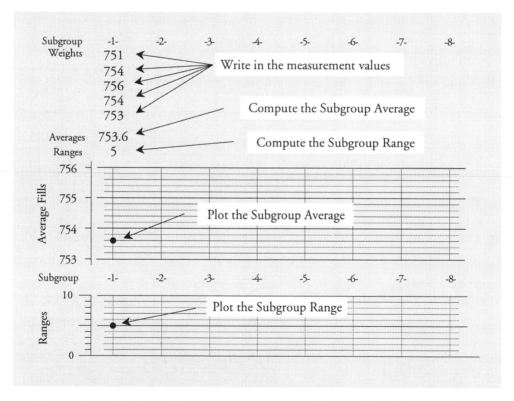

Figure 12.1: The First Subgroup on the Average and Range Chart for Fill Weights

The second hour you again measure the fill weights for five bottles. You get values of:

757 ml, 755 ml, 756 ml, 754 ml, and 756 ml

These five values are written on the average and range chart, and the subgroup average and subgroup range are computed, entered, and plotted as shown in Figure 12.2.

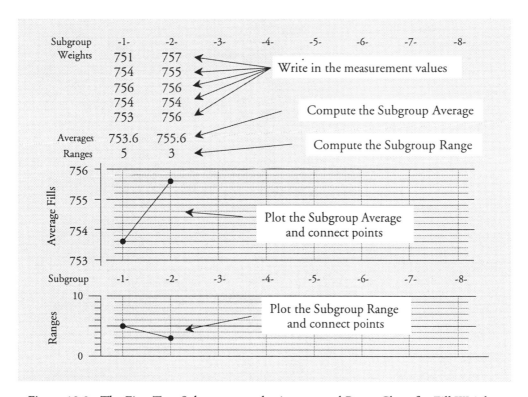

Figure 12.2: The First Two Subgroups on the Average and Range Chart for Fill Weights

Continuing in this manner, the measurements, subgroup averages, and subgroup ranges for one eight-hour shift are shown in Figure 12.3. With the addition of limits this figure will become an average and range chart.

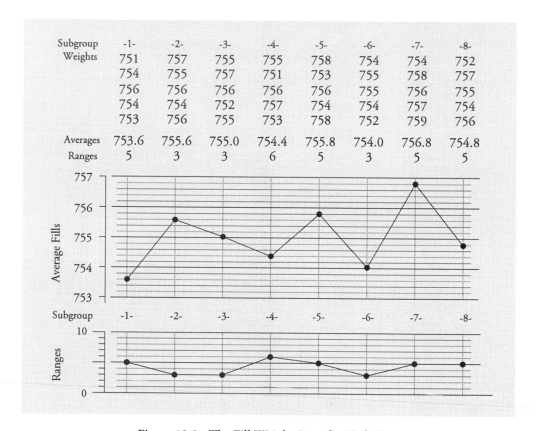

Subgroup Weights	-1-	-2-	-3-	-4-	-5-	-6-	-7-	-8-
	751	757	755	755	758	754	754	752
	754	755	757	751	753	755	758	757
	756	756	756	756	756	755	756	755
	754	754	752	757	754	754	757	754
	753	756	755	753	758	752	759	756
Averages	753.6	755.6	755.0	754.4	755.8	754.0	756.8	754.8
Ranges	5	3	3	6	5	3	5	5

Figure 12.3: The Fill Weight Data for Shift One

The two summary statistics used to compute limits for average and range charts are the grand average and the average range.

- The *grand average* is the average of the subgroup averages, and is commonly denoted by the symbol:

$$\bar{\bar{X}}$$

- The *average range* is the average of the subgroup ranges and is commonly denoted by the symbol:

$$\bar{R}$$

For the data in Figure 12.3 the grand average is the average of the 8 subgroup averages, which is 755.0 milliliters.

For the data in Figure 12.3 the average range is the average of the 8 subgroup ranges, which is 4.625 milliliters.

To convert these two summary statistics into the appropriate limits we again make use of certain scaling factors. There are three scaling factors needed for average and range charts:

A_2 is the scaling factor used to compute limits for the subgroup averages.

D_3 is the scaling factor used to compute the Lower Range Limit.

D_4 is the scaling factor used to compute the Upper Range Limit.

The values for these scaling factors will depend upon the subgroup size, n. Some values for these scaling factors are given in Table 12.1.

Table 12.1: Scaling Factors for Average and Range Charts

n	A_2	D_3	D_4
2	1.880	—	3.268
3	1.023	—	2.574
4	0.729	—	2.282
5	0.577	—	2.114
6	0.483	—	2.004
7	0.419	0.076	1.924
8	0.373	0.136	1.864
9	0.337	0.184	1.816
10	0.308	0.223	1.777
11	0.285	0.256	1.744
12	0.266	0.283	1.717
13	0.249	0.307	1.693
14	0.235	0.328	1.672
15	0.223	0.347	1.653

When n is 6 or less there will be no Lower Range Limit, and so no value for D_3 is given until n exceeds 6. Since Figure 12.3 has a subgroup size of $n = 5$ we will use the scaling factors of $A_2 = 0.577$ and $D_4 = 2.114$.

- The limits for the subgroup averages are commonly called "control limits." To compute these limits for the subgroup averages you begin by multiplying the average range by the appropriate value of A_2.

$$A_2 \bar{R} = 0.577 \times 4.625 \text{ ml} = 2.67 \text{ ml}$$

- The Upper Control Limit for averages will be found by adding this value to the grand average:

$$UCL = \bar{\bar{X}} + A_2 \bar{R} = 755.0 + 2.67 = 757.67 \text{ ml}$$

- In a similar manner, the Lower Control Limit for averages will be found by subtracting the value of 2.67 milliliters from the grand average:

$$LCL = \overline{\overline{X}} - A_2\overline{R} = 755.0 - 2.67 = 752.33 \text{ ml}$$

- To compute limits for subgroup ranges you multiply the average range by the appropriate values of D_3 and D_4. The Upper Range Limit for the data of Figure 12.3 is:

$$URL = D_4\overline{R} = 2.114 \times 4.625 \text{ ml} = 9.78 \text{ ml}$$

and there is no Lower Range Limit in this case (because $n = 5$).

When these limits are added to Figure 12.3 we get the average and range chart shown in Figure 12.4.

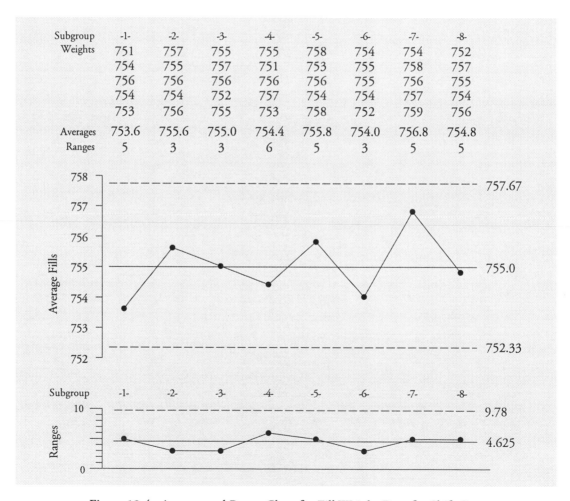

Subgroup	-1-	-2-	-3-	-4-	-5-	-6-	-7-	-8-
Weights	751	757	755	755	758	754	754	752
	754	755	757	751	753	755	758	757
	756	756	756	756	756	755	756	755
	754	754	752	757	754	754	757	754
	753	756	755	753	758	752	759	756
Averages	753.6	755.6	755.0	754.4	755.8	754.0	756.8	754.8
Ranges	5	3	3	6	5	3	5	5

Figure 12.4: Average and Range Chart for Fill Weight Data for Shift One

The average and range chart in Figure 12.4 shows a predictable process. With a grand average of 755.0 this process can be said to be averaging about 5 milliliters above the label value of 750 milliliters.

The limits on the average chart define the routine variation for the average fill weights of five bottles. In this case, as long as the *process* average remains close to 755, the *subgroup averages* may vary in the region of 752.3 to 757.7. Whenever a subgroup average falls outside this region it should be taken to be a signal that the process average has changed.

The limit on the range chart defines the routine amount of variation for the subgroup ranges. In this case, as long as the *process* variation does not change the subgroup ranges should fall in the region of 0 to 10.

12.2 What Average Charts Do Best

Figure 12.5 shows the average charts for the fill weights from Shifts One and Two. While the two charts are not identical, they do tell the same story. This consistency from time period to time period is characteristic of a predictable process. Since the process is uniform and unchanging, the different segments reveal the same basic story. While the details change, the big picture remains the same.

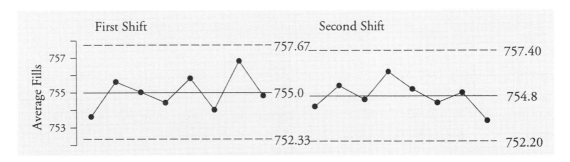

Figure 12.5: Average Charts for Fill Weights from Shifts One and Two

So what is the advantage of using subgroup averages rather than individual values? When it makes sense to arrange the data into subgroups you will gain sensitivity by doing so. This increased sensitivity may be seen in the comparison shown in Figure 12.6, where the 16 Hourly Average Fill Weights are shown next to the 80 Individual Fill Weights. The average chart and the X chart have the same central lines, but the average chart has considerably narrower limits.

The narrower limits for the subgroup averages allow them to be more sensitive to any given shift than the individual values will be. Thus, the advantage of using subgrouped data is the advantage of increased sensitivity to process changes. With an average and range chart you will be able to detect smaller process changes than would be the case with the *XmR* chart.

However, in order to achieve this greater sensitivity, it is imperative that the subgrouping used is a rational subgrouping.

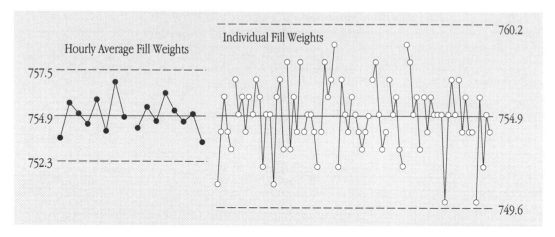

Figure 12.6: Average Chart and Individual Values Chart for the Fill Weight Data

12.3 When Does It Make Sense To Use Subgroups?

When you place two or more values together in a subgroup you are making a *judgment* that, for your purposes at least, you consider these values to have been collected under essentially the same conditions, and that the differences between the values represent nothing more, and nothing less, than routine, background variation.

>*Thus, the first requirement for rational subgrouping is that of*
>*internal homogeneity for the subgroups.*

One way to satisfy this requirement of internal homogeneity is to collect multiple measurements within a reasonably short time. While this is easy to do when making widgets, it becomes less feasible with continuous processes and administrative systems. In the example above we had one subgroup per hour and five pieces per subgroup. When we placed the five values from each hour together in one subgroup we were making a judgment that within each hour the five pieces could be considered to be essentially uniform.

This requirement of internal consistency means that you are willing to consider the variation within the subgroups as "background noise." The assumption that the values were collected under essentially the same conditions means that you are not concerned with the differences between the values. Thus these differences must be thought of as the background level of noise which is present in your system. And, as you may see from the computations, it is this background noise within the subgroups (as characterized by the average range) that is used to determine the limits for the average and range chart.

> *Thus, the second requirement for rational subgrouping is that*
> *the variation within the subgroups must truly represent*
> *the reasonable and proper amount of background variation for the process.*

In the previous example, when we computed the limits for the average and range chart, we were using the average variation within the subgroups to set limits on how much variation we should expect to see from subgroup to subgroup. We used the average variation among the five bottles collected each hour to determine how much variation should occur from hour to hour. And the only way to *judge* if this is appropriate is to know both the process and the way the measurements are made.

In other words, there has always been an element of judgment involved in subgrouping. Subgrouping cannot be automated. It is the conclusion of a *thought* process that combines the context for the data with the purpose of the process behavior chart and then organizes the data in such a way that the chart will answer the questions of interest.

12.4 Daily Department Store Sales

There are many situations where people will tend to collect administrative data into subgroups. Some typical examples follow.

Table 12.2 shows the daily sales figures for a department store over a three month period. These values are given to the nearest hundred dollars. Each week's worth of sales have been made into a subgroup and the weekly averages and ranges are included at the bottom of Table 12.2.

Table 12.2: Daily Department Store Sales

Day	Week 1	Week 2	Week 3	Week 4	Week 5	Week 6	Week 7	Week 8	Week 9	Week 10	Week 11	Week 12	Week 13
Sun.	66	67	69	71	77	122	67	76	108	76	87	126	82
Mon.	44	46	56	86	67	76	65	85	77	60	64	55	68
Tues.	54	54	44	53	45	64	64	76	65	85	54	47	44
Wed.	108	107	100	92	112	100	89	87	98	71	107	103	121
Thurs.	78	109	88	70	90	70	89	103	100	100	99	113	100
Fri.	107	86	127	111	65	85	109	88	74	111	114	75	100
Sat.	150	142	149	160	189	139	163	151	158	171	159	180	180
Averages	86.7	87.3	90.4	91.9	92.1	93.7	92.3	95.1	97.1	96.3	97.7	99.9	99.3
Ranges	106	96	105	107	144	75	99	75	93	111	105	133	136

The grand average is 93.84, and the average range is 106.5.

The scaling factors for subgroups of size $n = 7$ are: $A_2 = 0.419$, $D_3 = 0.076$, and $D_4 = 1.924$.

The control limits for the average chart are thus:

$$\bar{\bar{X}} \pm A_2 \bar{R} = 93.84 \pm (0.419 \times 106.5) = 49.21 \text{ to } 138.46$$

while the range chart limits are:

$$D_3 \bar{R} = 0.076 \times 106.5 = 8.1 \quad \text{and} \quad D_4 \bar{R} = 1.924 \times 106.5 = 204.9$$

These limits are shown in Figure 12.7.

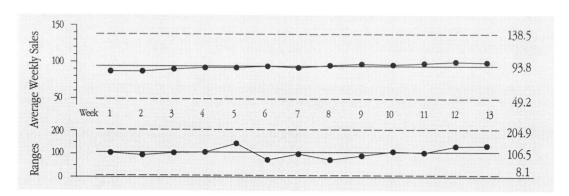

Figure 12.7: Average and Range Chart for Daily Department Store Sales

Does the subgrouping of the Daily Department Store Sales shown in Table 12.2 satisfy the two requirements of rational subgrouping? Are the subgroups internally homogeneous? Does the variation within the subgroups provide the proper yardstick for measuring the variation from subgroup to subgroup?

Even a cursory reading of the data in Table 12.2 shows that there are substantial differences in the sales volumes of different days of the week, with Mondays and Tuesdays being low and Saturdays being highest. Therefore, when the seven days of one week are subgrouped together we have a collection of unlike things. This represents a violation of the first requirement of rational subgrouping.

In addition, the variation within the subgroups is the day-to-day variation, while the variation between the subgroups is the week-to-week variation. Since the day-to-day variation is a completely different type of variation than the week-to-week differences, it is unreasonable to expect that the variation within the subgroups will provide an appropriate yardstick for setting the limits on the average chart.

Therefore, the weekly subgroups shown in Table 12.2 violate both requirements of rational subgrouping. While it is possible to perform the computations and to create a chart using the "subgrouping" of Table 12.2, the failure to organize the data into *rational* subgroups will result in a chart that is useless.

Well, if we cannot subgroup these data by weeks, could we subgroup them by days? Table 12.3 shows the data of Table 12.2 rearranged into seven subgroups of size $n = 13$. Each of these subgroups represent a day of the week. The seven subgroup averages and subgroup ranges are shown on the right side of the table.

Table 12.3: Daily Department Store Sales

Day	Week 1	Week 2	Week 3	Week 4	Week 5	Week 6	Week 7	Week 8	Week 9	Week 10	Week 11	Week 12	Week 13	Average	Range
Sun.	66	67	69	71	77	122	67	76	108	76	87	126	82	84.1	60
Mon.	44	46	56	86	67	76	65	85	77	60	64	55	68	65.3	42
Tues.	54	54	44	53	45	64	64	76	65	85	54	47	44	57.6	41
Wed.	108	107	100	92	112	100	89	87	98	71	107	103	121	99.6	50
Thurs.	78	109	88	70	90	70	89	103	100	100	99	113	100	93.0	43
Fri.	107	86	127	111	65	85	109	88	74	111	114	75	100	96.3	62
Sat.	150	142	149	160	189	139	163	151	158	171	159	180	180	160.8	50

The grand average is still 93.84. The average range is 49.7.

With subgroups of size 13 the scaling factors are: $A_2 = 0.249$, $D_3 = 0.307$, and $D_4 = 1.693$.

The control limits for the average chart are thus:

$$\bar{\bar{X}} \pm A_2 \bar{R} \ = \ 93.84 \pm (0.249 \times 49.7) \ = \ 81.46 \ \text{to} \ 106.22$$

while the range chart limits are:

$$D_3 \bar{R} \ = \ 0.307 \times 49.7 \ = \ 15.3 \ \text{and} \ D_4 \bar{R} \ = \ 1.693 \times 49.7 \ = \ 84.1$$

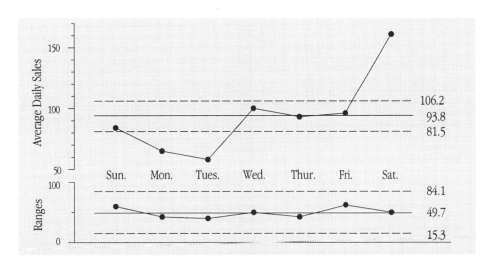

Figure 12.8: Another Average and Range Chart for Daily Department Store Sales

But do the subgroups of Table 12.3 satisfy the requirements of rational subgrouping? Is each subgroup internally homogeneous? Is it logical to assume that the sales volumes on a given day of the week are essentially the same from week to week? If there were substantial week-to-week differences, then would not these differences inflate the variation within each subgroup and thereby affect the limits computed?

While the subgrouping in Table 12.3 is not as severely flawed as that of Table 12.2, there are still potential problems with this second arrangement of these data. For example, while this subgrouping does allow you to distinguish the weekly sales pattern, it does not allow you to track your process over time.

How then can we track these sales over time? Could we plot these 91 values in a running record of Daily Sales? Yes. Should we turn this running record of 91 Daily Sales values into an *XmR* chart? Probably not.

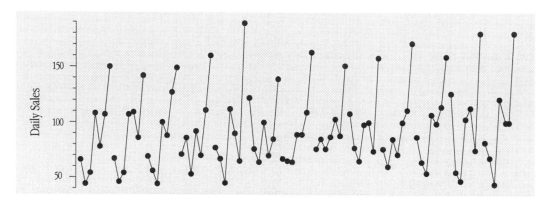

Figure 12.9: Running Record for Daily Department Store Sales

If we placed the 91 values from Table 12.2 on an *XmR* chart, the strong daily cycle of sales would inflate the moving ranges, which would in turn inflate the limits. The principles of rational subgrouping require successive values on an *XmR* chart to be collected under conditions that are, at least most of the time, reasonably similar. When your data display a recurring pattern this requirement is not satisfied. The name given to recurring patterns like the one in Figure 12.9 is seasonality. The next chapter will discuss ways of working with data that display such seasonal patterns.

Could we plot the weekly totals on an *XmR* chart? Yes. This will probably be the most satisfying way of tracking these data over time.

12.5 Regional Sales by Quarter

Table 12.4 shows the quarterly sales for each of six regions for the past five years. These values have been arranged into 20 subgroups of size 6 so that each quarter is a subgroup. What type of variation occurs *within* the subgroups in Table 12.4? What type of variation occurs *between* subgroups in Table 12.4?

Table 12.4: **Quarterly Sales for Five Years**

Quarter	Region A	Region B	Region C	Region D	Region E	Region F	Averages	Ranges
1	924	1,412	1,056	539	397	431	793.2	1015
2	928	1,280	1,048	558	391	470	779.2	889
3	956	1,129	1,129	591	414	439	776.3	715
4	1,222	1,181	1,073	556	407	431	811.7	815
5	748	1,149	1,157	540	415	471	746.7	742
6	962	1,248	1,146	590	442	496	814.0	806
7	983	1,103	1,064	606	384	506	774.3	719
8	1,024	1,021	1,213	643	448	573	820.3	765
9	991	1,085	1,088	657	441	403	777.5	685
10	978	1,125	1,322	602	366	440	805.5	956
11	1,040	910	1,256	596	470	371	773.8	885
12	1,295	999	1,132	640	426	405	816.2	890
13	765	883	1,352	691	445	466	767.0	907
14	1,008	851	1,353	723	455	536	821.0	898
15	1,038	997	1,466	701	363	551	852.7	1103
16	952	878	1,196	802	462	670	826.7	734
17	1,041	939	1,330	749	420	588	844.5	910
18	1,020	834	1,003	762	454	699	795.3	566
19	976	688	1,197	807	447	743	809.7	750
20	1,148	806	1,337	781	359	702	855.5	978

The grand average for the subgroups of Table 12.4 is 803. The average range is 836. The average and range chart for these 20 subgroups is shown in Figure 12.10.

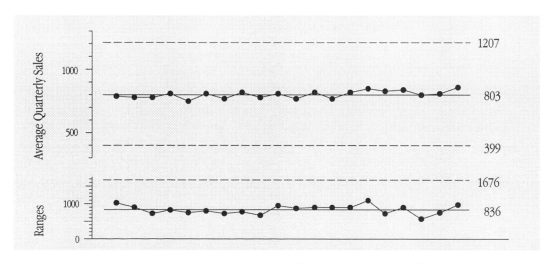

Figure 12.10: **Average and Range Chart for Quarterly Sales in Table 12.4**

What is the problem with the subgrouping in Table 12.4? Are the subgroups internally homogeneous? It is the region-to-region variation that occurs within the subgroups in Table 12.4, while the quarter-to-quarter variation shows up between the subgroups. Is the region-to-region variation the proper yardstick for characterizing the variation from quarter to quarter? Would it not make more sense to acknowledge that the six regions are different, and then to track each region separately on an *XmR* chart (as was done in Chapter 9)?

12.6 More on Peak Flow Rates

In Chapter Seven some peak flow rates were used to illustrate a clinical use of the *XmR* chart. As was mentioned there, the patient was asked to obtain a peak flow rate four times each day: (1) in the morning before taking any medication, (2) in the morning fifteen minutes after taking medication, (3) in the evening prior to taking any medication, and (4) in the evening fifteen minutes after taking medication. Table 12.5 shows a set of peak flow rate data for one patient for a two-week period.

One article, published in a medical journal, in an attempt to describe the clinical use of process behavior charts, arranged data like these into daily subgroups of size four—that is, each column in Table 12.5 was made into a subgroup. Each subgroup combined the a.m. pre-med, the a.m. post-med, the p.m. pre-med, and the p.m. post-med values for a single day.

Table 12.5: Two Weeks of Peak Flow Rates

Day	1	2	3	4	5	6	7	8	9	10	11	12	13	14
morning pre-med	282	264	276	252	356	310	326	322	290	371	376	330	351	376
morning post-med	412	376	381	351	406	391	444	432	406	438	432	426	456	444
evening pre-med	322	386	314	302	421	432	396	396	314	456	371	391	438	391
evening post-med	411	396	416	361	421	432	426	450	342	486	468	468	429	432

Does this subgrouping satisfy the conditions for rational subgroups? Would these subgroups be internally homogeneous? Would the variation within these subgroups be the proper yardstick for evaluating the day-to-day variation?

Since the 56 values in Table 12.5 constitute a time series (as shown in Figure 12.11) another person suggested that these values should be placed on an *XmR* chart. Would this be appropriate? What "process" would the "Natural Process Limits" for this chart represent? What would the moving ranges characterize? *

---

* The answers to the six questions on this page are, respectively: No., No., No., No., No single process., and, The variation between the different conditions—a.m. versus p.m. and pre-med. versus post-med.

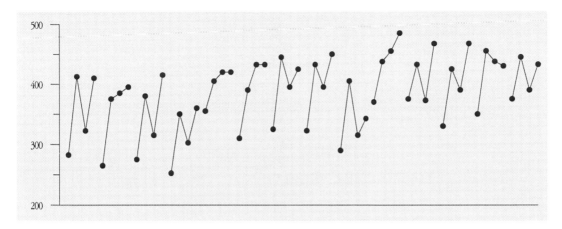

Figure 12.11: Four Peak Flow Rates Obtained Each Day

12.7 Administrative Average and Range Charts

When unlike things are subgrouped together the subgroups are said to be stratified. The problem of stratification will be apparent on the average and range chart because it will result in limits that look too wide for the graph. This phenomenon may be seen in Figures 12.7 and 12.10. When the computations for an average and range chart result in limits that look far too wide for the graph, check to see if unlike things have been grouped together. To understand this problem, return to the examples for Figures 12.7 and 12.10 and see how unlike things were subgrouped together in these two cases.

The average and range chart, for all of its power and sensitivity, requires data which contain multiple measurements collected under essentially the same conditions. This requirement is rarely satisfied in service and administrative applications, where data tend to come along one value at a time. This means that it will be difficult to find ways of using average and range charts to directly monitor service and administrative data. As outlined above, there are many ways to arrange data into what look like subgroups, but not all of these will result in charts that are appropriate, useful, or meaningful. If the subgrouping is not rational, then the chart will not work correctly, and you will be in danger of misleading yourself and others.

While it is difficult to use an average and range chart to directly track administrative data over time, there are indirect ways of using the average and range chart to gain insight into this kind of data. One way is to evaluate and estimate seasonal effects which might be present in your data. This use of the average and range chart will be illustrated in the next chapter.

12.8 Exercises

EXERCISE 12.1:

The fill weights for Shift Two are given in Table 12.6.

Table 12.6: Fill Weights for Second Shift

Hour	Weights					Average	Range
9	755	754	753	754	755	754.2	2
10	757	758	755	753	754	755.4	5
11	757	755	756	753	752	754.6	5
12	759	758	755	756	753	756.2	6
13	756	754	756	755	755	755.2	2
14	755	750	755	757	755	754.4	7
15	757	754	756	754	754		
16	750	756	752	755	754		

(a) Compute the subgroup averages and subgroup ranges missing from Table 12.6.
(b) Compute the grand average (the average of the averages) for the data in Table 12.6.
(c) Compute the average range for the 8 subgroups of size 5 in Table 12.6.
(d) Plot the subgroup averages and subgroup ranges on the next page.
(e) Compute and plot the appropriate limits for the average and range chart for these data.
(f) Compare your average chart with the right-hand portion of Figure 12.5.

Computation Worksheet:

Grand Average = _____   Average Range = _____

Subgroup Size = n = ____   Number of Subgroups = k = ____

Multiply Average Range by A_2 = _____

UCL = Grand Average + A_2 times Average Range = _____

LCL = Grand Average − A_2 times Average Range = _____

URL = D_4 times Average Range = _____

(Exercise 12.1 Continued)

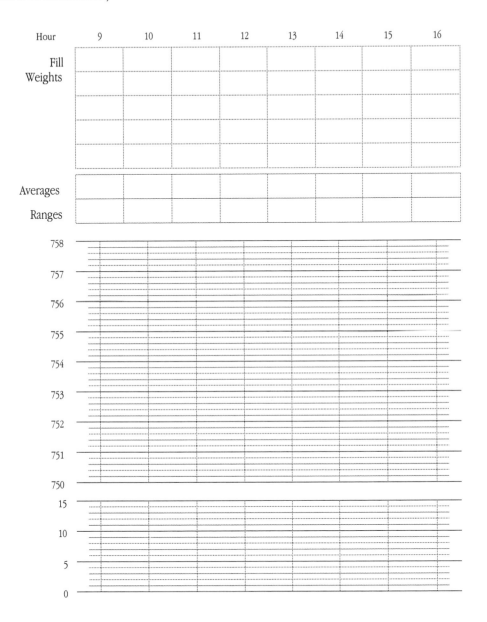

EXERCISE 12.2:

In the next chapter the average and range chart will be used to evaluate seasonal relatives. A seasonal relative is computed by dividing the sales for a given month by the average monthly sales value. These seasonal relatives can be analyzed to determine whether the sales show definite seasonal effects.

The data from one of the examples in Chapter 13 are given in Table 12.7. The entry for January of Year One is 0.316, which means that the sales for January of Year One were 31.6% of the average monthly sales for Year One.

Since the seasonal relatives are given for two years worth of data, they have been organized by months into $k = 12$ subgroups of size $n = 2$.

Table 12.7: Seasonal Relatives for Boutique Sales

Month	Year One	Year Two	Average	Range
January	0.316	0.355	0.3355	0.039
February	0.490	0.311	0.4005	0.179
March	0.749	0.422	0.5855	0.327
April	0.736	0.793	0.7645	0.057
May	1.075	1.276	1.1755	0.201
June	1.067	1.044	1.0555	0.023
July	0.959	0.857	0.908	0.102
August	1.094	1.179	1.1365	0.085
September	0.985	0.747	0.866	0.238
October	1.014	1.064	1.039	0.050
November	1.483	1.456	1.4695	0.027
December	2.032	2.495	2.2635	0.463

(a) Compute the grand average for the data in Table 12.7.
(b) Compute the average range for the 12 subgroups of size 2 in Table 12.7.
(c) Plot the subgroup averages and subgroup ranges on the next page.
(d) Compute and plot the appropriate limits for this average and range chart.
(e) Compare your average and range chart with that shown in Figure 13.14.

Computation Worksheet:

Grand Average = _____   Average Range = _____

Subgroup Size = n = ___   Number of Subgroups = k = ___

Multiply Average Range by A_2 = _____

UCL = Grand Average + A_2 times Average Range = _____

LCL = Grand Average − A_2 times Average Range = _____

URL = D_4 times Average Range = _____

(Exercise 12.2 Continued)

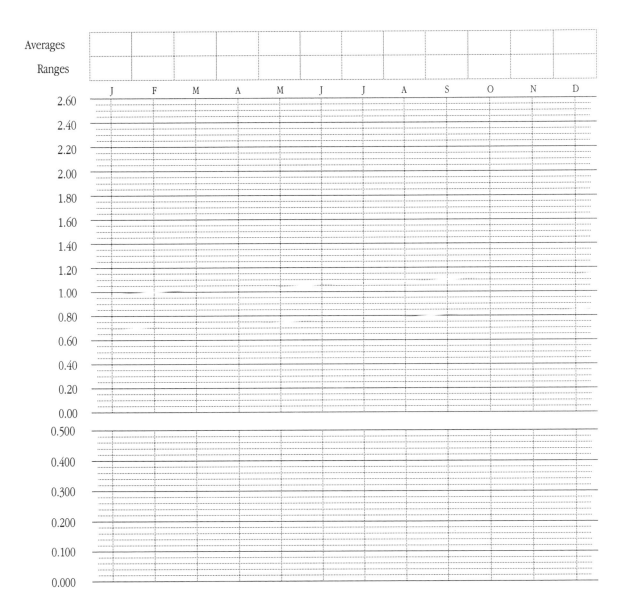

EXERCISE 12.3

The total sales for each week from Table 12.2 are, respectively:

607, 611, 633, 643, 645, 656, 646, 666, 680, 674, 684, 699, and 695.

Place these 13 weekly totals on an *XmR* chart.

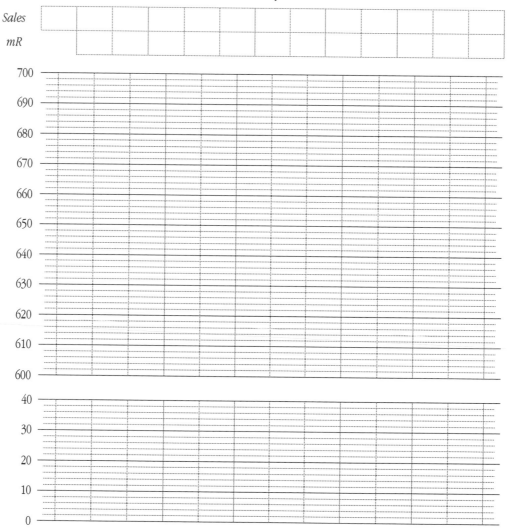

XmR **Chart for Weekly Total Sales**

EXERCISE 12.4

The total sales for the 13 weeks from Table 12.2 are, respectively:

607, 611, 633, 643, 645, 656, 646, 666, 680, 674, 684, 699, and 695.

Place the data above on an X chart with trended limits:

(a) Use the first six weeks values and the last six weeks values to construct a trend line.
(b) Estimate the amount by which this trend increases each week.
(c) Plot the Weekly Total Sales values, the trend line, and the trended limits on the graph.
(d) Estimate the total sales for week 14.
(e) How low would the sales for week 14 need to be to signal lower sales growth?
(f) How high would the sales for week 14 need to be to signal increased sales growth?

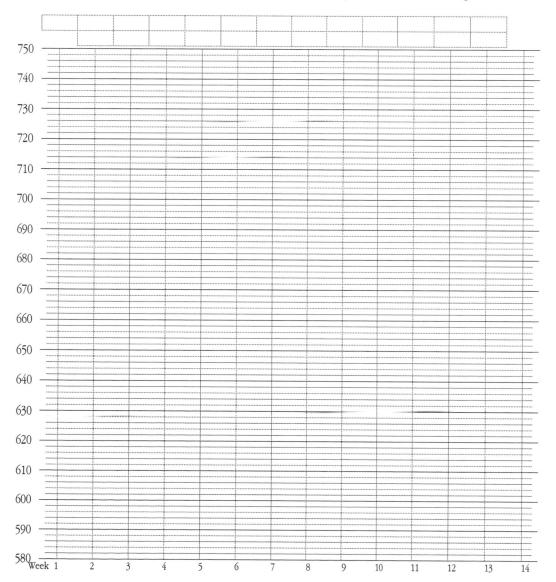

EXERCISE 12.5

For the subgrouping of Table 12.4 the grand average is 803; the average range is 836.

(a) Verify the limits shown in Figure 12.10.

(b) The median range is 850. Use the scaling factors from Table 4 in the Appendix to compute limits for Figure 12.10.

(c) No matter how you compute limits, the subgrouping in Table 12.4 is still stratified, and therefore not a rational subgrouping.
Computations cannot correct the defects of bad subgrouping.

Chapter Thirteen

Seasonal Data

Many time series display regular seasonal patterns and trends. These patterns and trends can be useful in your analysis and understanding of the data, but they also may obscure signals of changes which you would like to detect. Therefore, in order to get the most out of your data, you may need to be able to work with seasonal patterns and trends. Chapter Nine showed how to construct simple trend lines and trended limits for a time-series plot. In this chapter we will outline some ways of working with data which display seasonal patterns. Of course, the use of the term "seasonal" does not restrict us to working with quarterly data. Seasonality is a label for any regularly recurring pattern in a time series.

13.1 Moving Averages

Perhaps the simplest way to handle seasonal patterns is to average or smooth them out. Figure 12.9, on page 212, shows data with a pattern that repeats itself every week. In Exercise 12.3 the weekly averages for these data were plotted on an XmR chart, revealing the underlying trend without the clutter of the weekly pattern. But this method has the disadvantage of requiring that you wait until the end of the week to plot a point. While this may not represent too great an inconvenience, it can become a problem with annual patterns—we do not want to wait until the end of the year to see how we are doing.

A second way of removing a seasonal pattern is to use a year-long *moving average*. With quarterly data, a four-period moving average will always contain four quarters worth of data, and therefore will average out the seasonal effects to reveal the underlying average. (With monthly values a year-long moving average would become a twelve-point moving average.)

To illustrate a moving average we will begin with the quarterly sales values from Region C, shown in Table 13.1. To compute a four-period moving average you obtain the sum of each successive group of four periods. The sum of the sales for the first four periods is 4306. The sum for Periods 2, 3, 4 and 5 is 4407. The sum for Periods 3, 4, 5, and 6 is 4505, etc.

Table 13.1: Quarterly Sales for Region C

Year	Quarter	Period	Region C Sales	4-Period Sum	4-Period Moving Average
One	I	1	1056	—	—
	II	2	1048	—	—
	III	3	1129	—	—
	IV	4	1073	4306	1076.50
Two	I	5	1157	4407	1101.75
	II	6	1146	4505	1126.25
	III	7	1064	4440	1110.00
	IV	8	1213	4580	1145.00
Three	I	9	1088	4511	1127.75
	II	10	1322	4687	1171.75
	III	11	1256	4879	1219.75
	IV	12	1132	4798	1199.50
Four	I	13	1352	5062	1265.50
	II	14	1353	5093	1273.25
	III	15	1466	5303	1325.75
	IV	16	1196	5367	1341.75
Five	I	17	1330	5345	1336.25
	II	18	1003	4995	1248.75
	III	19	1197	4726	1181.50
	IV	20	1337	4867	1216.75

Next you divide each of the four-period sums by 4.0 to obtain the four-period moving averages shown in the last column of Table 13.1. While a moving average is not hard to compute, the computations can become tedious, which is where modern spreadsheet programs become useful. Figure 13.1 combines the individual values with the four-period moving average for Region C.

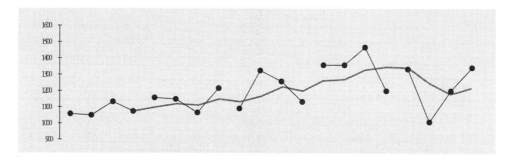

Figure 13.1: Sales for Region C and Four-Period Moving Average

The plot shown in Figure 13.1 is a very powerful summary. The individual values show the levels for each month, allowing you to look for seasonal patterns and abnormal events. At the same time the four-period moving average removes any seasonality that might be present. It also removes the month-to-month noise that complicates the interpretation of the individual values. The four-period moving average reveals the long-term trends in a way that is simple and easy to interpret. This estimate of the trend is automatically updated every time you compute the moving average. And the latest value of the moving average provides you with an instantaneous estimate of current sales levels, after making allowance for recent trends and removing seasonal influences. Finally, the four-period moving average provides a balanced view of the sales levels without being unduly influenced by the euphoria of a good quarter or the depression of a bad quarter.

For those measures that are merely report card measures it is hard to do better than to plot them in the format of Figure 13.1.

Moving averages are a way to smooth the data. They provide a floating central line for the plot in Figure 13.1. When you use a moving average you are characterizing the trend rather than looking for signals. For this reason we do not recommend computing limits for a year-long moving average.

The moving average is sometimes said to lag behind the time-series. This is because any moving average is constructed using historical values. We computed the first value of the four-period moving average at Time Period 4, and this is where we plotted it in Figure 13.1. In truth, the first value for the four-period moving average is the average for Time Periods 1, 2, 3, and 4, and might more properly be plotted at the mid-point of these four time periods, (Time Period 2.5). When this is done in Figure 13.1, it has the effect of shifting the moving average curve back 1.5 time periods. This shifted curve is shown in Figure 13.2, along with the trended limits found (back in Chapter 9) using the first four years of values. Notice how closely the shifted four-period moving average matches the trend line during Years One to Four.

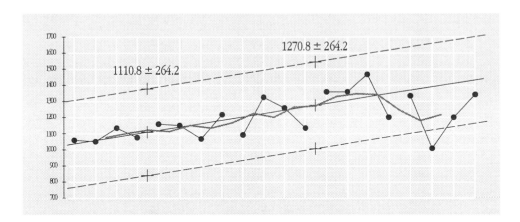

Figure 13.2: Sales for Region C and Four-Period Moving Average

To illustrate a 12-period moving average we will use the data from Table 13.2.

Table 13.2: Monthly Boutique Sales

Year	J	F	M	A	M	J	J	A	S	O	N	D
One	15.0	23.3	35.6	35.0	51.1	50.7	45.6	52.0	46.8	48.2	70.5	96.6
Two	20.1	17.6	23.9	44.9	72.2	59.1	48.5	66.7	42.3	60.2	82.4	141.2
Three	19.0	28.8	35.6	48.1	63.8	49.3	45.6	52.2	46.1	72.9	98.4	122.1

Table 13.3: 12-Period Moving Average for Boutique Sales

Time Period	Values Used (12-period moving subgroups)												Moving Average
12	15.0	23.3	35.6	35.0	51.1	50.7	45.6	52.0	46.8	48.2	70.5	**96.6**	**47.53**
13	23.3	35.6	35.0	51.1	50.7	45.6	52.0	46.8	48.2	70.5	**96.6**	20.1	47.96
14	35.6	35.0	51.1	50.7	45.6	52.0	46.8	48.2	70.5	**96.6**	20.1	17.6	47.48
15	35.0	51.1	50.7	45.6	52.0	46.8	48.2	70.5	**96.6**	20.1	17.6	23.9	46.51
16	51.1	50.7	45.6	52.0	46.8	48.2	70.5	**96.6**	20.1	17.6	23.9	44.9	47.33
17	50.7	45.6	52.0	46.8	48.2	70.5	**96.6**	20.1	17.6	23.9	44.9	72.2	49.09
18	45.6	52.0	46.8	48.2	70.5	**96.6**	20.1	17.6	23.9	44.9	72.2	59.1	49.79
19	52.0	46.8	48.2	70.5	**96.6**	20.1	17.6	23.9	44.9	72.2	59.1	48.5	50.03
20	46.8	48.2	70.5	**96.6**	20.1	17.6	23.9	44.9	72.2	59.1	48.5	66.7	51.26
21	48.2	70.5	**96.6**	20.1	17.6	23.9	44.9	72.2	59.1	48.5	66.7	42.3	50.88
22	70.5	**96.6**	20.1	17.6	23.9	44.9	72.2	59.1	48.5	66.7	42.3	60.2	51.88
23	**96.6**	20.1	17.6	23.9	44.9	72.2	59.1	48.5	66.7	42.3	60.2	82.4	52.88
24	20.1	17.6	23.9	44.9	72.2	59.1	48.5	66.7	42.3	60.2	82.4	**141.2**	**56.59**
25	17.6	23.9	44.9	72.2	59.1	48.5	66.7	42.3	60.2	82.4	**141.2**	19.0	56.50
26	23.9	44.9	72.2	59.1	48.5	66.7	42.3	60.2	82.4	**141.2**	19.0	28.8	57.43
27	44.9	72.2	59.1	48.5	66.7	42.3	60.2	82.4	**141.2**	19.0	28.8	35.6	58.41
28	72.2	59.1	48.5	66.7	42.3	60.2	82.4	**141.2**	19.0	28.8	35.6	48.1	58.68
29	59.1	48.5	66.7	42.3	60.2	82.4	**141.2**	19.0	28.8	35.6	48.1	63.8	57.98
30	48.5	66.7	42.3	60.2	82.4	**141.2**	19.0	28.8	35.6	48.1	63.8	49.3	57.16
31	66.7	42.3	60.2	82.4	**141.2**	19.0	28.8	35.6	48.1	63.8	49.3	45.6	56.92
32	42.3	60.2	82.4	**141.2**	19.0	28.8	35.6	48.1	63.8	49.3	45.6	52.2	55.71
33	60.2	82.4	**141.2**	19.0	28.8	35.6	48.1	63.8	49.3	45.6	52.2	46.1	56.03
34	82.4	**141.2**	19.0	28.8	35.6	48.1	63.8	49.3	45.6	52.2	46.1	72.9	57.08
35	**141.2**	19.0	28.8	35.6	48.1	63.8	49.3	45.6	52.2	46.1	72.9	98.4	58.42
36	19.0	28.8	35.6	48.1	63.8	49.3	45.6	52.2	46.1	72.9	98.4	**122.1**	**56.83**

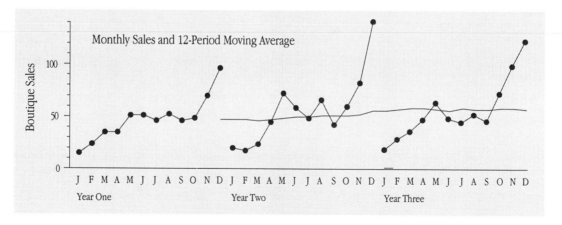

Figure 13.3: Boutique Sales and 12-Period Moving Average

The 12-period moving average is found by computing the average for each successive group of 12 values, as shown in Table 13.3. Since it will take 12 values to get started, the first value is computed at the 12th time period. Thus we get 25 moving averages from the 36 monthly values above. Figure 13.3 shows the monthly sales and the moving averages.

While the monthly values show the pronounced seasonality of the Boutique sales, the moving averages in Figure 13.3 remove these seasonal effects and show a gradual upward trend in sales. The current value of the moving average can always be converted into an annual sales amount by multiplying by 12. For example, the last value of 56.83 converts into total sales for the past 12 months of approximately 682 thousand dollars.

The advantages of combining the time-series plot of the individual values with a year-long moving average are simplicity, accessibility, and interpretability. The information contained in the data is conveyed to your readers with a minimum of fuss, with a minimum of effort, and without distracting details. For report card measures, this simple graph will often be sufficient.

13.2 Year-to-Date Plots

The problems of noise in the data and of seasonal effects have been appreciated for a long time. What has been lacking are effective ways of handling these problems in an understandable and straightforward manner. The year-long moving average superimposed on a plot of the individual values, as described in the previous section, is an effective way of dealing with both noise and seasonal effects. Moreover, it is far superior to the more common practice of plotting the year-to-date values.

Table 13.4: Appliance Store Sales

Monthly Sales

Year	J	F	M	A	M	J	J	A	S	O	N	D
One	86.9	78.3	97.2	77.3	113.5	99.5	75.0	81.8	113.4	122.3	74.4	80.4
Two	72.3	78.1	91.5	91.7	141.5	113.2	107.0	96.7	99.1	71.8	78.4	46.5

Twelve-Period Moving Averages

Year	J	F	M	A	M	J	J	A	S	O	N	D
One												91.7
Two	90.5	90.4	90.0	91.1	93.5	94.6	97.3	98.5	97.4	93.1	93.5	90.7

Year-to-Date Values

Year	J	F	M	A	M	J	J	A	S	O	N	D
One	87	165	262	340	453	553	628	710	823	945	1020	1100
Two	72	150	242	334	475	588	695	792	891	963	1041	1088

The first problem with year-to-date values is the naive comparisons which they encourage. For example, consider the year-to-date values for Year Two above. In January it is reported that sales are lagging behind last year's sales. They are behind in February. They are behind in March. They are still behind in April. What a disaster! But wait, in May they pull ahead of last year's sales level and the gloom is dispelled. They are ahead in June. They are ahead in July. They are ahead in August. What a great year! They are ahead in September. They are ahead in October. They are ahead in November. And yet they finish the year behind last year—so kiss the bonus good-bye. And that is how year-to-date values

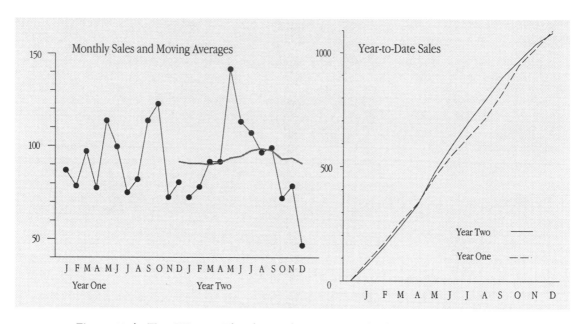

Figure 13.4: Two Ways to Plot the Appliance Store Sales for Years One and Two

are one of the major causes of man-made chaos. Whether we look at the year-to-date plot or the year-to-date values in the table we end up making the same naive comparisons because that is all these values will allow.

The second problem with year-to-date values is that they do not provide a simple and direct way of estimating the overall level of sales. Yet the moving averages show the sales level to be averaging in the vicinity of 90 to 100 thousand per month.

The third problem with year-to-date values is that they do not easily provide an estimate of the annual sales. Yet at any point in time, the current moving average times 12 is equal to the total sales over the previous 12 months.

The fourth problem with the year-to-date plots is that they replace the "levels" of the plot on the left with the "slopes" on the right. Since slopes are much more subjective to interpret, and since the lines are seldom straight, this shift is one that introduces more complexity than clarity.

The fifth problem with year-to-date plots is that they require an extremely compressed scale. This happens because the vertical scale has to allow for the annual total. As a consequence, even big swings in monthly values will result in small changes in angle. For example, the spike in sales in May of Year Two is easy to see on the left, but hard to find on the right. And the dramatic drop in sales in December of Year Two is only a slight change in angle on the year-to-date plot. While it is good to smooth out noise, the compressed scale of the year-to-date plot tends to obliterate more than just the noise.

Table 13.5: Year-to-Date Sales for Region C

	I	II	III	IV
Year One	1056	2104	3233	4306
Year Two	1157	2303	3367	4580
Year Three	1088	2410	3666	4798
Year Four	1352	2705	4171	5367
Year Five	1330	2333	3530	4867

As a second example consider the year-to-date values for Region C. Plotting more than two years' worth of year-to-date values on a single graph just creates more complexity. The problem with Figure 13.5 is that the dimension of time is buried. It goes into the paper, and therefore is unavailable to help the reader make sense of this plot. The years are different, but are things getting better or worse? Compare Figure 13.5 with Figure 13.1 to see the difference that plotting time-ordered data in a time series can make.

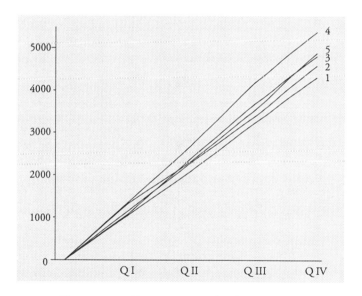

Figure 13.5: Year-to-Date Sales for Region C

Finally, the year-to-date values force you to make comparisons using different amounts of data at different points in time. The first time period you are just comparing Quarter I with Quarter I. The next time period you are comparing Quarters I and II with Quarters I and II, etc. Since the totals for two quarters will vary more than the totals for one quarter, the uncertainty of your comparison will increase with each passing period.

So year-to-date values will tell you that "when you're up you're up, and when you're down you're down, and when you're only half-way up you're neither up nor down." The running record and year-long moving average plot will generally provide more useful information, in a more accessible format, than will year-to-date plots.

13.3 The Problem of Seasonal Effects

The year-long moving average hides seasonal effects by averaging them out. Another way of working with seasonal effects is to explicitly adjust the data to allow for seasonality.

To illustrate data that have a strong seasonal pattern which is recurring from year to year we shall look at the monthly sales figures for a single store in a chain of department stores. The monthly sales, in thousands of dollars, are shown in Table 13.6, and the time series plot for these data is shown in Figure 13.6.

Table 13.6: Monthly Department Store Sales

	J	F	M	A	M	J	J	A	S	O	N	D
Year One	242.5	295.1	377.9	330.6	425.0	395.3	384.3	415.8	380.8	447.9	525.0	566.6
Year Two	241.0	287.2	365.0	322.1	418.8	400.2	403.7	410.9	382.8	449.8	520.7	549.1
Year Three	252.4	309.5	405.1									

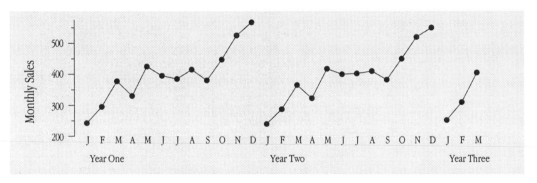

Figure 13.6: Monthly Department Store Sales

Clearly the dominant feature of the running record in Figure 13.6 is an annual pattern. This annual pattern effectively undermines simple comparisons from one month to another—January cannot be compared with December or February. So while we can use these data to compare January with January, and February with February, etc., we cannot compare months within a year.

If we should attempt to place these data on an *XmR* chart we would get something like Figure 13.7, which only reveals what we already knew—there is a detectable difference in sales volume from month to month throughout the year.

Now just how can the manager of this store interpret the sales for the First Quarter of Year Three? He has made changes in the store's advertising and he wants to know if it has had an impact. Can he use Figure 13.7 to tell if sales have changed? With the strong monthly pattern, and the large amount of month-to-month variation, it is difficult to make a reliable judgment using either Figure 13.6 or 13.7. We ought to be able to exploit the annual pattern to make our analysis more sensitive. And this is where deseasonalized data are helpful.

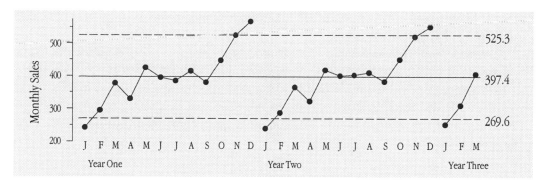

Figure 13.7: *X* Chart for Monthly Sales

13.4 Deseasonalized Values

A value is deseasonalized by removing the average seasonal effect. (A way of determining the seasonal effects is outlined in the next section.) Deseasonalized monthly sales are obtained by dividing each monthly sales value by the corresponding seasonal factor.

$$\text{Deseasonalized Monthly Sales} \ = \ \frac{\text{Monthly Sales}}{\text{Seasonal Factor}}$$

For the Department Store Sales, the actual sales for January of Year One are 242.5 thousand. However, the sales in January are typically about 61% as big as the average monthly sales for the year:

(Average Monthly Sales for Year) x (0.61) = Average January Sales Value

So if we divide our current January Sales figure of 242.5 thousand by the seasonal factor of 0.61 we will obtain an estimate of our average monthly sales for this year:

$$\frac{242.5 \text{ thousand}}{0.61} \ = \ 397.5 \text{ thousand}$$

Sales of 242.5 thousand in January are equivalent to an average monthly sales level of 397.5 thousand per month, or a annual sales level of:

$$12 \ \text{x} \ 397.5 \ = \ 4{,}770{,}000$$

The actual sales for February of Year One were 295.1 thousand. In the past the sales in February have been about 73% of the average monthly sales for the year. Therefore, sales of 295.1 thousand in February are equivalent to an average monthly sales level of:

$$\frac{295.1 \text{ thousand}}{0.73} = 404.2 \text{ thousand}$$

Notice how the different sales values for January and February (242.5 and 295.1 differ by 18%) become quite similar when adjusted for seasonal effects (397.5 and 404.2 differ by 1.7%). Thus, a deseasonalized value (also known as a seasonally adjusted value) is one that has been converted into an estimated average value.

When you deseasonalize a set of values you are dividing those numbers that tend to be large by a large seasonal factor, and you are dividing those numbers that tend to be small by a small seasonal factor, with the result that "things even out" and the adjusted values may reasonably be compared. You may see this happening in Table 13.7 which contains: (1) the monthly sales, (2) the seasonal factors, and (3) the deseasonalized monthly sales for the Department Store Sales for Years One and Two.

Table 13.7: Deseasonalized Monthly Department Store Sales

	J	F	M	A	M	J	J	A	S	O	N	D
Yr One Monthly Sales	242.5	295.1	377.9	330.6	425.0	395.3	384.3	415.8	380.8	447.9	525.0	566.6
Seasonal Factors	*0.61*	*0.73*	*0.93*	*0.82*	*1.06*	*1.00*	*1.00*	*1.04*	*0.96*	*1.13*	*1.32*	*1.40*
Yr I Deseasonalized	397.5	404.2	406.3	403.2	400.9	395.3	384.3	399.8	396.7	396.3	397.7	404.7
Yr Two Monthly Sales	241.0	287.2	365.0	322.1	418.8	400.2	403.7	410.9	382.8	449.8	520.7	549.1
Seasonal Factors	*0.61*	*0.73*	*0.93*	*0.82*	*1.06*	*1.00*	*1.00*	*1.04*	*0.96*	*1.13*	*1.32*	*1.40*
Yr II Deseasonalized	395.1	393.4	392.5	392.8	395.1	400.2	403.7	395.1	398.8	398.1	394.5	392.2

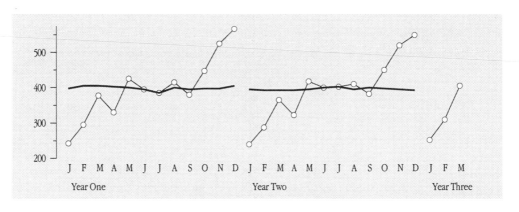

Figure 13.8: Monthly Sales and Deseasonalized Monthly Sales

Figure 13.8 shows the deseasonalized monthly sales superimposed upon the monthly sales. Clearly when you deseasonalize a time series you remove the average annual pattern. This allows you to look for other interesting signals which may be contained in the data. The vertical scale of Figure 13.9 is such that about all we can tell from the deseasonalized data is that they approximate the annual average for each year. To learn more from the deseasonalized data we will have to look at them on a different vertical scale, and that is why we place them on an *XmR* chart in Figure 13.9.

By using an *XmR* chart for the deseasonalized data we can separate potential signals from probable noise. The deseasonalization step removes the average annual pattern, and this makes month-to-month comparisons possible. However, before we get carried away making comparisons between months, we must remember that some of the variation between the deseasonalized monthly values will be noise. So we filter out the noise by placing the deseasonalized values on an *XmR* chart.

The limits shown in Figure 13.9 were computed using the deseasonalized values from Year One. The impact of removing the annual pattern from these data can be seen by comparing the width of the limits in Figure 13.7 (255.6 units) with the width of the limits on the *X* chart of Figure 13.9 (28.0 units). By deseasonalizing these data we have removed about 90% of the month-to-month variation, resulting in a much more sensitive analysis.

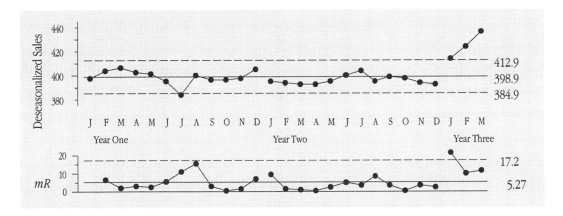

Figure 13.9: *XmR* Chart for Deseasonalized Monthly Sales

So how would we interpret the chart in Figure 13.9? First of all, Figure 13.9 shows a low point in July of Year One. Since this is a historical point, it may not be possible to identify the assignable cause of this signal. However, if it is possible, we might well learn something that can be advantageous in the future.

Second, the limits on the *X* chart, based on Year One, constitute a forecast of what to expect if there has been no change in the level of sales. The central line is about 399 thousand, and this value may be taken to be a forecast of what the average monthly sales are likely to be if nothing changes. The limits are ± 14 thousand on either side of the central line. These limits define the routine variation to be expected in the deseasonalized monthly sales values—14 thousand out of 400 thousand is about 3.5%, and this is the relative noise level in the deseasonalized data. Changes smaller than this will be hard to detect.

Figure 13.9 shows that there was no major difference between Years One and Two. While the total sales for Year Two were down about 3 thousand per month compared with Year One (less than 1% lower), and while 10 of the 12 deseasonalized values for Year Two are below the central line, there are no clear signals of a difference.

However, what about the new advertising campaign in Year Three? Did it have any impact upon sales? Should the manager continue this new approach, or drop it to save money? The deseasonalized values for the first quarter of Year Three show a detectable improvement in sales. Thus, it would seem that the change in advertising strategy was worthwhile. It is instructive to note how Figure 13.9 makes this change clear while Figures 13.6, 13.7, and 13.8 tend to obscure it.

Since we have evidence that Year Three is different from Years One and Two, we might want to revise our limits in Figure 13.9. We could use the average of the first three deseasonalized values from Year Three as our central line, and place our limits the same distance on either side as the old limits: with a central line of 424.5 thousand, and a spread of ± 14.0 thousand, we get limits of 410.5 thousand to 438.5 thousand.

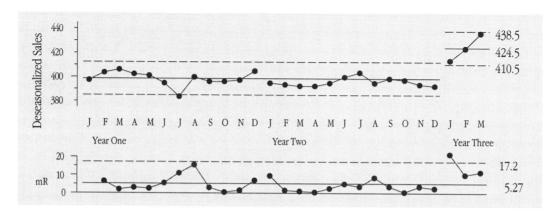

Figure 13.10: Revised Limits for Year Three of Deseasonalized Monthly Sales

These limits, shown in Figure 13.10, define a range where we might reasonably expect the remainder of Year Three's deseasonalized values to fall. They also constitute a forecast for the year. While this forecast was based upon a small amount of data, it nevertheless turned out to be a good number—the sales for Year Three averaged 427.5 thousand per month!

So, by deseasonalizing the monthly values as they occur, you can determine if some measure is behaving according to your forecast or not. If there is an indication that things have changed you can use the current deseasonalized values to revise your forecast.

Perhaps the best way to present data having a strong seasonal component is a combination graph like that shown in Figure 13.11. There we combine (1) the time-series plot of the original data, (2) the X chart for the deseasonalized values, and (3) the mR chart for the deseasonalized values. The time-series plot of the raw data shows the seasonality and the actual levels of the measure, while the deseasonalized data on the X chart allows your readers to spot interesting features in the data and prompts them to ask the right questions. In Figure 13.11 the X chart shows the increased level of sales for Year Three and provides a basis for making a forecast for Year Four. Both the X chart and the mR chart show the increased volatility of the sales in Year Three.

Table 13.8: Monthly Department Store Sales

	J	F	M	A	M	J	J	A	S	O	N	D
Year One	242.5	295.1	377.9	330.6	425.0	395.3	384.3	415.8	380.8	447.9	525.0	566.6
Year Two	241.0	287.2	365.0	322.1	418.8	400.2	403.7	410.9	382.8	449.8	520.7	549.1
Year Three	252.4	309.5	405.1	345.3	477.5	417.5	423.1	462.3	414.0	480.0	556.2	591.5

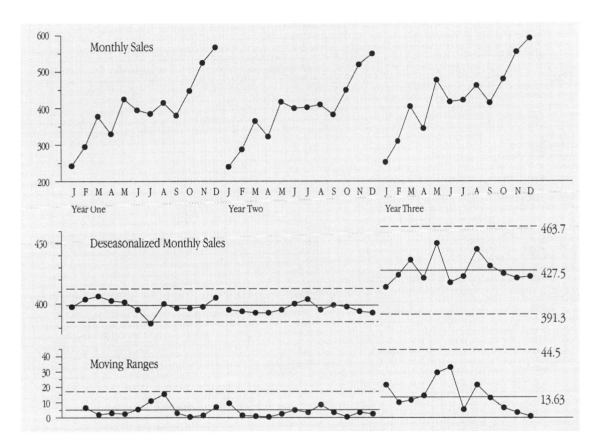

Figure 13.11: Department Store Sales for Years One, Two and Three

13.5 Finding Seasonal Factors

Now how do you find the seasonal factors? Since we will want to distinguish between noise in our data and actual seasonal effects we will need data for at least the past two years. Since we are not interested in ancient history we will rarely need more than three years worth of data.

The first step in constructing seasonal factors is to compute the seasonal relatives for each month. This is done by dividing each month's value by the average value for that year—the value for January of Year One would be divided by the average monthly value for Year One, etc. In Year One the department store had sales of 4,786.8 thousand. This corresponds to a monthly average of 398.9 thousand. The January sales were 242.5 thousand. The seasonal relative for January of Year One is thus:

$$\text{Seasonal Relative} = \frac{\text{this month's value}}{\text{average monthly value}} = \frac{242.5 \text{ thousand}}{398.9 \text{ thousand}} = 0.608$$

Since we are concerned with the approximate relationship between the monthly values and the annual average we will only record the seasonal relatives to three decimal places. This is illustrated in Table 13.9.

Table 13.9: Seasonal Relatives for the Department Store Sales

	J	F	M	A	M	J	J	A	S	O	N	D
Year One Sales	242.5	295.1	377.9	330.6	425.0	395.3	384.3	415.8	380.8	447.9	525.0	566.6
Average for Year 1	398.9	398.9	398.9	398.9	398.9	398.9	398.9	398.9	398.9	398.9	398.9	398.9
Seasonal Relatives	.608	.740	.947	.829	1.065	.991	.963	1.042	.955	1.123	1.316	1.420
Year Two Sales	241.0	287.2	365.0	322.1	418.8	400.2	403.7	410.9	382.8	449.8	520.7	549.1
Average for Year 2	395.9	395.9	395.9	395.9	395.9	395.9	395.9	395.9	395.9	395.9	395.9	395.9
Seasonal Relatives	.609	.725	.922	.814	1.058	1.011	1.020	1.038	.967	1.136	1.315	1.387

Next the seasonal relatives are placed on an average and range chart. All of the seasonal relatives for January would be placed in one subgroup, and all of the seasonal relatives for February are placed in a second subgroup, and so on until you have 12 subgroups of two (or three) seasonal relatives each. The limits for this average and range chart are computed in the usual manner, and averages that fall outside the limits are interpreted to be *detectable seasonal components*.

The grand average for the 12 subgroups in Figure 13.12 is 1.0000. (While the grand average for the seasonal relatives will often be close to 1.0, there is no guarantee that it must be exactly 1.0.) The average range for these 12 subgroups is 0.0169. Since we are using two years worth of data here, our subgroups are of size two. From Table 12.1, the scaling factors for subgroups of size $n = 2$ are $A_2 = 1.880$, and $D_4 = 3.268$. Thus, we compute limits to be:

$$UCL = 1.0000 + (1.880 \times 0.0169) = 1.032$$

$$LCL = 1.0000 - (1.880 \times 0.0169) = 0.968$$

$$URL = 3.268 \times 0.0169 = 0.055$$

These limits are shown in Figure 13.12. Ten averages and one range fall outside the limits, indicating very strong seasonality in these data. (Recall that when we deseasonalized these data in the previous section we removed about 90% of the month-to-month variation.)

By placing the seasonal relatives on an average and range chart we simultaneously obtain the average seasonal relatives and separate those average seasonal relatives which are likely to represent real seasonal effects from those that are obscured by the noise in the data.

The year-to-year variation between the seasonal relatives determines just how noisy the annual pattern happens to be, and the limits are set accordingly. Those average seasonal relatives which fall outside the limits represent detectable seasonal effects. Those average seasonal relatives that fall within the limits are not likely to represent real seasonal effects. Here every month except June and July appears to possess a real seasonal effect.

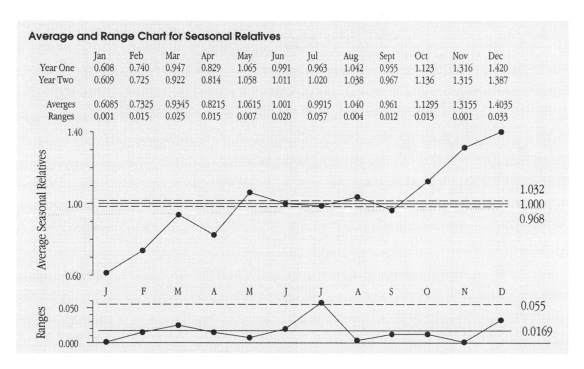

Average and Range Chart for Seasonal Relatives

	Jan	Feb	Mar	Apr	May	Jun	Jul	Aug	Sept	Oct	Nov	Dec
Year One	0.608	0.740	0.947	0.829	1.065	0.991	0.963	1.042	0.955	1.123	1.316	1.420
Year Two	0.609	0.725	0.922	0.814	1.058	1.011	1.020	1.038	0.967	1.136	1.315	1.387
Averges	0.6085	0.7325	0.9345	0.8215	1.0615	1.001	0.9915	1.040	0.961	1.1295	1.3155	1.4035
Ranges	0.001	0.015	0.025	0.015	0.007	0.020	0.057	0.004	0.012	0.013	0.001	0.033

Figure 13.12: Average and Range Chart for Seasonal Relatives for Department Store Sales

The range chart checks for consistency within the subgroups. Any range values that fall above the upper limit indicate that the seasonal pattern for that month may be changing from year to year, or else that a special event changed the seasonal pattern for one of the years used. Here the month of July shows excessive variation from Year One to Year Two. (Remember the point outside the limit for June of Year One in Figure 13.9?) An explanation for this discrepancy between the July seasonal relatives should be sought. In this case, since we do not have a detectable seasonal effect for July, we do not have to make a judgment about which year to use for our seasonal pattern.

Seasonal factors do not need to be known to high degrees of precision. Generally two or three decimal places will be sufficient. We are going to use the seasonal factors to characterize the relative inflation or deflation that is expected for each month. Rarely do we need to know this type of adjustment to more than the nearest percent. So, based upon the average seasonal relatives which appear to represent real seasonal effects, we will come up with a set of seasonal factors.

To obtain seasonal factors:
1. Round off to two decimal places those average seasonal relatives that fall outside the limits;
2. Replace with a value of 1.00 those average seasonal relatives that fall inside the limits;
3. Add up these 12 "rounded average seasonal relatives;"
4. Adjust the rounded average seasonal relatives so that they sum up to 12.00.

Adjustment of the rounded average seasonal relatives can be done in different ways. The objective is to get a reasonable set of values which average 1.000.

One way to adjust the rounded average seasonal relatives would be to divide each of the rounded average seasonal relatives by the average of the 12 values. When this is done the results should still be rounded off and these rounded values should be checked to see that they do sum to 12.000.

Another way is to simply add up the rounded average seasonal relatives and observe by how much this sum differs from 12.00. If the sum is 11.98, then you need to add 0.02 to the set of seasonals, and this is most easily done by adding 0.01 to a couple of the values, or perhaps 0.005 could be added to four of the values. It is basically a matter of judgment, but it is probably best to start by adjusting the smallest and largest rounded average seasonal relatives first. If the sum is 12.05, then you would need to judiciously subtract 0.05 from the set of values.

Table 13.10: Average Seasonal Relatives Converted into Seasonal Factors

	J	F	M	A	M	J	J	A	S	O	N	D
Averages	.6085	.7325	.9345	.8215	1.0615	1.001	.9915	1.040	.961	1.1295	1.3155	1.4035
Rounded	.61	.73	.93	.82	1.06	1.00	1.00	1.04	.96	1.13	1.32	1.40

Since the rounded values in Table 13.10 sum to 12.00 we need make no further adjustment, and we can use these values as seasonal factors. We therefore estimate that January sales are typically 61% of the average monthly sales for the year, while December sales are typically 140% of the average monthly sales for the year. Since we had no detectable seasonal effect for June and July, we estimate that June and July's sales are typically about the same as the average monthly sales for the year. These seasonal factors were used in Table 13.7 to deseasonalize the Department Store Data.

13.6 Not All Data Show Strong Seasonality

The Department Store Sales data in the previous section displayed strong seasonality. But not all sales data have such a consistent pattern from year to year. Here we shall return to the data shown in Table 13.2: the sales for a small retail boutique. These values are in thousands of dollars per month, and are shown in Table 13.11.

Table 13.11: Monthly Boutique Sales

Year	J	F	M	A	M	J	J	A	S	O	N	D
One	15.0	23.3	35.6	35.0	51.1	50.7	45.6	52.0	46.8	48.2	70.5	96.6
Two	20.1	17.6	23.9	44.9	72.2	59.1	48.5	66.7	42.3	60.2	82.4	141.2

Figure 13.13: Monthly Sales for Boutique

While each year shows a general trend of increasing sales throughout the year, Figure 13.13 does not show the same degree of parallelism from year to year that we saw in Figure 13.6.

The average monthly sales for Year One were 47.533; for Year Two they were 56.592. Dividing the monthly sales by these averages we obtain the seasonal relatives shown in Figure 13.14.

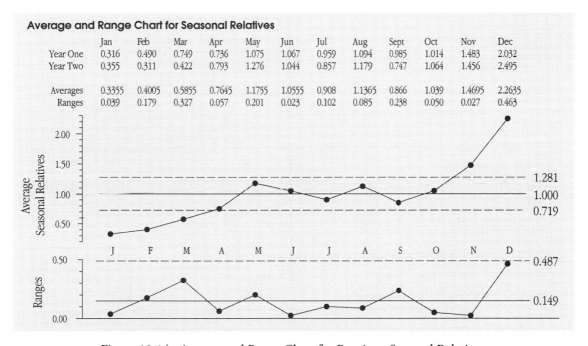

Average and Range Chart for Seasonal Relatives

	Jan	Feb	Mar	Apr	May	Jun	Jul	Aug	Sept	Oct	Nov	Dec
Year One	0.316	0.490	0.749	0.736	1.075	1.067	0.959	1.094	0.985	1.014	1.483	2.032
Year Two	0.355	0.311	0.422	0.793	1.276	1.044	0.857	1.179	0.747	1.064	1.456	2.495
Averages	0.3355	0.4005	0.5855	0.7645	1.1755	1.0555	0.908	1.1365	0.866	1.039	1.4695	2.2635
Ranges	0.039	0.179	0.327	0.057	0.201	0.023	0.102	0.085	0.238	0.050	0.027	0.463

Figure 13.14: Average and Range Chart for Boutique Seasonal Relatives

Even though the seasonal relatives in Figure 13.14 are generally further from 100% than those in Figure 13.12, only five months show detectable seasonal effects (January, February, March, November, and December). The large amount of variation between the seasonal relatives from year to year makes it hard to detect seasonal effects here. The limits suggest that effects smaller than 28% of the average sales level are indistinguishable from routine variation. Using three years worth of data does not substantially change things. The Boutique Sales data are noisy, and most of that noise cannot be accounted for by seasonal effects.

The average seasonal relatives shown in Figure 13.14 are listed as the first row of Table 13.12. Since seven months did not show any detectable seasonal effect, these seven average seasonal relatives were replaced with 1.00 in Table 13.12. The other five average seasonal relatives will be rounded off to two decimal places. This gives the second row of Table 13.12.

Table 13.12: Average Seasonal Relatives Converted into Seasonal Factors

	J	F	M	A	M	J	J	A	S	O	N	D
Averages	.3355	.4005	.5855	0.7645	1.1755	1.0555	.908	1.1365	.866	1.039	1.4695	2.2635
Rounded	.34	.40	.59	1.00	1.00	1.00	1.00	1.00	1.00	1.00	1.47	2.26
Adjusted	.336	.395	.583	1.00	1.00	1.00	1.00	1.00	1.00	1.00	1.453	2.233
SEASONALS	0.34	0.40	0.58	1.00	1.00	1.00	1.00	1.00	1.00	1.00	1.45	2.23

Since the five rounded values (.34, .40, .59, 1.47, and 2.26) sum to 5.06, we need to make an adjustment. The average of these five values is 1.012. Dividing each by this value we get 0.336, .395, .583, 1.453, and 2.233. This is the third row of Table 13.12. Rounding these adjusted values off gives a reasonable set of seasonal factors for the Boutique Sales Data.

Table 13.13 gives (1) the Monthly Boutique Sales for Years One and Two, (2) the seasonal factors for these data, and (3) the Deseasonalized Boutique Sales for Years One and Two.

Table 13.13: Monthly Boutique Sales and Deseasonalized Sales

	J	F	M	A	M	J	J	A	S	O	N	D
Yr I Monthly Sales	15.0	23.3	35.6	35.0	51.1	50.7	45.6	52.0	46.8	48.2	70.5	96.6
Seasonal Factors	0.34	0.40	0.58	1.00	1.00	1.00	1.00	1.00	1.00	1.00	1.45	2.23
Yr I Deseasonalized	44.1	58.3	61.4	35.0	51.1	50.7	45.6	52.0	46.8	48.2	48.6	43.3
Yr II Monthly Sales	20.1	17.6	23.9	44.9	72.2	59.1	48.5	66.7	42.3	60.2	82.4	141.2
Seasonal Factors	0.34	0.40	0.58	1.00	1.00	1.00	1.00	1.00	1.00	1.00	1.45	2.23
Yr II Deseasonalized	59.1	44.0	41.2	44.9	72.2	59.1	48.5	66.7	42.3	60.2	56.8	63.3

The Deseasonalized Boutique Sales for Years One and Two are shown in Figure 13.15. The wide limits in Figure 13.15 mean that there is a lot of month-to-month variation that is not directly attributable to seasonal effects.

One way to characterize the contribution of seasonal effects is to compare the limits computed for the actual values with those computed for the deseasonalized values. Figure 13.16 shows an X chart for the Monthly Boutique Sales and the X chart for the Deseasonalized

Boutique Sales. The limits on the first chart are 93.2 units wide, while those on the second chart are 56.2 units wide. Dividing 56.2 by 93.2 gives 0.603. This means that the deseasonalized values have 60 percent of the variation of the original values. So by deseasonalizing these data we have removed about 40 percent of the month-to-month variation.

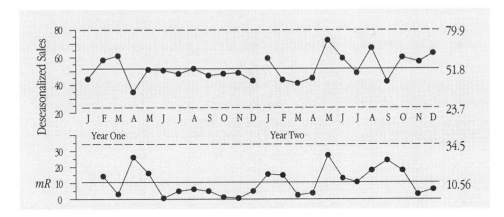

Figure 13.15: *XmR* Chart for Deseasonalized Boutique Sales

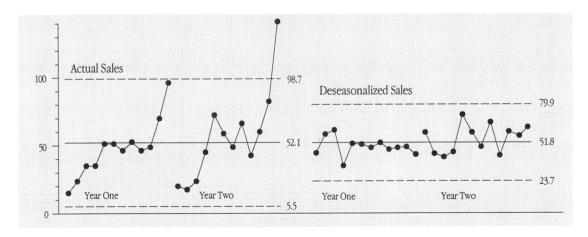

Figure 13.16: Limits for Boutique Sales and Deseasonalized Boutique Sales

While it helped to deseasonalize these data, we still have a highly variable time series. Figure 13.15 shows that the deseasonalized values can vary anywhere from 23.7 to 79.9 without indicating a change in sales levels. This means that even when they have a very good month, or a very bad month, it may not indicate a change for the better or for the worse. For example, the sales for February of Year Three were 28.8 thousand. This was 64% better than February of Year Two, and 24% better than sales in February of Year One. Generally such an improvement would be considered to be a good omen—sales are improving! Moreover, when we divide the 28.8 thousand by the February seasonal of 0.40 we get a deseasonalized value of 72.0 thousand—another good number. (Year Two only averaged 56.6 thousand a month in sales, so surely this deseasonalized value of 72.0 thousand represents an improvement!) However, a deseasonalized value of 72.0 thousand is still within the limits shown in Figures 13.15 and 13.16. Therefore it falls within the range of routine variation, and it would be a mistake to think that sales have increased based upon this one value.

If you cannot separate the potential signals from the probable noise, you will continually misinterpret your data. The XmR chart for the deseasonalized values allows you to make this critical distinction and focus your attention on those points that are meaningful.

The combined chart for the Boutique Sales for Years One, Two, and Three is shown in Figure 13.17. The X chart for the deseasonalized sales for Year Three gives the impression that sales for Year Three were up compared to the central line. While this is true (Year Three averaged 56.8), it is hard for the chart to *detect* changes of this size simply because these data are so full of noise.

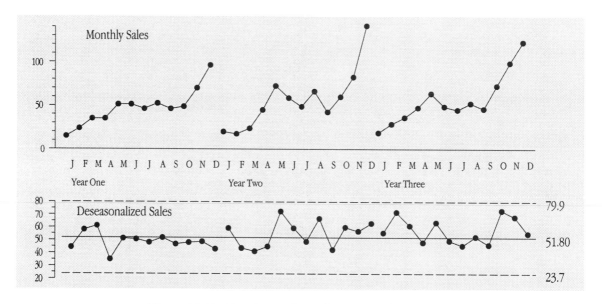

Figure 13.17: Boutique Sales and Deseasonalized Values

So how can the manager of the boutique track his sales in the face of seasonality and noise? While it helps to remove the seasonality, he still has the problem of making sense of the current values in spite of the noise. When the data are noisy, a year-long moving average will allow you to smooth out both seasonal effects and noise so that you can see the underlying trend. The data of Figure 13.17 were shown with a twelve-period moving average in Figure 13.3. There the gradual upward trend in sales is made visible.

13.7 The Appliance Store Data

The monthly sales for an appliance store will serve as an example of data where seasonal effects are weak and noise is substantial.

Table 13.14: Monthly Appliance Store Sales

Year	J	F	M	A	M	J	J	A	S	O	N	D	Average
One	86.9	78.3	97.2	77.3	113.5	99.5	75.0	81.8	113.4	122.3	74.4	80.4	91.67
Two	72.3	78.1	91.5	91.7	141.5	113.2	107.0	96.7	99.1	71.8	78.4	46.5	90.65
Three	82.0	117.1	98.0	85.5	105.6	69.8	63.7	81.9	78.8	96.1	70.1	58.9	83.96

When you work Exercise 13.1 you should find that the only average seasonal relative which falls outside the limits on the average and range chart is the one for May (1.352). Strictly speaking, this means that only one month has a detectable seasonal effect. However, the average seasonal relative for December (0.697) is very close to the limit. Therefore you might choose to include it as a second seasonal effect when obtaining your seasonal factors (it is easier to get seasonals when there are both highs and lows to cancel out). The other 10 months show no detectable seasonal effect. Therefore, the seasonal adjustment of the data in Table 13.9 would only change three (or six) of the 36 values by any appreciable amount, and there would be little difference between the raw data and the deseasonalized data.

The limits on the average and range chart for seasonal relatives show that a seasonal effect would have to be bigger than ± 31% in order to be detectable above the noise present in these data. In other words, these data contain weak seasonal effects and a lot of noise.

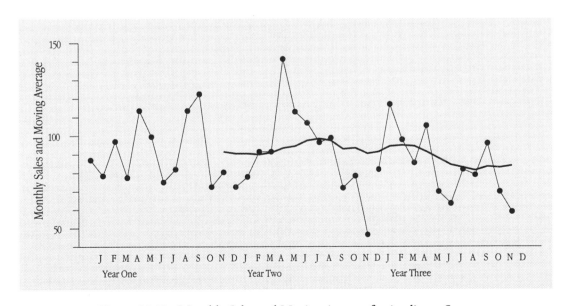

Figure 13.18: Monthly Sales and Moving Average for Appliance Store

Table 13.15: 12-Period Moving Averages for the Appliance Store Sales

Year	J	F	M	A	M	J	J	A	S	O	N	D
One												91.7
Two	90.5	90.4	90.0	91.1	93.5	94.6	97.3	98.5	97.4	93.1	93.5	90.7
Three	91.5	94.7	95.3	94.7	91.7	88.1	84.5	83.3	81.6	83.6	82.9	84.0

On the other hand, the 12-period moving average shows the overall trend for these sales data. Figure 13.18 contains both the individual values and the 12-period moving average for this store. The 12-period moving average shows that the appliance store sales have declined slightly over this three-year period.

13.8 The Claims Per Day Data

The claims processing division of a large health insurance company kept track of its productivity by dividing the number of claims processed each month by the total number of man-days worked that month. This ratio was known as "Claims Per Day" and was used, along with similar measures from other divisions, to evaluate and rank the division managers. The Claims Per Day values are shown in Figure 13.19. These values are aggregate values based upon the data from the eight regional offices.

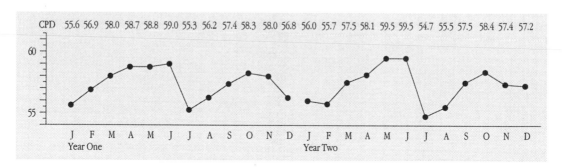

Figure 13.19: Claims Per Day Values for Years One and Two

The relative parallelism between these two years suggests that strong seasonal effects are present in these data. The managers had an explanation for this seasonality—it was said to be a consequence of variable staffing in response to the seasonal variation in claims. While there was a core of full-time personnel who processed claims, there was another group of personnel who were used on a part-time basis to help when the number of claims went up in the winter and when regular personnel were on vacation in the summer. Since the part-time personnel were not as efficient as the full-time personnel, the productivity measure suffered when they were used. The seasonal relatives for these two years are shown on the average and range chart in Figure 13.20.

As can be seen in Figure 13.20, seven or eight months can be said to have detectable seasonal effects. If a point does not fall outside the limits on the average chart, then there is no detectable seasonality for that period, and any seasonal adjustment for that month simply adds noise to the data. Therefore, the appropriate seasonals for March, September, November and December will be 1.00. The other eight months have detectable seasonal effects.

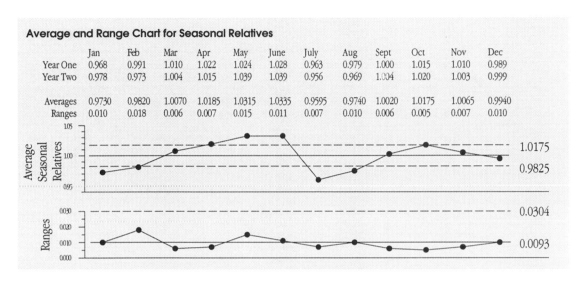

	Jan	Feb	Mar	Apr	May	June	July	Aug	Sept	Oct	Nov	Dec
Year One	0.968	0.991	1.010	1.022	1.024	1.028	0.963	0.979	1.000	1.015	1.010	0.989
Year Two	0.978	0.973	1.004	1.015	1.039	1.039	0.956	0.969	1.004	1.020	1.003	0.999
Averages	0.9730	0.9820	1.0070	1.0185	1.0315	1.0335	0.9595	0.9740	1.0020	1.0175	1.0065	0.9940
Ranges	0.010	0.018	0.006	0.007	0.015	0.011	0.007	0.010	0.006	0.005	0.007	0.010

Average and Range Chart for Seasonal Relatives

Figure 13.20: Average and Range Chart for Seasonal Relatives for the Claims Per Day Data

The average seasonal relatives are converted into seasonal factors in Table 13.16. The sum of the rounded values is 11.98, so an adjustment is needed. Since the detectable seasonals were all so close to 1.00 it was decided to make the seasonal factors for March and November into 1.01 rather than to adjust the eight months with detectable seasonals.

Table 13.16: Converting Average Seasonal Relatives into Seasonals

	J	F	M	A	M	J	J	A	S	O	N	D
Averages	0.9730	0.9820	1.0070	1.0185	1.0315	1.0335	0.9595	0.9740	1.002	1.0175	1.0065	0.9940
Rounded	0.97	0.98	1.00	1.02	1.03	1.03	0.96	0.97	1.00	1.02	1.00	1.00
Seasonals	0.97	0.98	1.01	1.02	1.03	1.03	0.96	0.97	1.00	1.02	1.01	1.00

Once we have our seasonals we can use them to deseasonalize both the old values and new values as they occur. The deseasonalized Claims Per Day values for Years One and Two are given in Table 13.17 and shown on an *XmR* chart in Figure 13.21.

Table 13.17: Claims Per Day Values and Deseasonalized CPD Values

	J	F	M	A	M	J	J	A	S	O	N	D
Year One	55.6	56.9	58.0	58.7	58.8	59.0	55.3	56.2	57.4	58.3	58.0	56.8
Seasonals	*0.97*	*0.98*	*1.01*	*1.02*	*1.03*	*1.03*	*0.96*	*0.97*	*1.00*	*1.02*	*1.01*	*1.00*
Adj Yr One	57.3	58.1	57.4	57.6	57.1	57.3	57.6	57.9	57.4	57.1	57.4	56.8
Year Two	56.0	55.7	57.5	58.1	59.5	59.5	54.7	55.5	57.5	58.4	57.4	57.2
Seasonals	*0.97*	*0.98*	*1.01*	*1.02*	*1.03*	*1.03*	*0.96*	*0.97*	*1.00*	*1.02*	*1.01*	*1.00*
Adj Yr Two	57.7	56.8	56.9	57.0	57.8	57.8	57.0	57.2	57.5	57.3	56.8	57.2

Figure 13.21 shows that, adjusted for seasonal effects, an average of 57.3 claims are processed per employee per day. The routine variation from month to month, after adjusting for the seasonal effects, can make this number vary from 56.3 to 58.4 claims per day.

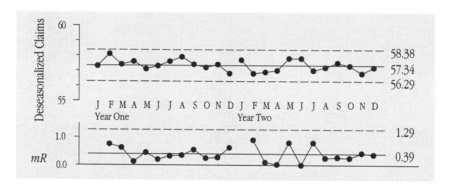

Figure 13.21: *XmR* Chart for Deseasonalized Claims Per Day Values

So what should you predict for Year Three? Since the past data appear to be predictable, we can reasonably use the past as an indicator of what to expect in the future. For prediction purposes, the average value of 57.3 should suffice. For interpretation of future values, as they occur, those values, when deseasonalized, should fall between 56.3 and 58.4. By plotting future deseasonalized values on the *XmR* chart you can tell if a change occurs in this process.

The Claims Per Day values for Year Three and the deseasonalized values are shown in Table 13.18.

Table 13.18: Claims Per Day Values and Deseasonalized CPD Values for Year Three

	J	F	M	A	M	J	J	A	S	O	N	D
Year Three	55.4	54.7	56.8	58.5	58.4	57.6	54.4	54.0	55.7	57.1	56.8	55.6
Seasonals	*0.97*	*0.98*	*1.01*	*1.02*	*1.03*	*1.03*	*0.96*	*0.97*	*1.00*	*1.02*	*1.01*	*1.00*
Adj Yr Three	57.1	55.8	56.2	57.3	56.7	55.9	56.7	55.7	55.7	56.0	56.2	55.6

The top portion of Figure 13.22 shows the time series for Claims Per Day. These are the actual values without any seasonal adjustment. While the first two values for Year Three

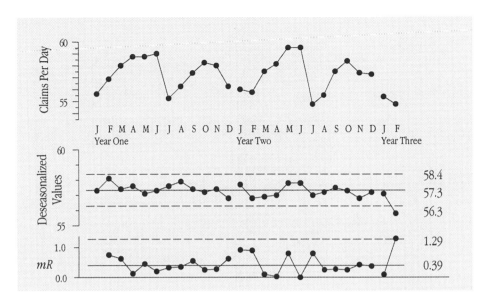

Figure 13.22: Claims Per Day Values and *XmR* Chart for Years One, Two and Three

appear to be a little low, it is not clear from this graph if there has been a change in productivity.

The middle portion of Figure 13.22 is the X chart for the deseasonalized Claims Per Day data. On this chart, which uses the limits based upon Years One and Two, there is a clear indication of a change in productivity by February of Year Three. The deseasonalized value of 55.8 claims per day is below the lower limit of what could occur due to routine variation. Something has changed for the worse, and the X chart allows you to detect this change.

The bottom portion of Figure 13.22 is the mR chart for the deseasonalized values. The moving range for February of Year Three is 1.3, which is just above the Upper Range Limit. This suggests that the change was sudden, rather than gradual, and that it took effect in February. So they should be looking for an assignable cause of reduced productivity which took effect in February (or late January) of Year Three.

The advantage of a composite plot like Figure 13.22 is that the reader can see both the original values and the seasonally adjusted values. This helps the reader to avoid confusing the seasonally adjusted values with the actual measures. It also facilitates the interpretation of the graphs, and allows everyone to visually check for consistency of the seasonal effects from year to year. Figure 13.23 shows the rest of the data for Year Three.

While the simple time series graph for the original Claims Per Day values does show a downward shift for Year Three, it is the X chart for the deseasonalized values that reveals the shift most clearly. Beyond any doubt, there was a drop in productivity in Year Three. The only explanation for this drop that they could find was the implementation of new corporate policies and procedures. While we might expect a temporary dip associated with a learning curve, the graph in Figure 13.23 shows a sustained drop in productivity. In other words, the "improvements" put in place at the beginning of Year Three actually made things worse.

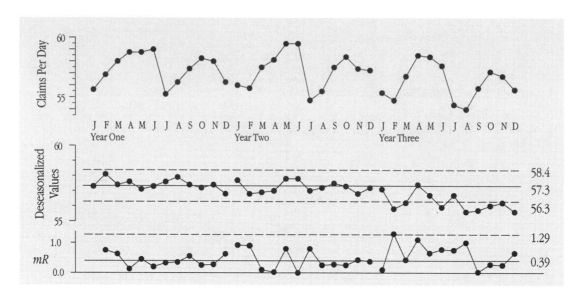

Figure 13.23: Claims Per Day Values and *XmR* Chart for Years One, Two and Three

Having identified a clear change in this process, and having found a possible explanation for this change, the question is now—what limits should be used for Year Four? Since these data are report-card data it makes sense to revise the limits to reflect the current process behavior. To this end we shall use the deseasonalized values from Year Three to recompute the limits. The average for these values is 56.25, while the average moving range is 0.608. This gives Natural Process Limits of 57.87 and 54.63, and an Upper Range Limit of 1.99. Since the deseasonalized values for Year Three all fall within these limits, we might use these limits to forecast Year Four. Namely, if they do not change things for the better, and if they do not change things for the worse, the claim processing division should expect to average about 56 claims per day per operator during Year Four. To expect the process to do better than this is unrealistic. Improvement does not tend to happen spontaneously.

Well, the management of this health insurance company decided that they needed to take action to remedy this drop in productivity—it was time to reengineer the organization. A thorough reorganization was undertaken, along with a thinning of the ranks of mid-level managers. Goals were set for each area of operations, and Year Four was declared to be the year of the turn-around. Everyone knew that it was just a matter of time until the benefits of the reshuffling became evident.

The claim processing division was given a goal of 60 claims per day. Since the average in Year Three was about 56 claims per day, they were expecting the reorganization to yield an increase of about 4 claims per day.

Before we deseasonalize the data for Year Four it is appropriate to reevaluate the Seasonals. (It is recommended that you reevaluate the seasonals each year to keep them up to date.) In this case the similarity of the yearly shape (see the top graph in Figure 13.23) suggests that there will be little change, but the only way to know for sure is to do the calcu-

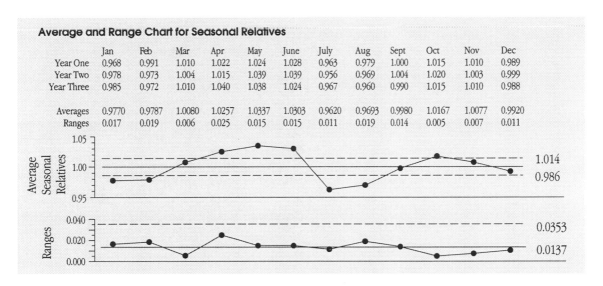

Figure 13.24: Average and Range Chart for Seasonal Relatives

lations. Figure 13.24 shows the seasonal relatives for Years One, Two, and Three on an average and range chart.

Once again, March, September, November and December are the only months that fail to display a detectable seasonal effect. In Table 13.19 the average seasonal relatives are converted into seasonals. (Since the rounded values already sum to 12.00 there is no need to make adjustments and the rounded values are taken to be the seasonals.) The seasonals in Table 13.19 are only slightly different from those in Table 13.16.

Table 13.20 shows the Claims Per Day values for Year Four, along with the deseasonalized values. These values are shown in a composite running record and *XmR* chart in Figure 13.25 on the following page.

Table 13.19: Converting Average Seasonal Relatives into Seasonals

	J	F	M	A	M	J	J	A	S	O	N	D
Averages	0.9770	0.9787	1.0080	1.0257	1.0337	1.0303	0.9620	0.9693	0.9980	1.0167	1.0077	0.9920
Rounded	0.98	0.98	1.00	1.03	1.03	1.03	0.96	0.97	1.00	1.02	1.00	1.00
Seasonals	0.98	0.98	1.00	1.03	1.03	1.03	0.96	0.97	1.00	1.02	1.00	1.00

Table 13.20: Claims Per Day Values and Deseasonalized CPD Values

	J	F	M	A	M	J	J	A	S	O	N	D
Year 4	51.9	52.7	55.4	54.7	54.1	54.1	50.6	50.5	51.6	51.3	51.0	51.8
Seasonals	*0.98*	*0.98*	*1.00*	*1.03*	*1.03*	*1.03*	*0.96*	*0.97*	*1.00*	*1.02*	*1.00*	*1.00*
Adj Yr 4	53.0	53.8	55.4	55.1	52.5	52.5	52.7	52.1	51.6	50.3	51.0	51.8

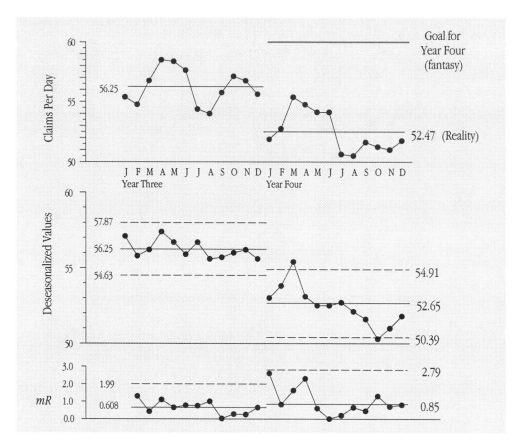

Figure 13.25: Claims Per Day, and *XmR* Chart for Deseasonalized Values

The fairy tale was that the productivity would go up about four units with the new system. The reality was that the productivity went down about four units—which is the usual result of wishful thinking.

The question that you should always ask whenever goals or targets are proposed is, "By what method?" The setting of goals or targets is no substitute for studying the process to discover how to improve it by removing assignable causes of excessive variation.

So what can we learn from Figure 13.25 about the assignable cause of this decrease in productivity? The drop in productivity was apparent in January of Year Four (the *X* chart for the deseasonalized values shows January of Year Four to be below the lower limit for Year Three). That this drop is the result of the reengineering is also made clear by the moving range chart, which shows the first moving range for Year Four to be above the limit for Year Three. This is an indication of a sudden change, a break from the past, and the reengineering took effect in January of Year Four.

So who is to blame for this drop in productivity? Who caused it? The responsibility for this drop in productivity must be placed upon the shoulders of those who decided it was time to reengineer the process. Goals, targets, and reorganizations are frequently signs of desperation—admissions that managers do not have a clue as to what to do to change things for the better. They just roll the dice and hope things will improve.

Process behavior charts provide an alternative to this everlasting game of chance. They give a way of learning about processes and systems so that we can improve them. They identify the opportunities for improvement, and they identify processes that are operating up to their potential. Knowing the difference is crucial. Not knowing the difference is a disaster.

Those who sponsor improvements often come to believe their own claims. The best antidote to this form of self-delusion is to listen to the Voice of the Process.

In the absence of effective ways of analyzing the data you may be subject to being misled by unsubstantiated claims of improvement. The best antidote to this form of misinformation is to listen to the Voice of the Process.

Without the Voice of the Process, it's just an opinion—and that opinion is likely to be based upon wishful thinking. And that is why, without process behavior charts, you are doomed to live and work in dreamland.

13.9 Working with Seasonal Data

When you suspect that your data contains seasonal patterns you may use the list below as a step-by-step guide on how to remove the seasonal effects.

1. Plot your data in a running record. If a repeating pattern is apparent, then go to step two. Otherwise go to Step 7.

2. Use a few complete cycles of the seasonal pattern to obtain seasonal relatives.

3. Place seasonal relatives on an average and range chart where each subgroup represents a single "season."

4. Points outside the limits on the average chart will indicate detectable seasonal effects. Points inside the limits on the average chart will indicate periods where the noise dominates the seasonal effect.

5. Estimate the seasonal factors for those periods with detectable seasonal effects. The seasonal factors for a five-day cycle must sum to 5; for a seven-day cycle, the seasonals must sum to 7. Quarterly seasonals must sum to 4, while monthly seasonals must sum to 12.

6. Deseasonalize past and future values by dividing each value by the seasonal factor for that period. Place these deseasonalized values on an *XmR* chart. Interpret this chart in the appropriate manner. Signals of assignable causes should be followed up by an investigation to determine the nature of the assignable cause. By removing the effects of assignable causes you will improve the consistency of your process. In the absence of signals the process may be considered to be predictable. The central line

will provide your best forecast for the future, while the limits place bounds on the uncertainty of this forecast. Since this *XmR* chart uses deseasonalized values, the forecast will be in terms of deseasonalized values. Multiplying deseasonalized forecasts by the appropriate seasonal factor will result in forecasts for the actual values.

7. Place the individual values on an *XmR* chart. If this chart is useful then interpret it in the usual way. If the limits on the X chart are so wide that they do not provide any useful information about your process (except the fact that noise is dominant), go to Step 8.

8. When noise dominates a time series it essentially becomes a report card on the past. In this case it can still be helpful to plot a running record of the individual values with a year-long moving average superimposed to show the underlying trends.

To help you with the judgment about the possibility of seasonal patterns in your data the following figures are provided. They are a recap of the figures in this and previous chapters. In general, whenever a recurring pattern exists there is a possibility of seasonality. If the shape of the pattern is changing from cycle to cycle the seasonality is likely to be moderate. If the shape of the pattern persists then the seasonality will be strong.

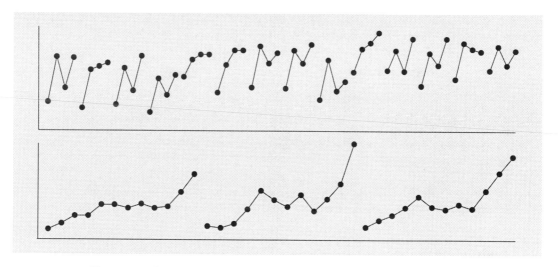

Figure 13.26: Some Time Series Which Display Moderate Seasonality

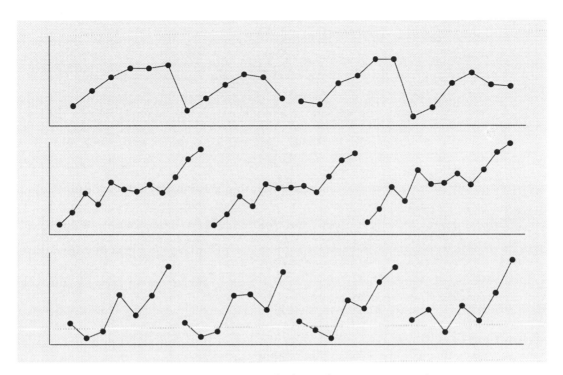

Figure 13.27: Some Time Series Which Display Strong Seasonal Patterns

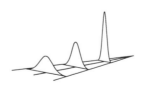

13.10 Exercises

EXERCISE 13.1

Three years worth of monthly sales for an appliance store are shown in Table 13.21.

Table 13.21: Monthly Appliance Store Sales

Year	J	F	M	A	M	J	J	A	S	O	N	D	Average
One	86.9	78.3	97.2	77.3	113.5	99.5	75.0	81.8	113.4	122.3	74.4	80.4	91.67
Two	72.3	78.1	91.5	91.7	141.5	113.2	107.0	96.7	99.1	71.8	78.4	46.5	90.65
Three	82.0	117.1	98.0	85.5	105.6	69.8	63.7	81.9	78.8	96.1	70.1	58.9	83.96

Use the worksheet on the next page to do the following:
1. Compute the seasonal relatives for the 36 months shown in Table 13.21. (As shown in the text, three decimal places will suffice.)
2. Consider these 36 seasonal relatives to be 12 subgroups of size 3 and compute the average seasonal relatives and the subgroup ranges.
3. Compute the limits for this average and range chart.
4. What months show detectable seasonal effects?

(You may compare your results with those described in Section 13.7.)

Seasonal Relatives

	Year 1	Year 2	Year 3	Average	Range
January	____	____	____	____	____
February	____	____	____	____	____
March	____	____	____	____	____
April	____	____	____	____	____
May	____	____	____	____	____
June	____	____	____	____	____
July	____	____	____	____	____
August	____	____	____	____	____
September	____	____	____	____	____
October	____	____	____	____	____
November	____	____	____	____	____
December	____	____	____	____	____

Computation Worksheet:

Grand Average = _____   Average Range = _____

Subgroup Size = n = ___   Number of Subgroups = k = ___

Find A_2 and D_4 from Table 3 in the Appendix:

Multiply Average Range by A_2 = _____

UCL = Grand Average + A_2 times Average Range = _____

LCL = Grand Average − A_2 times Average Range = _____

URL = D_4 times Average Range = _____

EXERCISE 13.2

While spreadsheet programs make the computation of moving averages quite easy, it is still helpful to know the easy way of doing these computations by hand. This exercise will use the data of Table 13.21 to illustrate how to keep a 12-period moving average with minimum effort.

Table 13.21: Monthly Appliance Store Sales

Year	J	F	M	A	M	J	J	A	S	O	N	D
One	86.9	78.3	97.2	77.3	113.5	99.5	75.0	81.8	113.4	122.3	74.4	80.4
Two	72.3	78.1	91.5	91.7	141.5	113.2	107.0	96.7	99.1	71.8	78.4	46.5
Three	82.0	117.1	98.0	85.5	105.6	69.8	63.7	81.9	78.8	96.1	70.1	58.9

Use the worksheet below to compute the first seven 12-period moving averages for the data in Table 13.21.

1. Add up the sales for the first 12 months shown in the table, and write this number down.
   This sum is the first 12-period total.
2. Divide the first 12-period total by 12 to get the first 12-period moving average.
3a. Subtract the sales for January of Year One from the first 12-period total.
3b. Now add the sales for January of Year Two to the value above to get the second 12-period total.
3c. Write down the second 12-period total.
3d. Divide the second 12-period total by 12 to get the second 12-period moving average.
4a. Subtract the sales for February of Year One from the second 12-period total.
4b. Now add the sales for February of Year Two to the value above to get the third 12-period total.
4c. Write down the third 12-period total.
4d. Divide the third 12-period total by 12 to get the third 12-period moving average.
5. Continue repeating the operations a, b, c, d as appropriate.

Worksheet for the Twelve-Period Moving Averages for Appliance Sales Data:

For the 12-month period ending:

	Dec. Year 1	Jan. Year 2	Feb. Year 2	Mar. Year 2	Apr. Year 2	May Year 2	Jun. Year 2
Total Sales	___	___	___	___	___	___	___
Moving Average	___	___	___	___	___	___	___

(You may compare your results with those in Table 13.15.)

As long as you keep track of the moving total you can update any moving average with one subtraction, one addition, and one division.

Part Three

Building Continual Improvement

Chapter Fourteen

Collecting Good Data

In Chapters Six through Thirteen we have outlined a methodology for making sense of data. The techniques given there are based on the *XmR* chart, the average and range chart, and special cases of these two charts. However, in order to use these techniques effectively, you will need to practice the way of thinking that is the foundation for these techniques—that all processes can be characterized as either predictable or unpredictable depending on the behavior of the data they generate.

This means that the techniques will always involve an element of judgment. They derive their power from the way they stimulate you to think about your processes. It is the interaction of the charts with the user that generates the thinking that result in Continual Improvement. We have tried to show this aspect of these techniques in the many case histories included in the first two parts of this book.

Continual Improvement is a journey. It consists of frequent, intermittent improvements, interspersed with alternating periods of predictable and unpredictable performance. Which is why it will not happen without a constancy of purpose on the part of those involved. This constancy of purpose is present when the way of learning becomes a way of life, and this will only happen when the tools and techniques in this book are used routinely throughout an organization.

Now we must address some of the issues concerning the collection of data, and some of the problems, pitfalls, and just plain nonsense that you will encounter when you embark on this journey.

14.1 What Are You Trying To Do?

The following comes from *Real People, Real Work* by Lee Cheaney and Maury Cotter.

One day, I noticed that Sara was really grinding away at putting numbers on spreadsheet paper in a black binder. Sara was a hard worker. She prided herself in her excellent productivity and her impeccable accuracy. All that day she worked on the binder. She worked from large piles of computer printouts that were stacked around her. Her fingers were a blur as they flew over her adding machine.

I didn't get a chance to chat with Sara the first day I noticed her working on the binder. I only noticed because it wasn't a task I had seen her perform before. On the second day she was still busy, head bent over the black binder. I went over to her area. "Hi Sara," I said. "What are you working on?"

"These are my stats," said Sara. I asked if she pulled this data together for the monthly production schedules that ultimately came to me.

"No, these numbers don't go in those schedules," she replied.

"Oh," said I, "you must be pulling these numbers together to serve as a quick reference in answering the dozens of calls you get each day."

"No," Sara explained, "I don't need the binder for them."

"Oh, you must run these tabulations for Roy, and then he uses them in his unit."

"No, these aren't used over there."

"Sara, who uses this binder?"

"I don't know."

"Do you keep this binder here in your area?"

"Yes."

"Does anyone ever come here and look in this binder?"

"No."

"Sara, do you ever use the information in this binder?"

"Nope," said Sara.

In the next few moments, I learned about a complexity existing in one of the systems within my jurisdiction. Complexity is work or tasks that people do which do not add any value to the product or service the organization provides. *Complexity is not real work.* Sara told me proudly that she had gotten the length of time necessary to do these monthly tabulations down to two days. She told me she had been doing these tabulations and recording the results in the black binder for almost ten years. That's two days a month, twelve months a year, for almost ten years.

When I asked her why she did this, she told me about a dead guy—a guy I had never met, but had heard of. Well, the guy had asked Sara, back when she worked for him, to pull together a certain kind of data in a black binder because he had a hunch that another party might call and ask for the numbers and he wanted to be prepared—just in case. Then he died. He never told her to stop. Neither did anyone else.

Sara was doing things right. She was accomplishing the task perfectly. There never was a doubt about Sara's accuracy, speed, dependability. But she wasn't doing the right work.

—◆—

So for those traditional measures which your organization routinely collects you should begin by asking, "Who uses these numbers?" Then you should ask, "How do they use them?" The answer to these two questions will help to focus your data collection efforts. If no one is using a measure, and you are not required to keep and report this measure, then it should be dropped. For those measures that are being used, or are required, how are they used?

The data you collect should serve as a basis for insight into your process, so that you can take action to make the process better in the future.

In this book we have outlined a methodology for making sense of any type of data. It looks at the variation that is present in all measures and breaks that variation into two types: routine variation and exceptional variation. We have illustrated a technique for examining any sequence of values so as to detect evidence of exceptional variation, while filtering out the routine variation.

The only limitation on this technique is the limitation of the data themselves. If the values are not collected in a consistent way, then they will not be comparable. This means, among other things, that the pedigree of your data will need to be known before you can make much use of them.

In order to be useful, data need to satisfy three conditions:
1. the data must be the right data,
2. the data must be analyzed and presented in an understandable manner, and
3. the results must be interpreted in the context of the original data.

What is your purpose in collecting data? Who is going to use the data? How are they going to use it? How are the values obtained? What assumptions were made in obtaining the values?

Collecting good and focused data is a prerequisite for creating a useful graph. The issues of discovery, investigation, communication, and persuasion are all promoted by effective and useful graphs, but the graphs cannot be any better than the original data.

14.2 Operational Definitions

Operational definitions are needed everywhere you have decisions to make. Say you are asked to count how many people are in your building? Sounds simple doesn't it? But what do you mean by "in your building?" Do you count anyone that enters the building throughout the day? Or do you count the people who are in the building at a specific time? And when would that be, 8:30 p.m.? Let's say you are told, "Just count those who are routinely in the building." Do you count the mail man? The delivery men? The customers? The consultants?

Whenever you are asked to collect some data the problems of what to measure, how to measure, and when to measure all raise their heads. An operational definition puts written and documented meaning into a concept so that it can be communicated and understood by everyone involved. It is an agreed upon way of making decisions so that consistent results can be obtained by different people at different times.

Many years ago, W. Edwards Deming wrote that an operational definition consists of three parts:

1. A criterion to be applied,
2. A test of compliance to be applied, and
3. A decision rule for interpreting the test results.

You may specify anything you like—weight, color, performance—but a specification, a goal, or a target is not enough for an operational definition. An operational definition must also contain a way of determining when you meet the goal.

Returning to the problem of counting the people in your building, until you have a criterion on who to count you cannot even get started.

Once you have a criterion, then you have to have a *method* of counting. How would you count everyone in your building? How long will it take you to simply walk around the building? Different methods of obtaining the count could result in different values.

Finally, a way to decide who to count and who to exclude from the count will be needed to avoid confusion.

Now, what if your sister division is given the same job of counting how many people are in their building. Without an operational definition of how to perform the count, is it likely that they will count their people the same way you counted yours?

While you may think this example is silly, it is the problem faced by the Census Bureau every decade. How many people live in Atlanta? While this question is easy to ask, *there is no exact answer to this question.* Which is why it is nonsense to claim that "this census was the most accurate ever." The census uses a given method to obtain a count. Change the method and you will change the count. A particular method may do a better job, or a poorer job, of counting people in a given segment of the population than will an alternative method. Nevertheless, there is no way to claim that one method is more accurate than another method. The number you get will be the result of the method you use.

This is why you need to know how the data are going to be used in order to define how the data will be collected. If all you want is a number that is correct to the nearest million, call the Atlanta Chamber of Commerce.

This is also why it is rarely satisfactory to use data which have been collected for one purpose for a different purpose. One plant manager was frustrated to be told that his productivity figures were the lowest in the company. According to his calculations he was doing better than several other plants. Yet, every month in the company report, his plant was listed last in productivity. After a particularly bad month he went to the Comptroller and found that the productivity figures were obtained by dividing the revenues for a plant by the headcount for that site. Since this manager's plant also housed the engineering division, his numbers were always deflated by the calculation. The headcount number used was not collected for purposes of computing the productivity.

A healthy appreciation of operational definitions is fundamental to being able to do business. Much of the confusion and mistrust about nonconforming materials and not meeting standards comes from a failure to use, in advance, operational definitions of conformance or performance.

An operational definition puts communicable meaning into an adjective. Adjectives like good, reliable, uniform, prompt, on-time, safe, unsafe, finished, consistent, and unemployed have no communicable meaning until they are expressed in operational terms of criterion, test, and decision rule. Whatever they mean to one person cannot be known to another until both agree on a communicable definition. A communicable definition is operational, because it involves doing something, carrying out a test, recording the result, and interpreting the result according to the agreed upon decision rule. This means that there can be different operational definitions for the same thing. It is not a matter of being right or wrong, but rather a matter of agreement between the parties involved. The result of an operational definition is consistency. The result of not having an operational definition is a lack of consistency.

When you have figured out how to collect your data, process behavior charts are an operational definition of "has a change occurred?" The criterion is that whenever the process changes the data will display exceptional variation. The process behavior chart is the test procedure for detecting exceptional variation, and the decision rules for interpreting the chart detect exceptional variation when it occurs. Thus, the process behavior chart is an operational definition of when a change has occurred in your process. This is why it provides the basis for taking action on the process.

Taking action on any other basis is arbitrary and capricious.

14.3 Counts and Categories

When you get into the counting game there is always the problem of counting events which have different degrees of severity. Many times this problem has been addressed by creating categories for the different degrees of severity and then awarding different numbers of "demerits" for the different categories. While it may be helpful to create such categories, you should resist the temptation of adding up the demerits. An example of the absurdities that can result from adding demerits comes from the University of Texas, where, in the 1960s, the campus police could issue tickets to students. The tickets came in three flavors; minor, major and flagrant. Four minor violations would get you expelled. The list of minor violations included such things as jaywalking and littering. Major violations consisted of more serious infractions, such as parking in a faculty space, or hitting a pedestrian with your car. Two major violations would get you expelled. And then there was the flagrant category. One flagrant citation and the Eyes of Texas would no longer shine upon you. The only infraction listed for a flagrant citation was moving a campus police barricade. So, if you had to make a choice between hitting a barricade or a jaywalker, you chose the pedestrian every time—you got two of them for each barricade.

Of course the problem illustrated here is that of using numbers to denote severity even though there is no logical, or proper, definition of *distance* for the numbers. When working with counts, four is twice as many as two. But when working with demerits, is flagrant (four demerits) twice as bad as major (two demerits)? Simply assigning numbers does not create what mathematicians call a "metric."

Ordinal Data

While numbers may be used to denote an ordering among categories, such numbers do not possess the property of distance. The term for numbers used in this way is ordinal data. This type of data is often seen when the responses to a survey question are spread out on a five-point scale. There is no guarantee that the distance between "strongly agree" (5) and "agree" (4) is the same as the distance from "agree" (4) to "neutral" (3), yet on the number line the distance from 3 to 4 is the same as from 4 to 5. About all such data will allow in terms of analysis is to look at the proportion of positive (or negative) responses (on that one question). Occasionally you might compute a pseudo-average for a single survey question, but this is on the edge of what is appropriate. (Grade point averages would be an example of this type of pseudo-average based upon ordinal data.)

For an example of survey data we shall use a question from one company's annual internal employee survey:

	strongly disagree	disagree	neutral	agree	strongly agree
This company is a good place to work.	1	2	3	4	5

Figure 14.1: Typical Internal Survey Question

Out of 7262 employees who answered this question, 496 strongly disagreed, 232 disagreed, 992 were neutral, 3024 agreed and 2518 strongly agreed. Thus a total of 5542 out of 7262 gave a positive response, which is 76.3 percent. The pseudo-average response is:

$$\frac{496\,(\,1\,)\,+\,232\,(\,2\,)\,+\,992\,(\,3\,)\,+\,3024\,(\,4\,)\,+\,2518\,(\,5\,)}{7262} = 3.94$$

Both the 76.3 percent and the 3.94 could be used to track the responses to this question over time.

Another example of survey data comes from an evaluation form used at a conference. The attendees at each presentation were asked to fill out forms, which were summarized in the manner shown in Figure 14.2.

The summary in Figure 14.2 would be better if it reported the number of responses for each category, rather than using percentages. There were a total of 33 evaluations filled out, and so a single response would correspond to 3%. While this is not a serious instance of over-reporting, what would the percentages mean if there were only 10 evaluations filled out? By using percentages the reader is automatically shifted to think in parts per hundred, even when that might not be supported by the data. When the actual counts are used, this shift does not occur and the data are presented with greater integrity.

	excellent	very good	average	below average	poor
1. Usefulness of subject.	67%	33%	0%	0%	0%
2. Organization and clarity of presentation	76%	21%	3%	0%	0%
3. Speaker's knowledge of subject	91%	9%	0%	0%	0%
4. Use of audio-visual aids	52%	33%	15%	0%	0%
5. Overall evaluation of presentation	67%	30%	3%	0%	0%
TOTAL AVERAGE	70%	25%	4%	0%	0%

Figure 14.2: Summary of Evaluation Form Questions

Another issue that is obscured by the use of percentages in Figure 14.2 is the fact that not every person will fill out every item in a survey. Some questions might have only 30 responses rather than 33. Once again, reporting the counts rather than the percentages would correct this problem.

Finally, what are we to make of the Total Average line in Figure 14.2? Item five has already asked the respondents for an overall summary evaluation. While we can certainly total the counts for each category across the different questions, what do these totals mean? And while we can convert these totals into percentages, what sense can we make of this fruit salad? The Total Average line in Figure 14.2 is essentially a triumph of computation over common sense. It should be deleted from the summary.

If we assigned values of 0 to poor, 1 to below average, 2 to average, 3 to very good, and 4 to excellent, we would have the familiar grade-point scale. The 33 evaluations could be summarized by a single number for each item. For example, this speaker received an average rating of 3.67 for usefulness of subject; an average rating of 3.72 for organization and clarity of presentation; an average rating of 3.91 for knowledge of subject; an average rating of 3.36 on use of audio-visual aids; and an average rating of 3.64 for the overall evaluation of the presentation. Of course, given numbers like these, who can resist averaging them into a single number of 3.66? While such global pseudo-averages may be appealing, their meaning is slippery at best. This final average rating is equivalent to the pseudo-average for the Total Average line in Figure 14.2, and contains more arithmetic than meaning. The computations are not even possible until a pseudo-distance is defined by assigning values to the five categories, and therefore the results of the computations are dependent upon this assignment. Different assignments will result in different values. Are you really sure that the distance from poor to below average should be the same as the distance from below average to average? Shouldn't there be a category of good between average and very good? If so, shouldn't it be twice as far from average to very good as it is from very good to excellent?

Pseudo averages are very convenient, but they are essentially an arbitrary scoring system which is used with ordinal data. They have limited meaning, and should not be over-interpreted.

And do not even think about using ordinal data to compute a measure of dispersion (such as a range or a standard deviation). The lack of a definition of distance will undermine all measures of dispersion.

Nominal Data

In the scheme of things, the next step below ordinal data would be "numbers used as labels." Telephone numbers are examples of this use of numbers. Numbers as labels do not possess either the property of *order* or *distance*. About the only type of analysis that is appropriate for such "numbers" is a tally of occurrences for each label. This was illustrated in Figure 3.6, where the operator numbers were used as labels for a bar graph. "Numbers as labels" have been called nominal data, but they are not data at all. If letters would work as well, then you are merely using numbers as symbols.

This is why you need to know the context for a set of numbers before you have any idea how to use them.

14.4 The Problems of Aggregation

When a measure is obtained for different locations, or different categories, and the values for this measure are combined across locations or categories, the result is said to be an aggregated measure. Aggregated measures are common in all types of business, but they do complicate the issue of making sense of the data. Two examples of the problems of aggregation follow.

The first example of aggregated data comes from the Chief Medical Officer of a health maintenance organization. Whenever members of the HMO are referred to physicians outside the HMO, the HMO has to pay the outside physicians. Every month the Chief Financial Officer of the HMO carefully computes and reports this cost of outside referrals. When it goes down he is happy, and when it goes up he is unhappy. The plot of these values for the past twelve months is shown in Figure 14.3.

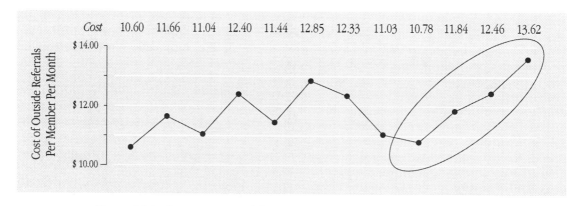

Figure 14.3: Running Record for Costs of Outside Referrals for an HMO

In a meeting the Chief Financial Officer got out his red pencil, circled the last four points, and said, "Over the past four months the cost of outside referrals has gone from $10.78 per member per month to $13.62 per member per month." He continued, "This amounts to $1.42 million per month in extra expenses." And then he looked at the Chief Medical Officer and added, "What are you going to do about this?"

The Chief Medical Officer, who had already looked at these data on an XmR chart, responded, "What would you like for me to do? Run around the block naked? That might be as helpful as anything. This is routine variation, and that is just the way it is!"

The Chief Medical Officer's X chart is shown in Figure 14.4. He was right. So what can the HMO do? The limits in Figure 14.4 are very wide, and represent a huge difference in costs. How can they live with this much uncertainty?

The answer is that they are already living with this amount of uncertainty, whether they like it or not. Routine, month-to-month variation in this process can cause this cost to vary between a low near $10.00 to a high near $14.00. Values in this range are not exceptional, no matter who takes exception to them. All the X chart does is make the uncertainty visible, instead of leaving everyone in the dark.

The question is not "how can we live with such wide limits?" The question is whether you know the difference between routine variation and exceptional variation. The fact is that their process has averaged about $12.00 per member per month for outside referrals, and unless the system is changed in some fundamental way, it can be expected to continue at this level in the near future. If the HMO fees do not have at least $12.00 per member per month budgeted for this expense, they will be losing money on these referrals. Even better would be $15.00 per member per month, which would cover the expected expenses with a little left over for profit. Good management requires planning, not reacting.

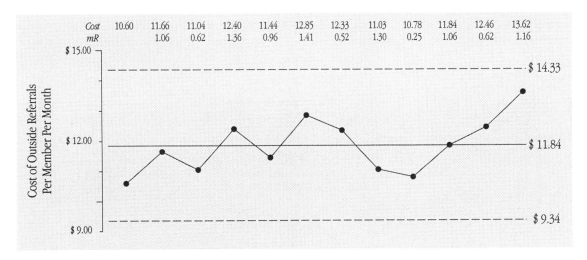

Figure 14.4: X Chart for Costs of Outside Referrals for an HMO

You may think your limits are far too wide to be of any practical use, but the limits only reflect the routine variation of your process. Some measures, and some processes, are full of noise. Crying about the noise does not do anything to change it.

Wide limits can occur when the measure on the chart is highly aggregated. As measures are combined from different categories the noise associated with each value is also aggregated, so that the totals end up displaying a large amount of routine variation.

When you combine values across categories, across departments, or across regions, you are essentially combining different variables even though they all measure the same thing.

When you summarize a measure across time you are combining multiple observations on a single variable.

Thus there are two major dimensions present in service and administrative data—time and categories. We could, for example, measure revenues for a single category at different time periods. We could also measure revenues for different categories at the same time period.

Table 14.1: Revenues by Category and Time Periods

| | Period ... | | | | | | |
	1	2	3	4	5	6	7
Category A	X_1	X_2	X_3	X_4	X_5	X_6	X_7
Category B	Y_1	Y_2	Y_3	Y_4	Y_5	Y_6	Y_7
Category C	Z_1	Z_2	Z_3	Z_4	Z_5	Z_6	Z_7

When you combine revenues across categories you will obtain an *aggregated* measure of the form:

$$X + Y + Z$$

When you combine revenues across time periods you will obtain a *summary* measure of the form:

$$X_1 + X_2 + X_3$$

As you combine measures in either manner you will also accumulate the noise that is associated with every measure. When a summary measure is converted into an average, which is commonly done, the accumulated noise is deflated by the act of averaging. However, aggregated measures are commonly used as totals, and when this happens the accumulated noise has its full effect. This is why aggregated measures will sometimes end up having wide limits on an X chart. The more highly aggregated a value, the greater the amount of noise that has been accumulated, and the more likely it becomes that the values will fall within the computed limits.

So when a highly aggregated measure shows evidence of an assignable cause, you can be confident that there really is an assignable cause. But when a highly aggregated measure behaves predictably, that does not mean that all of the components of that measure are predictable. Figure 14.6 shows the X chart for the total sales for all six regions combined. Figure

14.5 shows the *X* charts for each of the six regions for the same time periods. To facilitate comparisons, the vertical and horizontal scales are the same in both Figures 14.5 and 14.6. While Figure 14.6 shows the totals to be predictable, with wide limits, Figure 14.5 shows that four of the six regions contain signals of changes. In addition to these changes the different regions display different levels of noise in their sales values. For example, Regions A, B, and C have similar averages, but their limits are of different widths, with Region C showing the greatest amount of noise.

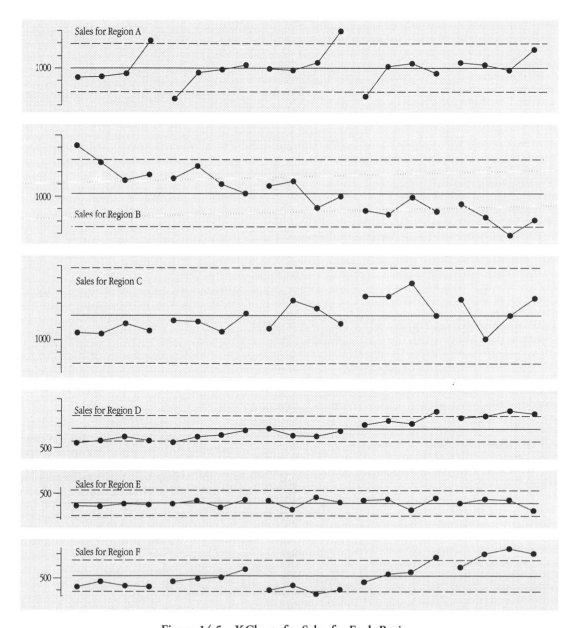

Figure 14.5: *X* Charts for Sales for Each Region

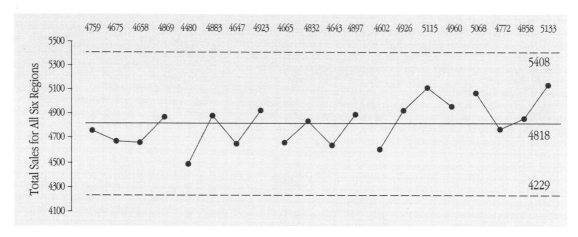

Figure 14.6: *X* **Chart for Total Sales (Aggregated Across All Six Regions)**

So while highly aggregated measures may give you nice "report-card" charts, you may well need to disaggregate your measures to identify the opportunities for improvement.

Then why would we ever put highly aggregated measures on an *XmR* chart? In order to know the answer to the question "Has a change occurred?" When highly aggregated measures are predictable, it does not mean that you cannot improve the process. It just means that you will need to look at your data in a less highly aggregated manner in order to detect signals of exceptional variation.

14.5 Ratios of Aggregated Measures

Another of the perils of aggregation is illustrated by the data for the number of Hospital Days per Million Member Days introduced in Chapter Eleven. Over a two-year period the *X* chart for these values showed a favorable downward trend. This chart is reproduced in Figure 14.7.

The healthcare plan represented by these values was sponsored by two hospitals located in two cities in one state in the midwest. The members of this healthcare plan were primarily residents of these two cities. In Table 14.2 the membership, number of hospital days, and the hospitalization rate per million member days are shown for each city.

Figure 14.8 shows the *X* chart for the Hospitalization Rate per Million Member Days for City A. The average is 240. The average moving range is 8.8. The Natural Process Limits for this hospitalization rate are 217 to 264. Over this two-year period all of the observed rates fall within these limits, although the last 8 values do fall below the central line, suggesting a weak but sustained drop in the hospitalization rate in City A.

Comparison of Figures 14.7 and 14.8 leads to the conclusion that the drop in the hospitalization rate cannot be fully explained by what happened in City A.

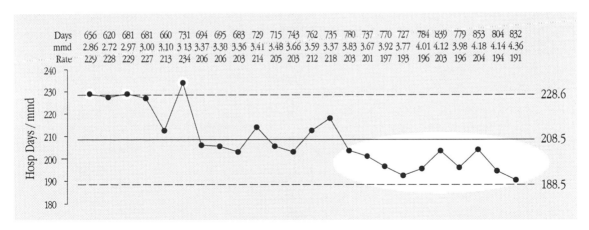

Figure 14.7: Hospital Days per Million Member Days Over a Two-Year Period

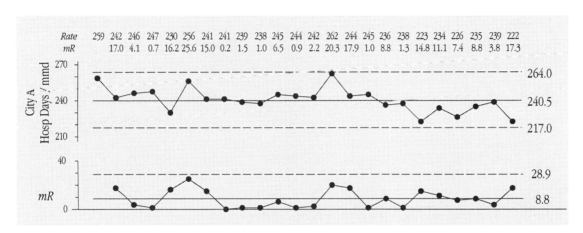

Figure 14.8: Hospital Days per Million Member Days for City A

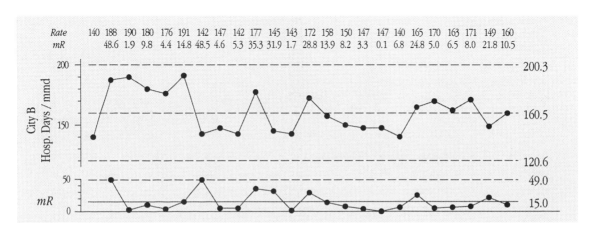

Figure 14.9: Hospital Days per Million Member Days for City B

Figure 14.9 shows the *X* Chart for the Hospitalization Rate per Million Member Days for City B. The Average is 160. The Average Moving Range is 15. The Natural Process Limits for this hospitalization rate are 121 to 200. Over this two-year period there are no signals of any changes in this rate.

So where did the drop shown in Figure 14.7 come from? City A shows a slight drop, but nothing as dramatic as seen in Figure 14.7. And City B shows no change at all. So what caused the overall hospitalization rate, shown in Figure 14.7, to decline over this two-year period?

The measure plotted in Figure 14.8 is a simple ratio of the form:

$$\frac{\text{Hosp Days City A}}{\text{mmd City A}}$$

Table 14.2: Hospital Days Per Million Member Days

Month	Total No. of Hosp. Days	Total No. of Member Days	Total Hosp. Rate/ mmd	CityA No. of members	CityA No. of Hosp. Days	CityA Hosp. Rate/ mmd	CityB No. of members	CityB No. of Hosp. Days	CityB Hosp. Rate/ mmd
Jan.	656	2,864,648	229.0	69,306	556	258.7	23,102	100	139.6
Feb.	620	2,725,604	227.5	71,347	483	241.7	25,996	137	188.2
Mar.	681	2,972,063	229.1	67,038	511	245.8	28,835	170	190.1
Apr.	681	3,000,390	227.0	70,434	521	246.5	29,579	160	180.3
May	660	3,102,449	212.7	67,633	483	230.3	32,446	177	175.9
Jun.	731	3,125,700	233.9	68,897	529	255.9	35,293	202	190.7
Jul.	694	3,366,972	206.1	70,281	525	240.9	38,331	169	142.2
Aug.	695	3,381,294	205.5	68,205	509	240.7	40,869	186	146.8
Sept.	683	3,362,310	203.1	70,637	507	239.2	41,440	176	141.5
Oct.	729	3,406,373	214.0	66,480	491	238.2	43,403	238	176.8
Nov.	715	3,480,510	205.4	70,263	516	244.7	45,754	199	144.9
Dec.	743	3,657,287	203.2	70,236	531	243.8	47,741	212	143.2
Jan.	762	3,589,304	212.3	67,024	502	241.6	48,760	260	172.0
Feb.	735	3,371,676	218.0	69,396	509	261.9	51,021	226	158.1
Mar.	780	3,833,863	203.5	70,327	532	244.0	53,346	248	149.9
Apr.	737	3,667,800	200.9	67,471	496	245.0	54,789	241	146.6
May	770	3,917,966	196.5	70,314	515	236.2	56,072	255	146.7
Jun.	727	3,773,580	192.7	67,906	484	237.5	57,880	243	139.9
Jul.	784	4,006,316	195.7	68,926	476	222.7	60,310	308	164.7
Aug.	839	4,121,853	203.5	70,074	508	233.8	62,889	331	169.7
Sept.	779	3,978,360	195.8	68,311	464	226.4	64,301	315	163.2
Oct.	853	4,182,985	203.9	68,832	502	235.2	66,103	351	171.2
Nov.	804	4,137,480	194.3	69,016	495	239.0	68,900	309	149.4
Dec.	832	4,365,730	190.6	69,833	480	221.7	70,997	352	159.9

The measure plotted in Figure 14.9 is a simple ratio of the form:

$$\frac{\text{Hosp Days City B}}{\text{mmd City B}}$$

But the measure plotted in Figure 14.7 is a ratio of aggregated values having the form:

$$\frac{\text{Hosp Days City A } + \text{ Hosp Days City B}}{\text{mmd City A} + \text{mmd City B}}$$

When you have a ratio, a change in either the numerator or the denominator can create a signal on the process behavior chart. When you have a ratio of aggregated values the number of ways in which changes can occur increase dramatically, making interpretation more complicated. In this case, the signals seen in Figure 14.7 are due to the enrollments. Inspection of Table 14.2 shows that the enrollments in City B were increasing during this time period, while those in City A were fairly steady. Since City B had a lower average hospitalization rate than City A, this shift in enrollment caused an overall drop in the combined hospitalization rate. As this growth in City B tapers off, the "improvement" seen in Figure 14.7 will evaporate.

Ratios of aggregated measures can be hard to interpret. When aggregated measures are placed on an *XmR* chart, and a signal is found, it is best to look at the disaggregated measures separately in order to determine what is happening.

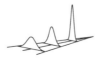

Chapter Fifteen

The Learning Way

Improvement doesn't have to be hard.
Improvement doesn't have to be profound.
Improvement just has to be done.

Flowcharts and cause-and-effect diagrams help you to visualize your process—to see it as a whole and to gain the perspective that is needed to improve your processes and systems. Bar charts allow you to make descriptive comparisons across categories.

Running records allow you to see how a measure is changing over time—to spot trends and sudden changes that can be crucial to know about.

What do all of these techniques have in common? They are all graphical representations. The flowchart and cause-and-effect diagram are graphical representations of relationships. Bar charts and running records provide pictures of your data. In each case you obtain a picture that displays relationships or data in their context. In many cases these contextual displays will be sufficient, in connection with your own insight into the relationships, processes, and systems represented, to suggest improvements that can be made immediately.

This is why context is the beginning of improvement. But what happens when context is not enough? What comes next? The next step is to characterize your process behavior so you can choose an appropriate improvement strategy. And to this end you will need a way of visualizing your process behavior. You will need a way of interpreting the graphs, and you will need a guide as to how to go about making improvements. This is where the process behavior chart comes in.

Process behavior charts tell you when your process has changed. The allow you to separate the noise of the routine variation from the signals of exceptional variation. In short, they are very powerful tools for understanding and using data.

Throughout this book we have tried to emphasize the importance of interacting with the tools in a process of discovery. The ultimate power of all of these techniques is the power to stimulate your imagination. Which brings us back to the Plan, Do, Study, Act cycle. The PDSA cycle provides a framework for organizing your use of these various tools. In this chapter you will see two extended examples of how people have used this cycle to build Continual Improvement into their processes.

15.1 Mail Order Improvement

In Chapter Two we told how a small mail order company used flowcharts as part of an improvement effort. Since they were working with an existing process they began at the "Study" step of the PDSA cycle—they created a complete flowchart of their existing order process. Why would they take the time to do this when they were planning to purchase software that would automate the order entry system? Because without a good understanding of the current system they could easily end up with a new system that would not suit their needs.

Following the preparation of the current process flowcharts, the managers used those flowcharts to identify areas that could be improved. For example, they identified several places where different people did things differently, and some places where no one knew what to do.

After this exercise in studying the current process, the managers were ready to purchase a program that would meet their current needs, that could be set up according to the nature of their business, and which would allow them to do things that their current system could not do.

After they purchased and set-up the new order-entry and accounting system they then had to plan how to introduce the new system. Here they began in a small way. Since the old system was a manual system, using nothing more sophisticated than a typewriter, there was a considerable degree of anxiety about the computerization of the system. In addition, there were concerns about the possibility of layoffs.

To meet the concerns about layoffs the managers met with each of the employees and explained that they did not envision a reduction in personnel, simply because they were currently understaffed.

To meet the concerns about the new system they devised a simple training program. When the hardware and software were installed they set up a dummy system and let everyone learn on the dummy system, where a mistake did not have real consequences. A side benefit of this was that they also used the dummy system to learn how to fix mistakes. Each week every employee was given a set of dummy orders to process using the new system. They had to review these dummy orders with their supervisor each week. Of course, with the process flowchart to use, the dummy problems could be made to match the real types of orders that this company had to deal with. At first the exercises were simple. As proficiency grew, the complexity of the exercises was increased. Within two months this training program had everyone ready to switch over to the new system.

By practicing the use of the new system on a small scale, and with a dummy system, the actual change-over to the new system was extremely smooth. In fact, in the experience of the consultants from the software company, it was the most trouble-free changeover they had ever seen.

The new system was simpler than the old system. There were fewer steps, fewer decisions to make, and many of the decisions were automated—the system provided the operator with the appropriate information to facilitate the decision. In all, the order process was more standardized than it had ever been before. The direct labor cost of processing an order was cut by over one-third. The backlogs in invoicing and in the posting of accounts were eliminated. The new system provided much more effective inventory control, better accounting information, and more timely sales information than was formerly available.

The operators loved the new system. The customers got their orders faster, with fewer errors. The operators could respond to customer's questions more quickly, more completely, and with greater consistency. The standardization of procedures allowed flexibility of staffing that was formerly not available.

With the increased productivity, time was available to spend on crucial areas that had formerly been neglected. One such area was accounts receivable. Table 15.1 shows the accounts receivable as a percentage of the three-month sales for three years. The use of the new system began in February of Year Two.

Table 15.1: Accounts Receivable as Percentage of Three-Month Sales

	J	F	M	A	M	J	J	A	S	O	N	D
Year One	61.5	42.6	50.8	52.8	53.3	49.3	49.2	44.4	48.2	42.5	43.1	42.1
Year Two	44.2	46.1	45.8	46.1	61.0	44.5	41.4	41.1	41.7	39.6	43.3	42.9
Year Three	36.2	40.2	38.9	42.8	44.8	42.5	38.4	36.7	28.8	27.0	40.4	34.7

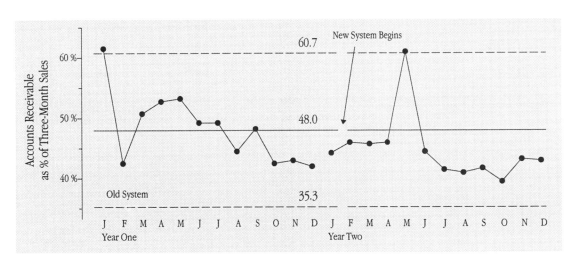

Figure 15.1: *X* Chart for Accounts Receivable for Years One and Two

Figure 15.1 shows the accounts receivable for the first two years. The limits shown were computed using the data from the old system. Under the old system their accounts receivable were averaging about 48 percent of the three-month sales value. When they began to use the new system, in February of Year Two, they had three points below 48%, one above, and then seven more below the old central line of 48%. While this does not satisfy the run-of-eight rule, I think that you will agree that the average is no longer 48%. Ten out of eleven successive values below the central line is compelling evidence of a weak but sustained shift. (The one large value in May of Year Two was due to a single large order that was current at the end of May.) When limits were computed for those months following the changeover they got Figure 15.2.

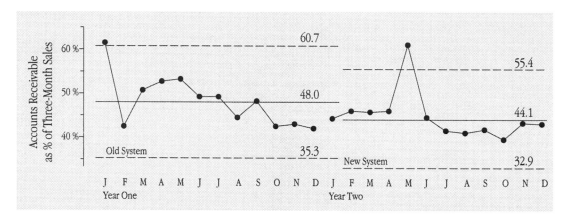

Figure 15.2: *X* Chart for Accounts Receivable Before and After the Change

After the change their accounts receivable averaged about 44 percent of the three-month sales value. A four percent reduction in working capital. The new system had paid for itself in short order.

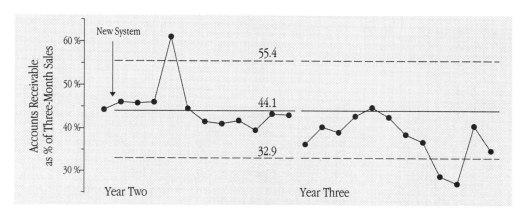

Figure 15.3: *X* Chart for Accounts Receivable Comparing Year Two and Year Three

Figure 15.3 shows the values for Year Three plotted against the limits from Year Two. Clearly, Something happened to the accounts receivable in Year Three. As a result of the increased productivity and the enhanced reporting capabilities of the new system, the supervisors had been able to systematically study the overdue accounts. As they began to characterize the accounts that were going overdue, they were able to suggest changes to the managers, and they could document their recommendations. Based on these suggestions the company made changes in their credit policies. It was these changes that resulted in the drop in accounts receivable seen in Year Three. Figure 15.4 shows that at the end of Year Three their accounts receivable were averaging about 36 percent of the three-month sales. Think about what this number means—36 percent of the three-month sales is approximately one month's sales. Overdue accounts are minimal. Most of the accounts receivable are current.

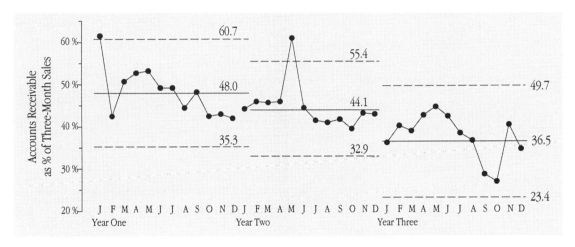

Figure 15.4: Accounts Receivable for Years One, Two and Three

15.2 Plan, Do, Study, Act

Continual Improvement involves a *cycle* of activities, which have been characterized as the Plan, Do, Study, Act cycle. This cycle provides a framework for learning about your process and then working to improve that process.

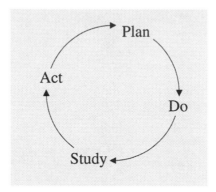

Figure 15.5: The PDSA Cycle

Plan: Determine the improvement to be made, the improvement method, and the method for evaluating the results. What do you want to accomplish? By what method will you achieve this objective? And how will you know when you have reached your objective? Until you have answered these questions you will not have completed the planning stage.

Do: Perform the activities defined in the plan. A pilot program is recommended. (Large starts lead to large consequences!)

Study: Compare the results with the desired results; learn from them. This step is sometimes referred to as "check" rather than "study."

Act: Take advantage of what you have learned. Make it part of your process, if appropriate, or decide what you will try next. Take action.

Implicit in the cycle is its repetition. After *Act*, it begins anew: *Plan* again, *Do* again, *Study* again, *Act* again; an unending cycle of learning, evaluating, and working on process improvement.

The mail order company in the previous example studied their accounts receivable, acted on what they learned, planned changes and then put these changes into place. By doing this they reduced their working capital and reduced the overdue accounts dramatically. Instead of merely reacting when things got bad, they studied their current system, learned what was happening, then planned and implemented changes to improve the system for the future.

While the story, and the work itself was virtually seamless, they still followed the Plan, Do, Study, Act cycle. To make this explicit, the steps in the previous example are listed below in the order they occurred and labeled according to which of the PDSA steps was used. Since they were working on an existing system, they began at the Study step:

Study: flowchart the current process
Act: purchase software and hardware and set up new system
Plan: prepare training program
Do: train operators
Study: review training exercises
Act: revise new system
Plan: extend and expand training
Do: train operators
Study: evaluate training
Act: decide on activation date
Plan: get ready for change-over
Do: start using new system
Study: monitor new system, look for opportunities
Act: continue using system, decide to work on overdue accounts
Plan: identify characteristics of overdue accounts
Do: change credit policies
Study: look for impact of new policies
Act: confirm new policies and enjoy the improvements

The Plan, Do, Study, Act cycle is a methodology for learning. It is a framework for getting things done. The four steps are not rigid rules to be slavishly followed. Instead they are guidelines for how to proceed in practice. They embody the feedback and follow-through that are essential for learning from your processes, and also for improving your processes. Whether they are explicit or implicit, they will be present whenever improvements are made. They are the essence of Building Continual Improvement. And that is why they will be part of the culture in those organizations that provide quality services and products.

Another facet of the Plan, Do, Study, Act cycle is the way that it facilitates, and even requires, standardized procedures. Standardized procedures are concerned with how you perform some action. They are the key to performing that action consistently. Since operational definitions are focused on making a decision, they may well be part of a standardized procedure, but we interpret standardized procedures more broadly than operational definitions.

In case after case, improvement begins with establishing operational definitions and standardizing procedures. In some cases these side effects of the work required by the PDSA cycle are the major improvements themselves.

15.3 "Let's Reduce Losses on Beer and Sake Sales"

This is the story of a project undertaken by a QC Circle at a nightclub in Osaka, Japan. Since the original document is in Japanese we will show direct translations in italics.

The name of the QC Circle at the Esquire Club was *"The Minnow Sisters Wanting to Become Carp."* They met regularly at the club, for about 45 minutes at a time, with an average attendance of 70%. This project was the second project this circle had undertaken, and the supervisor prepared the written summary shown.

Page One of the three-page summary of this project is shown in Figure 15.7 on the next page. The first paragraph in the summary describes the selection of the theme for the project.

> *This theme was chosen after a brainstorming discussion among our circle. Some of the problems discussed in this session were the timing of filling an order, properly recording the number of drinks ordered, properly recording the number of guests in a party, and keeping employee lockers clean. The losses on beer and sake sales were finally selected as a topic because it improved the communication with the waitresses while realistically analyzing the effectiveness of the operation. In addition, it was a topic which was important to the continued operation of the club.*

Following the selection of the theme, a time-line for seven additional phases of the project was prepared (see Figure 15.6). This graph shows both the planned times and the actual times for each phase. The scale at the top represents the months. This project started in February and was finished in June.

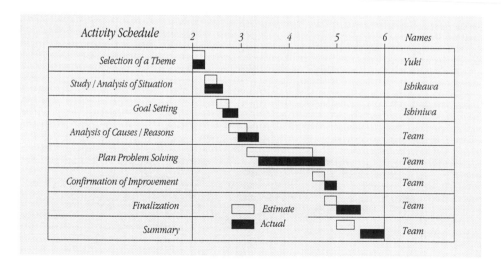

Figure 15.6: Time Line for Project

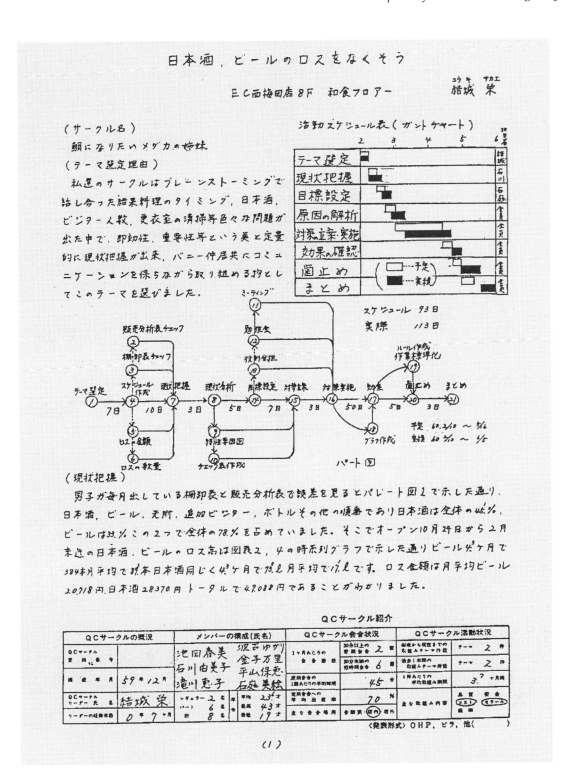

Figure 15.7: "Let's Reduce Losses on Beer and Sake Sales," Page One

283

While the time line shows the general progression of the project, it does not show the detail of the various steps, nor does it show the concurrency of these steps in the way that the PERT diagram does.

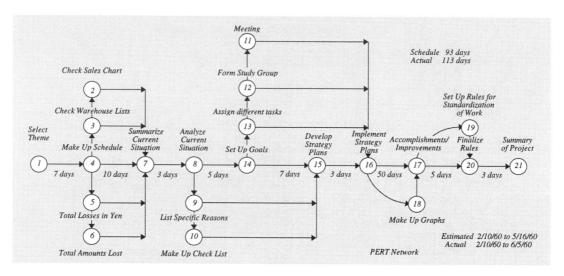

Figure 15.8: PERT Diagram for "Let's Reduce Losses on Beer and Sake Sales"

This PERT diagram was discussed in Chapter Two. It is essentially a flowchart of the work to be done on this project. They planned this project to last 93 days, and they actually completed it in 113 days. Notice the 50 day implementation period.

The next paragraph of text on Page One of the project summary is entitled "*Summary of the Current Situation.*"

> *By analyzing the difference between the list of warehouse deliveries and the list of actual sales produced by the "guys" at the warehouse every month it was possible to create a Pareto Chart for the losses.*
>
> *In total losses sake ranked first, beer second, followed by side orders, latecomers, and bottle losses as shown in Figure 1.*
>
> *Among these losses, sake accounted for 45% of the total loss in sales, and beer accounted for 33%, with a total of 78% for both sake and beer losses combined.*
>
> *The monthly amounts lost between October 24 and the end of February are shown in Figures 2 and 4. During this 4.3 month period, the total beer loss was 384 bottles, with an average of 89.3 per month, while the total sake loss was 73 liters, with an average of 17.1 liters per month. The average amount lost per month was 20,178 Yen for beer and 28,370 Yen for sake. This amounts to an average monthly loss on beer and sake sales of 49,088 Yen.*

Thus they summarize the Pareto chart which appears on Page Two of the summary.

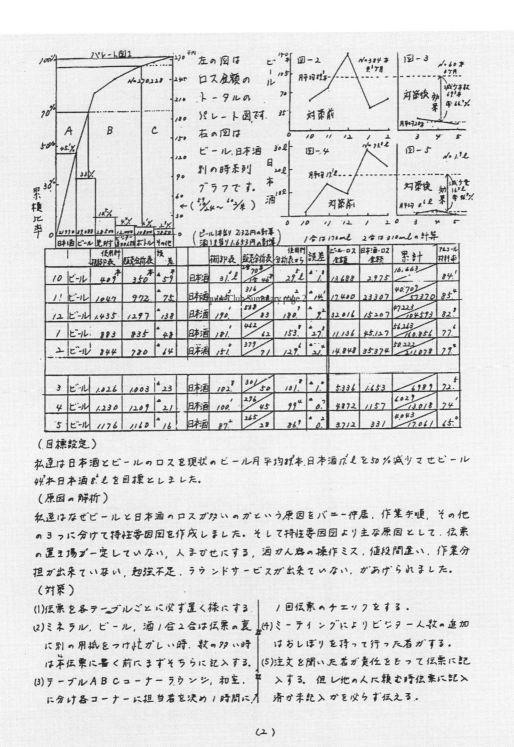

Figure 15.9: "Let's Reduce Losses on Beer and Sake Sales," Page Two

Since beer and sake losses were predominant, it was decided to concentrate on these two areas. The raw data for these losses were summarized in tables and running records.

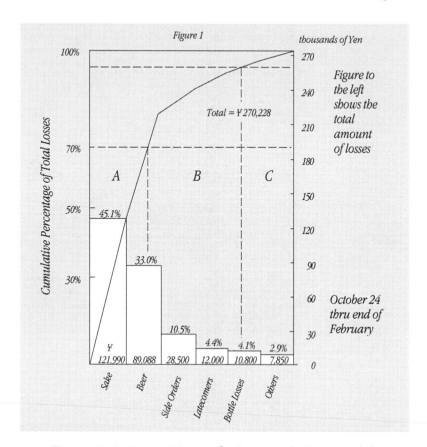

Figure 15.10: Pareto Diagram for Losses at the Esquire Club

Month		number of bottles used from warehouse	number of bottles sold	beer losses (bottles)		amount used from warehouse in liters	Single = 170 ml Double = 310 ml doubles.... singles sold	amount sold in liters	Sake Losses (Liters)
10	Beer	409	350	59	Sake	31.3	70 / 46	29.5	1.8
11	Beer	1047	972	75	Sake	125.3	316 / 78	111.2	14.1
12	Beer	1435	1297	138	Sake	190.1	538 / 83	180.9	9.2
1	Beer	883	835	48	Sake	181.1	462 / 62	153.8	27.3
2	Beer	844	780	64	Sake	151.0	379 / 71	129.6	21.4

Figure 15.11: Physical Losses for Beer and Sake

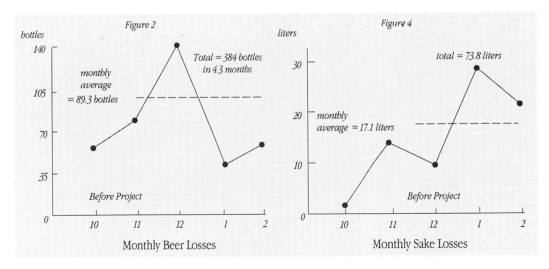

Figure 15.12: Running Records of Physical Losses for Beer and Sake

At this point the sequence of the project and the layout of the written summary diverge, mainly because of the spacing required to fit all of the information on the pages of the summary. It is apparent from the Pareto chart that they had also figured out the losses associated with the graphs and tables above. The running record for the losses for each month is tucked away on Page Three of the summary, while the table of values is on Page Two.

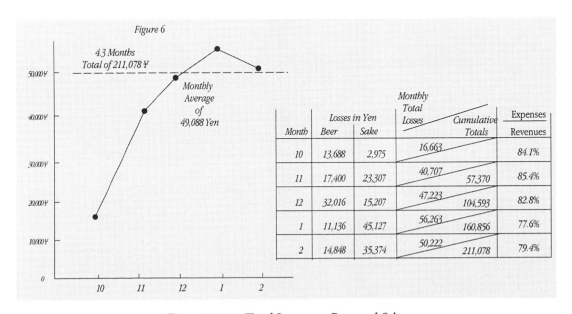

Figure 15.13: Total Losses on Beer and Sake

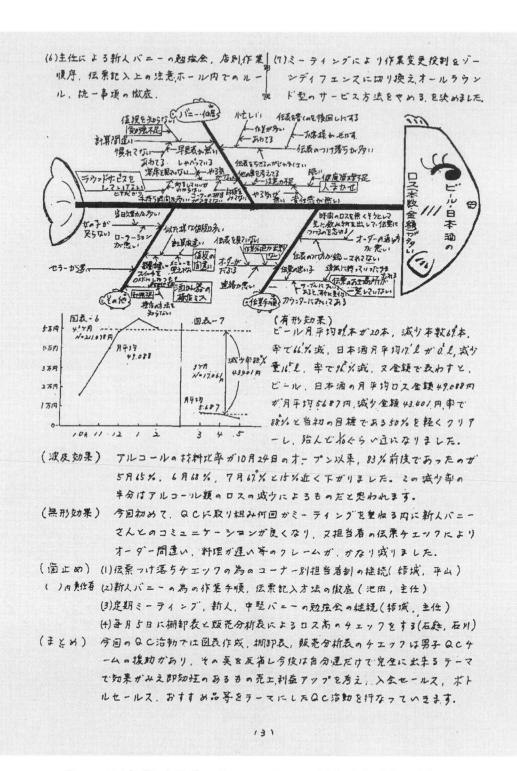

Figure 15.14: "Let's Reduce Losses on Beer and Sake Sales," Page Three

Following the summary and analysis of the current situation, the Minnow Sisters used a cause-and-effect diagram to organize their thoughts about the causes for the losses. Picking up the text from the middle of Page Two, the story continues:

> *(Establish Objectives)*
>
> *We established our goal to be the reduction of loss by 50%: from the current monthly average loss of 89 bottles of beer and 17 liters of sake to [no more than] 44 bottles of beer and 8 liters of sake, respectively.*
>
> *(Analysis of Causes)*
>
> *We analyzed the reasons why there are so many losses in beer and sake according to three separate analysis groups—waitresses, work procedures, and others.*

Waitresses, Work Procedures, and Others make up the three major branches of the fishbone (cause-and-effect) diagram.

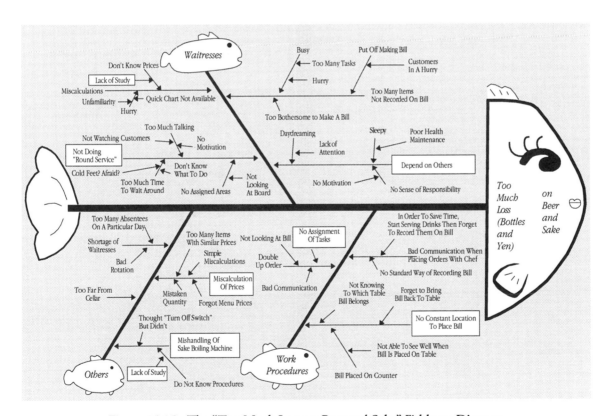

Figure 15.15: The "Too Much Loss on Beer and Sake" Fishbone Diagram

The Waitresses Branch had four sub-branches:

1. Miscalculations
    a. Don't know prices—lack of study
    b. Hurry—unfamiliarity / quick chart not available

2. Not doing round service
    a. Too much talking—not watching customers / no motivation
    b. Too much time to wait around—cold feet? Afraid /don't know what to do
    c. No assigned areas—not looking at board

3. Too many items not recorded on bill
    a. Put off making bill—customers in a hurry
    b. Busy—too many tasks / hurry
    c. Too bothersome to make a bill

4. Depend upon others
    a. Sleepy—poor health maintenance
    b. No sense of responsibility—no motivation
    c. Daydreaming—lack of attention

The Work Procedures Branch had three sub-branches:

1. Bad communication when placing orders with chef
    a. In order to save time, start serving drinks then forget to record them on bill
    b. No standard way of recording bill

2. No constant location to place bill
    a. Forget to bring back to table
    b. Bill is placed on counter—not able to see well when bill is placed on table
    c. Not knowing to which table bill belongs

3. Double up order
    a. Not looking at bill
    b. No assignment of tasks
    c. Bad communication

The Others Branch had four sub-branches:

1. Miscalculation of prices
    a. Too many items with similar prices
    b. Simple miscalculations
    c. Mistaken quantity
    d. Forgot menu prices

2. Shortage of waitresses
    a. Too many absences
    b. Bad rotation

3. Too far from cellar

4. Mishandling of sake boiling machine
    a. Thought "turn off switch" but didn't
    b. Do not know procedures—lack of study

Following the brainstorming session in which they created the fishbone diagram for the losses on beer and sake sales, the Minnow Sisters placed boxes around eight of the causes. These were the causes they felt were the major contributors to the losses. They listed these causes on the summary.

> *(Analysis of Causes)*
> *Based on this Cause-and-Effect Diagram we came up with the following main reasons/causes:*
> *No specific constant location to place the order/bill;*
> *Depend on others;*
> *Mishandling of the sake boiling kit;*
> *Miscalculations of the prices;*
> *Misassignments or no assignment of the work;*
> *Ill-prepared [lack of study shows up two places on the diagram];*
> *Low frequency for making the rounds of the customers.*

(The sake boiling kit is a water filled vessel which sits on a stove. The sake is placed in a bottle which is then placed in the hot water and heated. If the sake boiling kit is left turned on the sake will, of course, evaporate, to the tune of approximately $16 per liter.)

The *Corrective Actions* undertaken in order to fix the problems noted above were:

> *(1) Make sure to leave bill at each table, do not carry bill away.*
> *(2) During the busy periods mark mineral water, beer, and sake on the sheet that is attached to the back of the master bill before recording to the master—this should facilitate the recording and totaling of the bill.*
> *(3) Develop procedure for allocating work in all areas of club. Once each hour person in charge of each area must check all bills.*
> *(4) Person who brings out "oshibori"* [a steaming hand towel] *is responsible for recording any additional customers to a party.*
> *(5) Whoever takes the order is responsible to record it on the bill. If she must ask somebody else to take care of the order, make sure to communicate whether the order is already recorded or not.*
> *(6) Supervisor must provide training and study group for new employees.*
> *(7) Change table allocation to "zone defense" to make it clear who is responsible for each table.*

Looking back at the PERT diagram in Figure 15.8, they have now arrived at step number 16. They have identified the most likely causes of the losses, and they have implemented some fixes for these problems. Now, as shown on the PERT diagram, they will collect data for the next 50 days to see the impact of these changes.

The data for the physical losses are shown in Figure 15.16. The running records for the physical losses compare the losses before and after these changes were put in place, and are shown in Figure 15.17.

Month		number of bottles used from warehouse	number of bottles sold	beer losses (bottles)		amount used from warehouse in liters	doubles singles sold		amount sold in liters	sake losses (liters)
3	Beer	1026	1003	23	Sake	102.8	301	50	101.8	1.0
4	Beer	1230	1209	21	Sake	100.1	296	45	99.4	0.7
5	Beer	1176	1160	16	Sake	87.2	265	28	86.9	0.2

Figure 15.16: Physical Losses for Beer and Sake

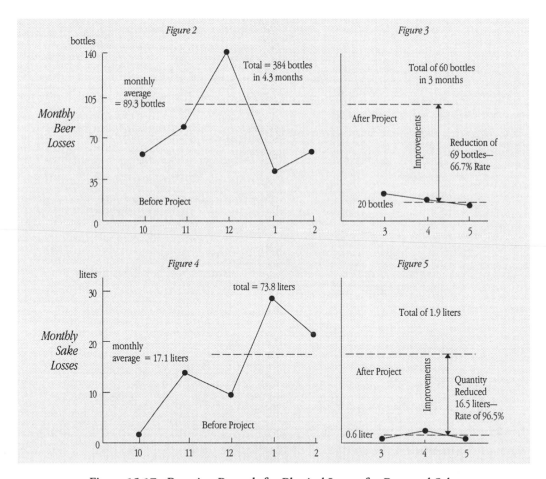

Figure 15.17: Running Records for Physical Losses for Beer and Sake

When these physical losses are converted into yen the running record of Figure 15.18 results.

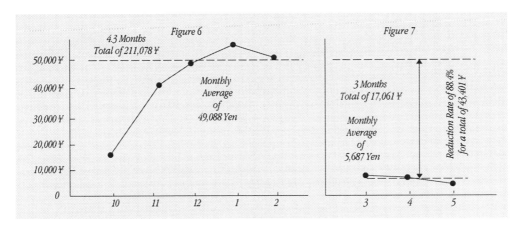

Figure 15.18: Running Records for Total Losses on Beer and Sake Sales

Beside this graph is a paragraph entitled *Improvements*:

> *In Yen, the beer and sake losses were reduced from a monthly average of 49,088 Yen to 5,687 Yen, for a reduction of 43,401 Yen, or 88%. This reduction easily exceeded our initial objective of a 50% reduction. In fact, the current losses are almost down to 10 percent of what they were previously.*

> *(Side Effects of the Project)*
> *Since the opening of the club on October 24, the operating expenses as a percentage of the revenues went down almost 15%—from 83% to 65% in May, 68% in June, and 67% in July. Half of this reduction can be attributed to the reduction of the losses on Beer and Sake sales.*

> *(Intangible Effects of the Project)*
> *In the course of several meetings dealing with the QC circle, there were several intangible improvements observed:*
> * *Improved communication with new waitresses;*
> * *Significant reduction in mistaken orders due to the bill checking system by the waitress in charge of each area;*
> * *Reduced complaints for delayed orders (Is my order ready yet?).*

So they have been successful. The targeted losses have been cut by about 90%, and the club is more profitable as a result. In addition, the customers are being better served. As is often the case, when procedures are standardized, when confusion is eliminated, when people are trained, and when steps are taken to avoid mistakes, we find that the quality goes up, the job gets easier to do, and everyone is better off.

Now how are they going to maintain these improvements in a business where turnover in personnel is the rule?

In the next to the last paragraph of the three-page summary, the Minnow Sisters list four things they are going to do to maintain these improvements. The names at the end of each item are those who are responsible for this item. Sakae Yuki is the supervisor and the leader of the Minnow Sisters QC circle. Ishiniwa and Ishikawa are the managers of the club.

> *(Final Checking Procedures)*
>
> (1)   *Continue assignment of particular waitress to a specific area in order to check that all orders are recorded on the bill.*
>
>

(Yuki, Hirayama)
>
> (2)   *Thorough training of new waitresses for work procedures, order taking, recording procedures, etc.*
>
>

(Ikeda, Chief Waitress)
>
> (3)   *Continue periodic meetings and study sessions for new and intermediate waitresses.*
>
>

(Yuki, Chief Waitress)
>
> (4)   *On the fifth day of every month continue to check the difference between the warehouse list and the sales list to determine the loss amounts.*
>
>

(Ishiniwa, Ishikawa)

Finally, they summarize where they are and where they plan to go in the future. Notice that there is no question about whether or not there will be another project. It is a foregone conclusion that there will be. It is part of the learning way known as Continual Improvement.

> *(Summary)*
>
> *During this project we received generous assistance from the warehouse QC team in the areas of graph development and the analyses of the warehouse charts and the sales charts. In the future we would like to plan a project which we can accomplish by ourselves. For example, promotion of new business meetings, improvement of bottle sales, and recommended side orders could be considered as an effective project to improve overall sales.*

Clearly this project could be organized according to the Plan, Do, Study, Act Cycle. There was a definite planning phase, followed by some changes in procedures. Next the effect of these changes were studied, and as a result certain specific actions were taken in the finalization phase of the project.

Another way to structure this project would be to use Hitoshi Kume's seven step breakdown of the PDSA cycle, sometimes known as the QC Story:

1. Problem: Define the problem clearly.
   The Selection of a Theme paragraph, along with the time-line and the PERT diagram would fit under this heading.

2. Observation: Investigate the problem from a wide range of different viewpoints.
   The Pareto diagram, the collection of data on the losses, and the preparation of the running records on the beer and sake losses would fit under this heading.

3. Analysis: Find out what the main causes are.
   The construction and interpretation of the cause-and-effect diagram would fit under this heading.

4. Action: Take action to eliminate the main causes.
   The identification of the corrective actions listed in the summary would fit under this heading.

5. Check: Make sure the problem is prevented from occurring again.
   Here the collection of new data during the 50 day observation period, the preparation of the running records, the summary of the improvements, the observed desirable side-effects, and the intangible effects would all fit under this heading.

6. Standardization: Eliminate the cause of the problem permanently.
   This is clearly what they were doing with the paragraph entitled *Final Checking Procedures*.

7. Conclusion: Review the problem-solving procedure and plan future work.
   This is seen in their final paragraph entitled *Summary*.

However you may wish to outline the steps taken by the Minnow Sisters, it should be clear that this is an effective way of approaching the problem of improvements. At each stage they used the techniques and graphs that provided them with the insight they needed to understand where they were and to see where to go next. Then they documented their gains so that others could learn from them, and the improvements could be maintained in the future.

So, if a bunch of 19 and 20 year-old kids can use these techniques so effectively, what possible excuse can the rest of us have for not using them?

15.4 What Should You Do Now?

There is an obstacle on the path from awareness to understanding. In order to move beyond awareness, you must begin to practice the use of these techniques. It is only after you use these tools that you begin to understand just how they work and why they work. Once this understanding has taken root, you can begin to actually explain the phenomena revealed by the tools. This feedback cycle continues and becomes the new way of thinking which is the basis for continual improvement. In short, you must first act—in order to understand—in order to explain—in order to be able to act effectively.

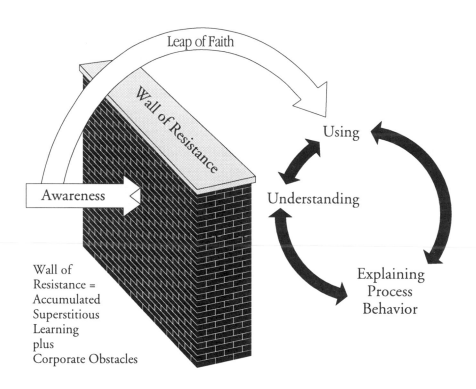

Figure 15.19: What You Have To Do

But there is one thing that you need before you take your flying leap. You need an operational definition of what you want to do. To create this operational definition you will need to answer three fundamental questions.

1. What do you want to accomplish? What is your objective? What do you want to improve? Is there a problem that you need to solve? Until you can answer this question, you will not be able to get started.

2. How will you measure your progress toward your objective? What direct or indirect measures are available that you? If you cannot measure progress toward your objective, you will be unable to document what you have done, and you will be unable to know if things have changed.

3. How will you judge that you have met your objective? How will you know when things have improved?

Of course, these three questions come from the three elements of the operational definition: the criterion, the test procedure, and the decision rule. Within this framework you can then begin the interactive use of the tools and techniques which is the heart of Continual Improvement.

Visualize your process with flowcharts and cause-and-effect diagrams. You may find that the very act of trying to draw a flowchart of your processes will reveal things that need to be worked on. When people finally start using flowcharts, they are generally amazed at what they can learn from this simple technique. Use cause-and-effect diagrams to visualize the contributing factors for a given problem.

Visualize your data using running records, bar charts, Pareto charts, and histograms as appropriate.

Visualize your process behavior using *XmR* charts and average and range charts as appropriate. These charts are the Voice of the Process—you can learn a lot by listening to your process.

Use the PDSA cycle as your guide to action. It is the learning way that leads to discovery, implementation, and improvement.

Improvement doesn't have to be hard.
Improvement doesn't have to be profound.
Improvement just has to be done.

Part III: Building Continual Improvement

298

Appendix

For Further Reading...

Balestracci, Jr., Davis, and Jeanine L. Barlow, *Quality Improvement; Practical Applications for Medical Group Practice, Second Edition,* Center for Research in Ambulatory Health Care Administration, Englewood, Colorado, 1994.

Cheaney, Lee, and Maury Cotter, *Real People, Real Work,* SPC Press, Inc., Knoxville, Tennessee, 1991.

Deming, W. Edwards, *Out of the Crisis,* Massachusetts Institute of Technology, Center for Advanced Engineering Study, Cambridge, Massachusetts, 1986.

Deming, W. Edwards, *The New Economics, Second Edition,* Massachusetts Institute of Technology, Center for Advanced Engineering Study, Cambridge, Massachusetts, 1994.

Ishikawa, Kaoru, *Guide to Quality Control,* Asian Productivity Organization, Tokyo, Japan, 1983.

Joiner, Brian L., *Fourth Generation Management; The New Business Consciousness,* The McGraw-Hill Companies, New York, 1994.

Kume, Hitoshi, *Statistical Methods for Quality Improvement,* The Association for Overseas Technical Scholarship, Tokyo, Japan, 1985.

Langley, Gerald J., Kevin M. Nolan, Thomas W. Nolan, Clifford L. Norman, and Lloyd P. Provost, *The Improvement Guide,* Jossey-Bass, Inc., San Francisco, 1996.

Mowery, Neal, Patricia Reavis, and Sheila R. Poling, *Customer Focused Quality,* SPC Press, Inc., Knoxville, Tennessee, 1994.

Neave, Henry R., *The Deming Dimension,* SPC Press, Inc., Knoxville, Tennessee, 1990.

Scherkenbach, William W., *Deming's Road to Continual Improvement,* SPC Press, Inc., Knoxville, Tennessee, 1991.

Scholtes, Peter, *The Team Handbook,* Joiner Associates, Madison, Wisconsin, 1988.

Scholtes, Peter, *The Leader's Handbook,* The McGraw-Hill Companies, New York, 1998.

Shewhart, Walter, (1931) *Economic Control of Quality of Manufactured Product,* republished by American Society for Quality, Milwaukee, Wisconsin, 1980.

Shewhart, Walter, (1939) *Statistical Method from the Viewpoint of Quality Control*, republished by Dover Publications, New York, 1986.

Tribus, Myron, *Quality First*, National Society of Professional Engineers, Washington, DC, 1987.

Tufte, Edward R., *The Visual Display of Quantitative Information*, Graphics Press, Cheshire, Connecticut, 1983.

Wheeler, Donald J., *SPC at the Esquire Club*, SPC Press, Inc., Knoxville, Tennessee, 1992.

Wheeler, Donald J., and David S. Chambers, *Understanding Statistical Process Control, Second Edition*, SPC Press, Inc., Knoxville, Tennessee, 1992.

Wheeler, Donald J., *Understanding Variation*, SPC Press, Inc., Knoxville, Tennessee, 1993.

Answers to Exercises

Pages 39 and 40: The cumulative value for Scotland's exports to Ireland, America, the West Indies, and Flanders combined was £ 687,000 or about 88% of their total. The cumulative value for Scotland's exports to Ireland, America, the West Indies, Flanders, and Denmark combined was £ 722,000 or about 92% of their total.

Page 45: The next two values are 14.2 and 11.7.
You would place a 2 after the 14, and a 7 after the 11.

Page 81: The average of the data set {10, 25, 12, 32, 26} is 21.
The median is 25. The range is 22.

Exercises 6.1 and 6.2:

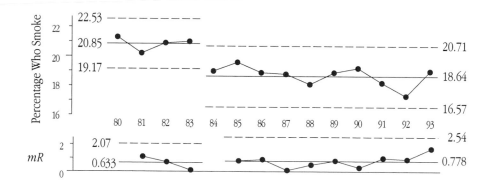

Exercise 6.3:

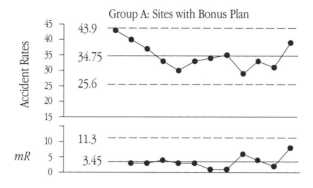

Group A: Sites with Bonus Plan

Exercise 6.4:

This accident process is predictable.

The prediction would be about 35 accidents per million man-hours.

The monthly values could range from 26 to 44.

To signal a reduction a single month's value would have to fall below 25.

Exercise 6.5:

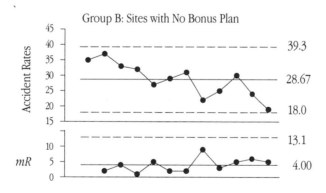

Group B: Sites with No Bonus Plan

Exercise 6.6:

This accident process is predictable.

The prediction would be about 29 accidents per million man-hours.

The monthly values could range from 18 to 39.

To signal a reduction a monthly value would have to drop below 18.

Exercise 7.1:

The average is 10.03. The average moving range is 3.067.
The *UNPL* is 18.19. The *LNPL* is 1.87. The *URL* is 10.0.

Exercise 7.2:

The average is 18.64. The median moving range is 0.8.
The *UNPL* is 21.15. The *LNPL* is 16.13. The *URL* is 3.1.

Exercise 7.3:

The average is 2.00. The average moving range is 2.96.
The *UNPL* is 9.87. The *LNPL* is – 5.87. The *URL* is 9.7.

Exercise 7.4:

The average is 2.0. The median moving range is 2.7.
The *UNPL* is 10.48. The *LNPL* is – 6.48. The *URL* is 10.4.

Exercise 8.1:

$$3\ Sigma(X) \quad = \quad 3\ \frac{\widetilde{mR}}{0.954} \quad = \quad \frac{3\ \widetilde{mR}}{0.954} \quad = \quad 3.145\ \widetilde{mR}$$

Exercise 8.2:

There are three successive values in the upper 25% of the limits.
This is a moderate signal.

Exercise 9.1:

The half averages are 410.5 and 430.1. The average moving range is 42.8. The upper range limit is 140. The three-sigma distance for the *X* chart is ± 114. The forecast for time period 21 would be about 440. The range of possible values for time period 21 would be about 330 to 550.

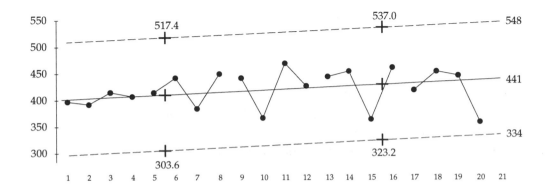

Exercise 9.2:

The half averages are 20.3 and 18.4.

The value for 1993 does not signal an end to the "downward trend."

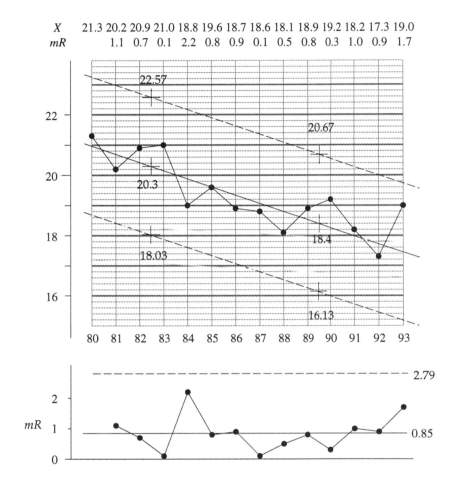

X	21.3	20.2	20.9	21.0	18.8	19.6	18.7	18.6	18.1	18.9	19.2	18.2	17.3	19.0
mR		1.1	0.7	0.1	2.2	0.8	0.9	0.1	0.5	0.8	0.3	1.0	0.9	1.7

Exercise 12.1:

The average for Hour 15 is 755.0. The range for Hour 15 is 3.
The average for Hour 16 is 753.4. The range for Hour 16 is 6.
The grand average is 754.8, and the average range is 4.5.

Second Shift Average and Range Chart

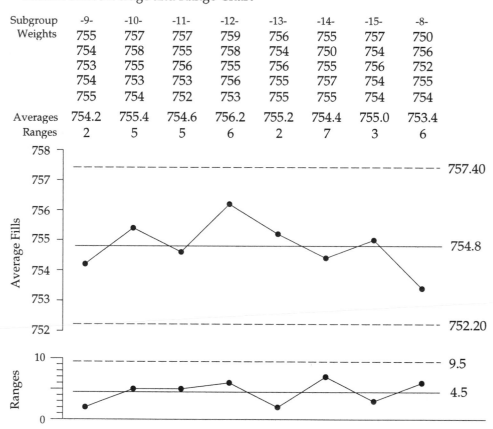

Subgroup	-9-	-10-	-11-	-12-	-13-	-14-	-15-	-8-
Weights	755	757	757	759	756	755	757	750
	754	758	755	758	754	750	754	756
	753	755	756	755	756	755	756	752
	754	753	753	756	755	757	754	755
	755	754	752	753	755	755	754	754
Averages	754.2	755.4	754.6	756.2	755.2	754.4	755.0	753.4
Ranges	2	5	5	6	2	7	3	6

Exercise 12.2:

Average and Range Chart for Seasonal Relatives

	Jan	Feb	Mar	Apr	May	Jun	Jul	Aug	Sept	Oct	Nov	Dec
Year One	0.316	0.490	0.749	0.736	1.075	1.067	0.959	1.094	0.985	1.014	1.483	2.032
Year Two	0.355	0.311	0.422	0.793	1.276	1.044	0.857	1.179	0.747	1.064	1.456	2.495
Averages	0.3355	0.4005	0.5855	0.7645	1.1755	1.0555	0.908	1.1365	0.866	1.039	1.4695	2.2635
Ranges	0.039	0.179	0.327	0.057	0.201	0.023	0.102	0.085	0.238	0.050	0.027	0.463

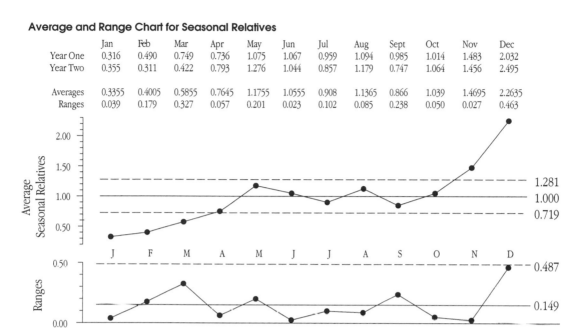

Exercise 12.3:

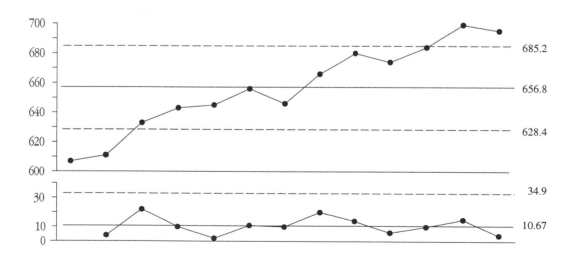

Appendix

Exercise 12.4:

The half-averages are 632.5 and 683.

The sales are trending upward by an average amount of;

$$\frac{683 - 632.5}{7 \text{ weeks}} = 7.2 \text{ units per week}$$

The estimated sales for week 14 would be about 709.

Sales below 680 would signal lower growth.

Sales above 737 would signal faster growth.

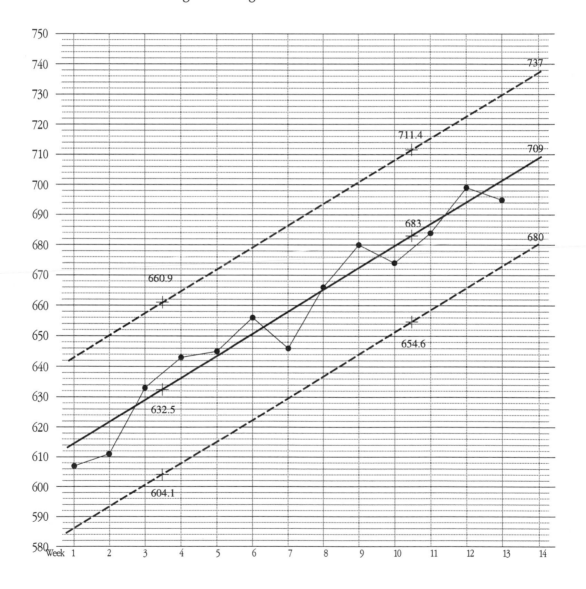

Exercise 12.5 (b):

$$UCL = 803 + 0.495\,(850) = 1224$$
$$LCL = 803 - 0.495\,(850) = 382$$
$$URL = 2.055\,(850) = 1747$$

Exercise 13.1:

	Seasonal Relatives				
	Year 1	Year 2	Year 3	Average	Range
January	.948	.798	.977	.9077	.179
February	.854	.862	1.395	1.0370	.541
March	1.060	1.009	1.167	1.0787	.158
April	.843	1.012	1.018	.9577	.175
May	1.238	1.561	1.258	1.3523	.323
June	1.085	1.249	.831	1.0550	.418
July	.818	1.180	.759	.9190	.421
August	.892	1.067	.975	.9780	.175
September	1.237	1.093	.939	1.0897	.298
October	1.334	.792	1.145	1.0903	.542
November	.812	.865	.835	.8373	.053
December	.877	.513	.702	.6973	.364

> Computation Worksheet:
>
> Grand Average = 1.0000   Average Range = 0.3039
>
> Subgroup Size = n = 2   Number of Subgroups = k = 12
>
> Find A_2 and D_4 from Table 3 in the Appendix: 1.023 and 2.574
>
> Multiply Average Range by A_2 =   0.311
>
> UCL = Grand Average + A_2 times Average Range =   1.311
>
> LCL = Grand Average − A_2 times Average Range =   0.689
>
> URL = D_4 times Average Range =   0.782

Only May shows any clear evidence of a seasonal effect. December is close.

Table 1: Bias Correction Factors

The values below are those factors which convert average ranges and median ranges into appropriate measures of dispersion, namely, either $Sigma(X)$, $Sigma(\overline{X})$ or $Sigma(R)$. *

n	d_2	d_3	d_4		n	d_2	d_3	d_4
2	1.128	0.8525	0.954		21	3.778	0.7272	3.730
3	1.693	0.8884	1.588		22	3.819	0.7199	3.771
4	2.059	0.8798	1.978		23	3.858	0.7159	3.811
5	2.326	0.8641	2.257		24	3.895	0.7121	3.847
6	2.534	0.8480	2.472		25	3.931	0.7084	3.883
7	2.704	0.8332	2.645		30	4.086	0.6927	4.037
8	2.847	0.8198	2.791		35	4.213	0.6799	4.166
9	2.970	0.8078	2.915		40	4.322	0.6692	4.274
10	3.078	0.7971	3.024		45	4.415	0.6601	4.372
11	3.173	0.7873	3.121		50	4.498	0.6521	4.450
12	3.258	0.7785	3.207		55	4.572	0.6452	4.521
13	3.336	0.7704	3.285		60	4.639	0.6389	4.591
14	3.407	0.7630	3.356		65	4.699	0.6333	4.649
15	3.472	0.7562	3.422		70	4.755	0.6283	4.707
16	3.532	0.7499	3.482		75	4.806	0.6236	4.757
17	3.588	0.7441	3.538		80	4.854	0.6194	4.806
18	3.640	0.7386	3.591		85	4.898	0.6154	4.849
19	3.689	0.7335	3.640		90	4.939	0.6118	4.892
20	3.735	0.7287	3.686		100	5.015	0.6052	4.968

Given k subgroups of size n:

$$Sigma(X) \text{ is found using either } \frac{\overline{R}}{d_2} \text{ or } \frac{\tilde{R}}{d_4}$$

$$Sigma(\overline{X}) \text{ is found using either } \frac{\overline{R}}{d_2\sqrt{n}} \text{ or } \frac{\tilde{R}}{d_4\sqrt{n}}$$

$$\text{while } Sigma(R) \text{ is found using either } \frac{d_3\overline{R}}{d_2} \text{ or } \frac{d_3\tilde{R}}{d_4}$$

For the average moving range, or the median moving range,
the effective subgroup size is $n = 2$.

---

* The *Sigma( )* notation used in this book is a generic representation of an adjusted dispersion statistic. Some of these formulas are shown above. While these statistics might be used to estimate the dispersion parameter of some probability distribution, they are not a representation of any such parameter. They are simply a convenient way of representing any one of a collection of within-subgroup measures of dispersion.

Table 2: Charts for Individual Values and Moving Ranges

When a *time series* has a logical subgroup size of $n = 1$ we can plot the individual values and use a two-point moving range to measure the dispersion. The average moving range or the median moving range may then be used to compute the Natural Process Limits for the individual values and the Upper Range Limit for the moving ranges according to the formulas:

$$
\begin{aligned}
UNPL &= \bar{X} + E_2\,\bar{R} & \text{or} && \bar{X} + E_5\,\tilde{R} \\
CL &= \bar{X} \\
LNPL &= \bar{X} - E_2\,\bar{R} & \text{or} && \bar{X} - E_5\,\tilde{R}
\end{aligned}
$$

$$
\begin{aligned}
URL &= D_4\,\bar{R} & \text{or} && D_6\,\tilde{R} \\
CL &= \bar{R} & \text{or} && \tilde{R}
\end{aligned}
$$

For two-period moving ranges these scaling factors are:

$$E_2 = \frac{3}{d_2} = 2.660 \qquad\qquad E_5 = \frac{3}{d_4} = 3.145$$

$$D_4 = \left[\, 1 + \frac{3\,d_3}{d_2} \,\right] = 3.268 \qquad\qquad D_6 = \frac{d_2 + 3\,d_3}{d_4} = 3.865$$

Moving ranges which fall above the upper range limit may be taken as indications of a potential break in the time series—some sudden shift which is so large that it is unlikely to have occurred by chance.

There is no advantage to using any other measure of dispersion besides a two-point moving range. Moving ranges based on any $n > 2$ will be harder to compute and less efficient than the two-point moving ranges. Mean square successive differences will be harder to compute and more prone to being inflated by extreme values while being no more efficient than the two-point moving range. Global measures of dispersion beg the question of predictability by making a strong assumption that the data are completely homogeneous (i.e. already predictable). That is why global measures of dispersion can never be properly used to compute limits for process behavior charts.

If the data do not come from a time series, i.e., if the individual values do not possess a definite and known time order, then the use of a moving range to measure the dispersion of the data is essentially arbitrary because the order of the data is arbitrary.

Moreover, if the individual values are *known* to come from different cause systems, as would be the case in a sequence of experimental runs, then the moving ranges may not be used to construct limits even when the data constitute a time series.

Table 3: Average and Range Charts:
Factors for Using the Average Range, $\bar{R}$

n	A_2	D_3	D_4	E_2	
2	1.880	--	3.268	2.660	Given k subgroups
3	1.023	--	2.574	1.772	each with n observations
4	0.729	--	2.282	1.457	with Grand Average, $\bar{\bar{X}}$
5	0.577	--	2.114	1.290	and Average Range, $\bar{R}$
6	0.483	--	2.004	1.184	use the tabled constants
7	0.419	0.076	1.924	1.109	with the formulas below to obtain
8	0.373	0.136	1.864	1.054	
9	0.337	0.184	1.816	1.010	• limits for Subgroup Averages,
10	0.308	0.223	1.777	0.975	• limits for Subgroup Ranges, or
11	0.285	0.256	1.744	0.945	• Natural Process Limits for X.
12	0.266	0.283	1.717	0.921	
13	0.249	0.307	1.693	0.899	
14	0.235	0.328	1.672	0.881	
15	0.223	0.347	1.653	0.864	

$$UCL_{\bar{X}} = \bar{\bar{X}} + A_2\,\bar{R} \quad = \textit{Grand Average} + A_2 \textit{ times the Average Range}$$

$$CL_{\bar{X}} = \bar{\bar{X}} \qquad\qquad = \textit{the Grand Average}$$

$$LCL_{\bar{X}} = \bar{\bar{X}} - A_2\,\bar{R} \quad = \textit{Grand Average} - A_2 \textit{ times the Average Range}$$

$$URL_R = D_4\,\bar{R} \qquad = D_4 \textit{ times the Average Range}$$

$$CL_R = \bar{R} \qquad\qquad = \textit{the Average Range}$$

$$LRL_R = D_3\,\bar{R} \qquad = D_3 \textit{ times the Average Range}$$

while Natural Process Limits for individual values may be obtained from:

$$UNPL_X = \bar{\bar{X}} + E_2\,\bar{R} \quad = \textit{Grand Average} + E_2 \textit{ times the Average Range}$$

$$CL_X = \bar{\bar{X}} \qquad\qquad = \textit{the Grand Average}$$

$$LNPL_X = \bar{\bar{X}} - E_2\,\bar{R} \quad = \textit{Grand Average} - E_2 \textit{ times the Average Range}$$

The formulas for these constants are:

$$A_2 = \frac{3}{d_2\sqrt{n}} \qquad D_3 = \left[1 - \frac{3\,d_3}{d_2}\right] \qquad D_4 = \left[1 + \frac{3\,d_3}{d_2}\right] \qquad E_2 = \frac{3}{d_2}$$

Table 4: Average and Range Charts:
Factors for Using the Median Range, $\tilde{R}$

n	A_4	D_5	D_6	E_5
2	2.224	--	3.865	3.145
3	1.091	--	2.745	1.889
4	0.758	--	2.375	1.517
5	0.594	--	2.179	1.329
6	0.495	--	2.055	1.214
7	0.429	0.078	1.967	1.134
8	0.380	0.139	1.901	1.075
9	0.343	0.187	1.850	1.029
10	0.314	0.227	1.809	0.992
11	0.290	0.260	1.773	0.961
12	0.270	0.288	1.744	0.935
13	0.253	0.312	1.719	0.913
14	0.239	0.333	1.697	0.894
15	0.226	0.352	1.678	0.877

Given k subgroups each with n observations with Grand Average, $\bar{\bar{X}}$ and Median Range, $\tilde{R}$ use the tabled constants with the formulas below to obtain
- limits for Subgroup Averages,
- limits for Subgroup Ranges, or
- Natural Process Limits for X.

$$UCL_{\bar{X}} = \bar{\bar{X}} + A_4 \tilde{R} = \text{Grand Average} + A_4 \text{ times the Median Range}$$
$$CL_{\bar{X}} = \bar{\bar{X}} = \text{the Grand Average}$$
$$LCL_{\bar{X}} = \bar{\bar{X}} - A_4 \tilde{R} = \text{Grand Average} - A_4 \text{ times the Median Range}$$

$$URL_R = D_6 \tilde{R} = D_6 \text{ times the Median Range}$$
$$CL_R = \tilde{R} = \text{the Median Range}$$
$$LRL_R = D_5 \tilde{R} = D_5 \text{ times the Median Range}$$

while Natural Process Limits for individual values may be obtained from:

$$UNPL_X = \bar{\bar{X}} + E_5 \tilde{R} = \text{Grand Average} + E_5 \text{ times the Median Range}$$
$$CL_X = \bar{\bar{X}} = \text{the Grand Average}$$
$$LNPL_X = \bar{\bar{X}} - E_5 \tilde{R} = \text{Grand Average} - E_5 \text{ times the Median Range}$$

The formulas for these constants are:

$$A_4 = \frac{3}{d_4 \sqrt{n}} \qquad D_5 = \frac{d_2 - 3d_3}{d_4} \qquad D_6 = \frac{d_2 + 3d_3}{d_4} \qquad E_5 = \frac{3}{d_4}$$

Glossary of Symbols

a_i	area of opportunity for the Poisson count from the ith sample, p. 171
A_2	a scaling factor: Table 3, p. 312
A_4	a scaling factor: Table 4, p. 313
$\bar{c}$	average count per sample for Poisson count data, p. 185
CL	the central line of a control chart, pp. 69, 138, 311-313
D_3, D_4	scaling factors: Table 3, p. 312
D_5, D_6	scaling factors: Table 4, p. 313
d_2	a bias correction factor for converting ranges into $Sigma(X)$, p. 310
d_3	a bias correction factor used in converting ranges into $Sigma(R)$, p. 310
d_4	a bias correction factor for converting median ranges into $Sigma(X)$, p. 310
k	the number of subgroups in a set of data, pp. 218, 312-313
LCL	Lower Control Limit for a control chart, pp. 180, 312-313
$LNPL$	Lower Natural Process Limit, pp. 91, 138, 311
mR	the moving range, pp. 89-90, 311
$\overline{mR}$	the average moving range, pp. 90, 138
$\widetilde{mR}$	the median moving range, pp. 123, 138
n	the number of items in a subgroup, p. 205
n or n_i	the area of opportunity for a binomial count, pp. 167, 179, 182
$\bar{n}$	average size of areas of opportunity, p. 191
$n\bar{p}$	central line for np-chart, p. 180
p	a parameter for the binomial probability model, p. 179
$\bar{p}$	average proportion nonconforming statistic for binomial data, p. 180

p or p_i	a sample proportion, pp. 173, 182
R	the range of a set of data, p. 71
$\bar{R}$	the average range, p. 204
$\tilde{R}$	the median range, p. 313
s	the sample standard deviation for a set of data, p. 73
s_n	the root mean square deviation of a set of data, p. 72
$Sigma(X)$	a measure of dispersion for individual values, pp. 137, 310
$Sigma(\bar{X})$	a measure of dispersion for subgroup averages, p. 310
$Sigma(R)$	a measure of dispersion for subgroup ranges, p. 310
u_i	the Poisson rate for the ith sample, p. 186
$\bar{u}$	the average rate of nonconformities per unit area of opportunity, p. 187
UCL	Upper Control Limit for a control chart, pp. 180, 312-313
$UNPL$	Upper Natural Process Limit, pp. 91, 138, 311
URL	Upper Range Limit, pp. 90, 138, 311-313
w_i	the scaling factor for chunky ratios, p. 191
$\bar{X}$	the average of a set of data, pp. 69, 138
$\bar{\bar{X}}$	the grand average, the average of the subgroup averages, p. 204
X or X_i	a single measurement, pp. 69, 120, 182
X chart	a chart for individual values, p. 91
$\tilde{X}$	a median for a set of data, p. 70
XmR	symbol for individual and moving range chart, p. 89
Y_i	an alternative for X, p. 120

Appendix

Index